THE ACTUAL AND THE REAL

THE ACTUAL AND THE REAL

Oscar Köllerström

Turnstone Books

© 1974 Oscar Kollerstrom

First published 1974

Turnstone Books
37 Upper Addison Gardens, London W14 8AJ

ISBN 0 85500 024 4

Set by Cold Composition Limited, Tunbridge Wells, Kent

Printed in Great Britain by Redwood Burn Limited,
Trowbridge and Esher

In memory of
two great-spirited women:

Marcella R. Clark,

who alone had faith in my vision.
I was a boy, and she understood,

And later,

Muriel, Countess De La Warr,

who, though I gave her no chance
to understand, yet did so.

ACKNOWLEDGEMENTS

I must thank Mr Verhulst of the Servire Press (The Hague) for permission to publish *The Son of Man and Every Son of Man;* the Editor of the *Liberal Catholic,* for the articles 'Can I know God?' and 'An Existential Moment', and for the extract from Bishop King's article; Mrs Aird and Messrs Heinemann & Co Ltd, for the quotation from Professor Ian Aird's biography *A Time to Heal;* the Vision Press and Miss Honegger (Groddeck's heir) for the quotations from Groddeck's works; Messrs Hodder and Stoughton for the quotations from Mr. Raynor C. Johnson's *Nurslings of Immortality;* the Editor of *The Golden Blade* for the quotation from Dr Guirdham's article 'Reincarnation in Clinical Practice'; Messrs Rider & Co for the quotation from Lama Anagarika Govinda's *Foundations of Tibetan Mysticism;* the Theosophical Publishing House for the quotations from Dr Besant's translation of *The Bhagavad Gita;* Mr C. R. Judd and the Editor of the *Times* for Mr Judd's letter to the *Times,* 1 April 1969; the Editor of the *Guardian* for a quotation from a report of the Inter Governmental Conference of Experts on the Scientific Cases for the National Utilisation and Conservation of Biospheric Resources; the Oxford University Press, for the quotation from *The Textbook of Psychiatry,* by Sir David Henderson and Dr Ivor R. C. Batchelor; Dr Joseph Bard for permission to quote my verse, 'The Tale of Any Prophet', from *The Island,* a quarterly he edited in 1930; Messrs May, Angel and Ellenberger, Basic Books Inc, for the quotation from the article by Dr Erwin W. Straus, 'Aesthesiology and Hallucination', included in *Existence, a New Dimension in Psychiatry and Psychology,* 1958.

I also wish to thank my friends Mr Christopher Gillie and Mr Charles Davy for permission to quote from their letters, and the latter for his careful reading of the whole text, and for all the generous encouragement of his correspondence about it. Others too have been at pains to help, both by encouragement, and by textual suggestions: Mrs. Wyn Henderson, with an early version of the script, and Mr Owen Barfield with my essay The Son of Man and Every Son of Man.

I have already spoken of my gratitude to Professor Wisdom, but now having studied his introduction, I am overwhelmed, I do not know how to express my thanks.

In conclusion I am overjoyed to be able to be in a position to thank Bridget, my wife, for the ever ready help of her remarkable judgement. Whenever I was in doubt about what to include, I have invariably been able to obtain from her a verdict that I at once recognised as right.

CONTENTS

PREFACE

My childhood was an experience of solitude; for although I lived at home with my parents, and with two sisters who were only a little younger than I, yet I was never close to them, indeed I had almost no communication with them. My mother and sisters formed a unit that, it seemed, had little place for me; though at weekends, when my father appeared, the unit included him. From earliest times my play was too rough for the little ones, and I was told to run outside and play, or simply to go away, or to leave the room. It was not that I was unloved: my parents did love me very dearly — and were splendid people — but they were stern moralists, and my mother was constantly in fear of the sexual behaviour to be expected of a little boy towards little girls. Seeing that I was some sort of suspect in my mother's eyes, the girls naturally allied themselves against me, and always supported each other against me before the bar of my mother's judgement. The situation lent itself to troublesome developments, and it soon came about that I was always regarded as the black sheep, and that I found it wiser to play alone and keep my own counsel. This solitariness no doubt encouraged a tendency that started when, aged four or five, early one spring morning, I went out into the garden and was astonished at the compelling force with which my gaze was caught and held by the still bare branches of an almond tree, motionless in the crystal air. I was taken out of myself, so that, not the 'I' left standing before the door, but the tree and the sky and the grass, and the ever brighter shining of it all — these were the reality, as I stood stock still, and the morning and the world were new. . . . It was not till I was much older that I came to identify the content of such experiences with the second person of the Trinity, the creator and sustainer of the universe — the cosmic Christ.

Aged ten I left home to start on a course that took me to the priesthood in the Liberal Catholic Church. I was ordained at a midnight mass on Christmas Eve in the church's beautiful international centre in

Holland. Never before or since has an occasion moved me more; yet subsequent events were to make it rather a culmination than a new beginning; for soon I was launched on what proved to be a very different career. Barely had I left home when my nature had awakened to new interests, and soon I had been unable to keep my eyes off the girls. And then, aged perhaps thirteen, or it may have been fourteen, I had fallen most ecstatically in love, and had had no eyes for any other girl. I can still remember the first time I touched her: we were standing close in a crowd when the outside of my hand brushed against her, and instantly my whole body and being were aflame: she was like a fairy, an angel; and her enchantment made each instant lyrical . . . at twenty-one I very nearly proposed to her.

Our church never proclaimed celibacy a virtue. Nor did I for a moment think that the heavenly passion I had for her could be inconsistent with my mature mysticism. Yet how could a young man given to such intensities – the ardours of love ever unrequited – reconcile these with what the world expected of a priest? Moreover, although freedom of belief was proclaimed in our church, a body of doctrine was preached. But alas, this did not give me anything I was able to use to help people in the ways I thought they needed helping. Like me, they needed the wings of faith, the spirit's flight into the empyrean, the going beyond the self's confines towards nature, the divine, all that is more than self; yet many of them seemed to me as if, having once known this need, they had forgotten it. Like me they too sought to lose the ego in personal relationships. Often, however, as I now saw so plainly, it was exactly here that they were thwarted by troubles that soured and confined them, and which I understood no better than they. And they, in their suffering, clung to doctrines, to the church as such; and they so rationalised it all that faith became mere belief, and the heavenly symbol of the church was at times made an idol. Faith and reason were at loggerheads: instinct and delight, like individuality and communality, were irreconcilable. Yes, although all sorts of questions were undoubtedly involved, this was the real root of the trouble, that one aspect of the self could not know the other.

Psychoanalysis was the obvious source for me to turn to. In this, I was fortunate indeed in finding Georg Groddeck, M.D. of Baden-Baden, 1866-1934, who was one of the originators of psychoanalysis, and to whom Freud attributed the theory of the It – called Id by English Freudians – and who started what is now known as psychosomatic medicine. Groddeck was once described (by D. Mitrinovic) as 'the only one of the originating analysts to have evolved a Christology.' His little essay 'The It and the Gospels', while not violating his humanist position, is yet profoundly reverential; and it breathes a sense of non-literalist faith. Lest my words make it seem strange, I must add that it is, throughout, exceedingly simple. It has enabled many who had lost their faith to realise

Groddeck's desideratum, that we should find again the faith of our childhood, but in a new way. He had found a language, that, for these readers, bridged the gulf beyond which reason had consigned their faith. And yet, elsewhere, Groddeck was more 'Freudian' than Freud. Thus he has shown us how, with complete consistency, we may express both the natural and the instinctive on the one hand, and on the other, all that is reverential in us. In this he is perhaps alone in our century. Nay, more: where else, and by whom, was this ever, ever shown? In living words he gives convincing assurance to those whose reverence so suffocates them that, to gain any freedom for their instincts, they must repress it. There are those who hate him for offering this double liberation.

Having trained as a psychoanalyst under Groddeck, I have practised in London since 1930. If I now say that the analyst's and the priest's worlds are a continuum, it is not that I would have analysts moralising at us, nor on the other hand, that I would in any sense betray or deny the full-blooded Freudian outlook, nor my commitment to the secular liberties of Western culture. Whether via psychoanalysis, poetry, or Taoism, or by any chanced path, there is always the fourth dimensional, world of the spirit to be discovered; and this must be cognised if we would truly know the other three. If you do not believe me, then read any novel by Dostoievsky, and note the extra dimension of meaningfulness surrounding every character; or read the Bible, and be aware of that ancient awareness that men had of their God.

A well-known psychiatrist described his son as 'gloriously ordinary'. Too many psychiatrists give the impression that the unconscious is packed with nothing but evil, and that any deviation from the ordinary is neurotic, or worse. This book is written in opposition to such an attitude. To Groddeck, the unconscious was full of riches; to Blake, heaven was beyond the janitors of sanity; for the Buddhist, the supreme attainment is dependent on ordinary consciousness being 'blown out' (a literal translation of *nirvana*) like a candle flame.

Anywhere that we step across a brittle frontier we are in a universe of meaning that is eternal.

In the pages ahead, I first present an outline of Groddeck as I saw him, and thereafter glance at a variety of facets of the spirit in the same light. He opened my eyes to a new mode of vision; to apprehend him at all necessitated this. Perhaps, it occurred to me, the presentation to the reader of the image of him that he awakened me to − this might evoke the reader's own ability to use the light of his understanding in a new way, and to turn it on to some of those facets of the spirit that I seek to illuminate. I have no wish to inculpate, or in any other way to involve, Groddeck in what I do; what he did was done by being completely himself, and that is therefore impossible for another to do, except in the sense that, by being so utterly himself, Groddeck made it difficult for others to be false. My hope is that my presentation may have something of that same effect.

In presenting facets of the spirit, I shall be seeking a transvaluation of beliefs commonly associated with them. *Transvaluation* was to have been the title of this book, for it is my subject: throughout, my aim and my method are the transvaluation of reality by the mystic's illumination. Professor Wisdom wrote the following sentence about me: 'Mr Köllerström believes that what the mystics speak of is the most important thing in the world, that without it, life is meaningless, and that with it, life can bring to us, in Spinoza's words, what "in the Scriptures is called 'glory', not without reason."' This is not what Groddeck would claim; moreover it was mine from long before I had ever heard of Groddeck. Yet Groddeck helped me in realising my claim; he facilitated my transvaluing. Everywhere in the unlikeliest places, in the most innocent disguises, transvaluation exposes an idol and reveals, in its place, a symbol, till we come to the tremendous understanding with which Goethe opened the last verse of his Faust: *"Alles vergängliche ist nur ein Gleichniss"* (All things transitory / But as symbols are sent). Without question mankind's greatest symbol is the mass, for it re-enacts the Incarnation, and is therefore its symbol. Yet the significance of this does not begin to be apparent till we understand that, in Groddeck's words: 'To the unconscious, symbol and what is symbolised are identical.'

I came to feel the entirety of my experience of the Church as itself a 're-happening' of the Incarnation, which itself is an ever-happening event — a view that has since come to the fore and is now widely held. But, of course, the all-important site for it is the heart of man. Science points to nature as our mentor; and nature mysticism is indeed the heart's realisation of its own content in responding to the cosmic Christ. Our church made much of the idea of the living Christ, which I took to mean that, increasingly, He would live again in the hearts of all who would open themselves to Him. Thus were we to understand the promise of a second coming. If only we could avoid falling away from such spiritual apprehensions into literalism — idolatry! For His ever new life in the heart is the divine event that is at the centre of the entirety of man's world, is that of which all else is a symbol, is the reality that everywhere makes sense of the actual (its multifarious symbol); it is this, His life rekindling in our hearts, that we call communion, and which so illumines a relationship that we can see another — and then any other — with new eyes that behold not only Oedipus but, also, the Son of Man.

To know another you must indeed see all the working of his grievances and his envy and his vanity, and of the perversity of his sexuality. But if you know nothing in him above these, you do not yet know him as human; for that you must know, too, something of the divine in him, of the acts of his spirit. If you know him on neither of these levels, you know him only as an object. But although what I have just written might be said to explain the culmination of the last paragraph, in truth it is little more than a concession to our current habit of thought, and which takes the heart, the fullness and the drive out of my meaning. For such explaining will never grant us the fuller vision, whereas what I wrote above might open the eyes of one ready to see.

Born with, or at least given by upbringing, a mouthful of silver spoons, I spat them out. If ever a youth was blessed in finding great teachers, it was surely mine; indeed nothing could have matched my serendipity in this but my near endless defiance and rebelliousness. However, this latter was so thorough-going and meticulous that I was driven by it to gain the most detailed understanding of my mentors; for how otherwise could I formulate full and detailed rebuttals of all I was taught — thereby making proper rebellions? Thus the upshot was that I did at least learn what I was taught; and when at long, long last, I had come to terms with the rebel in me, I had in me also what I needed to know. Perhaps too I had sharpened my wits in my prolonged struggles; or at least that is a pleasing thought — more pleasant than dwelling on my career of folly.- On re-reading the above I cannot say that I am greatly impressed by it, nor that it satisfies me as an account of my education, especially in view of my not really having had any ordinary schooling, and of the vast amount of time I have abandoned to dreaming.

Of all my mentors, the one I found it hardest, indeed impossible, to shake off, and who most influenced me — indeed gave me my career — was obviously Groddeck. I had visited five or six other psychotherapists, in different countries before I settled on him as my teacher, but my choice of him was made the instant I met him. Was it that I somehow recognised him as a fellow rebel? It was not till much later that I learned of his score in this field of honour, of its many details, such as that he was all but expelled from *Pfort, the* school in Germany, on the eve of his final examination, and that he "had long since far out-distanced all others in the number and the severity of the thrashings" he was given. Later came the more significant rebellions that shaped his life and career, and made these his own. By cutting him off from his external sources, they constrained him to be individual, to rely on his originality. Alas! I can claim nothing so heroic, nor anything so meaningful.

Inevitably this book begins with Groddeck, and it is in the light he shed that I proceed to consider other matters. After some preliminary impressions of him, comes my account of his therapy. This was read to the 1952 Club, a group of rather senior members of the Institute of Psychoanalysis, on 28 September 1967. Sensible of the honour of being asked to read a paper to this club, and as an outsider, I began with an assurance of my general attitude by the declaration that I regarded Freud as the presiding genius of our epoch, a view which I am sure was also Groddeck's.

Following this is a shorter chapter in which I seek to show how Groddeck, though soundly rooted in our safe and solid earth, has intuitions that are fed with breath as rare as spirit. I follow with chapters on the very different subject of mysticism, particularly as seen in Christianity. There is, however, nothing sectarian here; indeed, all my life I have taught that our understanding of Christianity is enriched by some knowledge of other faiths, particularly Zen Buddhism. In 1926 I visited Japan with an introduction to Professor Suzuki, and Zen has ever since coloured my thought.

The actual conception of this book was in a blessed moment of the harmony of the opposites. The four chapters comprising the section headed 'The Actual Dimension of the Matter' are edited tape-recordings of lectures delivered in 1958 under the title of *Transvaluation*. As I rose to address my audience at the first of these lectures, I was pleased to notice that the syllabus had succeeded in attracting both religious and irreligious listeners, some of both of whom I knew to be strongly partisan. As I left the hall, I assured myself that the evening must indeed have been a success, for though discussing such a debatable a topic as the after-life, I had given a degree of satisfaction to people in both camps. All parties contributed to a consensus. Following Groddeck, I had taken it that psychology provides a language that is not only for the mundane, but is one in which we can also discuss the spiritual, and without subtracting from or falsifying it. That was a happy hour, one of those moments in which we seem aware of a millennial promise, of mankind's dream of Babel's fall.

But I have no millennial hopes for this book. The magic made by that hour of talking will not shield my brazen, naked print. To every side I shall be an intrusion, and a puny challenge — except only to those who, belonging to no side, are yet seeking. And, indeed, I have no mission to compete with any man's faith, nor the animus to undo those assured that there is no place for faith. In this sphere, both proof and disproof seem of Alice-land. I am not here concerned so much with what is believed or disbelieved, as with a way of thinking about eternity and its problems. All I seek is to extend a little that first happy hour, and to find a few more, here and there, between whom communication may become — if only momentarily — of prime significance. In themselves, believing and disbelieving never seem to me as important as our attitude in considering.

But I write for more than this.

I write to proclaim that, without raising a foot from the most solid earth, we may yet breathe again the spirit of eternal life. Perhaps, while not renouncing thought's integrity, in some way each seeker may find again — or only feel — something of what Groddeck characterised as the one true faith, the faith of one's childhood. Perhaps he might catch its spirit, and this without a side-step from the course of his everyday logic.

When a man steps down from a kerb instead of trying to walk straight off it, he shows a kind of believing — in gravity — which is absent when he declares a belief that the dead have harps. He will never do anything about the latter 'belief', nor will it — or the harps — ever affect him. The 'thinking' he might wish to show has no steps in logic to the harps. Yet without such wanton steps, and with his own life-experience as sole vantage-ground, a man can trace and follow a genuine if tortuous way — or is it Chesterton's gloriously cock-eyed 'rolling English road' — a way from the kerb stones and solid feet and daily earth to where the angels sing — if unaccompanied by harps?

I present the attempted 'thinkings' and conceptions comprising this book as showing one man's stumblings down such a path. But though I do not prescribe this way for others, yet nevertheless I would not go quite to the lengths of Groddeck, who directed: "If you want to follow me, do as I did, and go your own ways." Or do you feel it best to seek a way through poetry?

Mystics of all cultures have sung to us their enchanted messages, always clearly in the faith that something of these, if not their entirety, would be received with understanding. And such messages, surely, we must regard as our essential sources of the knowledge of eternity. Throughout I have followed the example set by Aldous Huxley — that herald of happy enlightenment — in his *The Perennial Philosophy,* and have kept to pure mysticism without anything of spiritualism, nor of systems of belief based on clairvoyant revelations and investigations, although much of interest and of value may be found in these. An outstanding exemplar of our great seers, one who did much to portray such a system, was the Rt. Rev. C.W. Leadbeater, who was also one of the originators of the Liberal Catholic Church. He was widely known for his accounts of spiritual phenomena. For example, he described coloured emanations that constituted auras surrounding people, from which he could read their characters and their emotional changes. Although he had unquestioning certainty in the objective reality of everything he thus saw, an aspect of his great-hearted attitude was shown in accounts he gave of the vision of a woman who could read the same results as those he read, but from a geometric figure she saw over a person's head. What he was telling us, of course, was that there might be a variety of ways of apprehending what may lie beyond the veil. There is a further pertinent consideration advanced by Victor Cofman, a scientist and a thinker of great profundity, that the realm of the mystics must be thought of as infinite and eternal, and that we should therefore not be surprised if its explorers give us differing or even contradictory accounts of it.

To my mind it behoves each seeker to function according to his own natural bent, realising, as Groddeck put it, that no man can grasp the whole, and that one's perceptions are as individual as one's thumb-print. Any attempt to learn to 'see' what another has 'seen', or to corroborate another, can lead to a delusional 'success', from which very great harm can result. (Could it be that, with the forces of attention so far removed from the customary, the normal powers of criticism are overwhelmed by the will to be in happy agreement?) I have both seen this happening in others, and have myself experienced it — individually, and in association with a group. One day I shall give in detail the whole story of this group, composed of well-known, sincere and devout seekers, which was thus misled — in the interpretation of the *Parousia.* I trust my account will be a sufficient warning to others. Bishop Leadbeater, I may add, had nothing to do with anything like this. Indeed he could not have, at least during the years when I knew him, for he kept his seership individual, and always remained true to his gift and to its conditions, never relaxing from the ascetic and saintly rules he believed necessary to its maintenance. Indeed there was no false note in him; every least aspect of his life was completely dedicated, which is perhaps why one increasingly hears it said that he has been proved right in so much that he said.

But having thus made my bow, I return to my theme, that of pure mysticism. I referred to Aldous Huxley and must therefore add something approaching a caution. In his *Doors of Perception,* he has shown that ordinary people could at times experience something at least related to the mystic's experience, by means of drugs. Even yogis of certain schools, and followers of very different faiths, in other lands, have made use of drugs. I myself have not yet tried anything of the sort, though much recommended to me by professional (medical) colleagues who have done so. It would seem that a function of the normal brain — which would appear to be inhibited by such drugs — is to shut out these perceptions; thus the judicious use of appropriate drugs would seem to be reasonable. To me, however, what I can do purely of my own volition seems best; moreover I am loathe to violate nature. Further, it sometimes seems that experiences induced by drugs are sought purely as indulgence, whereas to my mind, the most ecstatic mystical experience is to be valued not for its own sake, but only as the medium of understanding what lies beyond the ego, and thereby gaining strength and enlightenment in one's life and work. The spirit of man exists for spirit's sake and for man's sake, but not for consumption by the pint, as in the four-ale bar — though an occasional visit there may preserve us from losing the common touch.

The mention in the first words of this section of the Preface of the four 'Actual Dimension' lectures was appropriate in that they gave rise to the idea of this book, and it was on these that Professor Wisdom's interest first centred. His kind interest has prevailed against my own very dubious feelings about my writings. Indeed, but for his interest — sustained through many a discussion, and even by correspondence – the book would never have appeared. Association with the great has results it is indeed hard to evaluate, yet it is clearly a major element in one's life and development. One can only be thankful for one's ability to venerate, for by means of it one may hope that the association will enrich one beyond the mere learning that it brings.

Throughout the ages, all ways of considering eternity have led, not to its explanation, but to confrontation with a mystery. Early in our relationship I mooted this topic with Professor Wisdom, and sought to develop my idea. He found my thought obscure. Then he went on to recall MacTaggart on the unreality of time and on reincarnation; Spinoza on the unreality of time, triumph over death, and overcoming human bondage; and Gide on what Dostoievsky thought was the meaning of Christ's words about eternal life. Professor Wisdom made it clear that he did not think any of all this was to be understood.

The tyro author may take comfort when even the great fail to communicate. With such a verdict, all one can hope to achieve is to re-state, or re-present, aspects of the mystery. Always they claim re-statement, and to my mind, the experiencing and the struggle that go to such re-formulation, and then its actual expression, make the most profoundly satisfying of all life's tasks. One is tempted to regard it as man's *magnum opus*. Yet is the outcome of it all to be not understood?

One may ask what is conveyed by the word 'understand'. A philosopher will sometimes want it to connote recognition of a reference precise or concrete enough for a scientist to handle. I suppose Professor Wisdom felt that no writings about eternity would be likely to pass such a test. We may however claim that they may be understood in the sense that poetry is. Yet it is more than this that we would claim. Granted that the subject is obscure, then to write about it all is to verge on the edge of what can be thought; but because one must use a philosophical concept here and there, it does not follow that one seeks to trespass on the philosopher's province. Far from it. There is an area which is still, in spite of all its literature, inadequately developed; this area is not that of the philosopher – though it needs philosophers to define it. I think of Psyche's world, more full of meaning for you and me than any other world. Does Psyche's tongue – only now given to us, by Freud, in this late epoch – enable us at last to speak of the eternal and be understood, at least to a degree?

The kind of faith – in both Christ and man – which I have sought to portray so far will not be fully comprehensible without a counterbalancing statement of my uproarious joy in doubt, and this must precede my prefatory comments on the individual items of the book, as follows. To begin with Groddeck: in spite of love for him, I could never happily settle to the practice of his methods as I understood them, till I had tried others. I therefore made a point of getting personal experience of various methods; indeed of any methods that were not too wildly at variance with the central Freudian approach. Thus, very early on I submitted to three months of Adlerian therapy, later to a Stekel course, and then to an analyst who, though not a Jungian, interpreted in Jungian terms whenever material that lent itself to such terms presented itself. I even, quite a lot later, went to a Freudian. Further, I went outside the fold to the extent of studying five or six distinct methods of relaxation and co-ordination. Here it is perhaps appropriate to mention that I had nearly eighteen months under F.M. Alexander, perhaps the only non-Groddeckian procedure about which I now have neither regrets nor reservations. For the sake of completeness I would mention that I even took a course of dianetics, though I could never feel any sympathy for its successor, scientology. Indeed I found it difficult to understand how the one could be regarded as the successor of the other in any logical sense.

Alas! In spite of all my systematic, indeed studious doubt, I kept being driven back to Groddeck. However, this is perhaps not so remarkable, since before settling on him, I had taken a great deal of trouble to find the right man.

Perhaps the foregoing account of my elaborate doubts in one sphere will be enough, as an example, to give the required picture to the reader without a superfluity of description.

The Gospel story always cries again for reinterpretation. Irrespective of whether we are believers or otherwise, the figure of Christ persists for us as a prime significator for our culture; and as our world turns, His meaning must always again be re-experienced. But the required effort of creative understanding is evaded alike by the traditionalist re-statement of established attitudes and by detractors and iconoclasts. While retaining a sense of His spiritual meaningfulness, I have sought whether a view of Christ through Psyche's eyes might enhance His reality for you and me. I must render thanks to Groddeck for this approach, though *The Son of Man, and Every Son of Man* involves much that I do not think Groddeck would have had me lay at his door. In what was essentially its present form, however, it was first presented at Het Oude Loo,* on 1 February 1957. A tape-recording of the lecture was then published as a booklet in Dutch.

An intention similar to that which motivated me in producing *The Son of Man, and Every Son of Man* resulted in my version of the mass, in 1942. Here, however, it was not merely the significance of the Gospel story, but the wider message of Christianity as a whole, that was my concern. Because of its length, the mass is perhaps unsuitable for actual use — though it is easily shortened. The idea that inspired it was that it should

---

*Het Oude Loo is the old royal summer palace in Holland, a moated medieval castle of fairyland beauty, which Queen Juliana makes available for certain lectures on spiritual themes.

set a ball rolling. Others — perhaps some among our poets — might feel moved to produce their versions. What a wonderful subject for a poet! And what a wonderful thing for our tired culture to be thus re-vitalised from its ancient sources! A whole series of such versions by our major contemporary poets might set off an illumination, both spiritual and literary, that could light our first steps out of the universal squalor engendered by materialist creeds, whether of Nazism, Communism, or the affluent society. In a recent number of the *Liberal Catholic,* a remark made to one of our priests by the Rt. Rev. J.I. Wedgwood, the real founder of our church, is quoted: he refers to 'a conviction that the last quarter of this century would experience an Advent, centring on the transforming work of the Holy Eucharist'. May this publication seem timely.

My version is based on that of the Liberal Catholic Church, and preserves all the 'ancient landmarks': the Canon, the manual acts, and so on. I should like to add that our Presiding Bishop, the Rt. Rev. Sir Hugh Sykes, Bart, has of course seen it, and although there was no question of his sanctioning it, he wished me well with it.

'An Existential Moment' was written and published in the *Liberal Catholic* in 1947. In it I direct attention to a particular view of Christ by means of comparing Him with Buddha.

The notes comprising the chapter headed 'Death', written in 1943, were the outcome of meditations on my Easter sermon in 1919. Although these notes do not recapture the original nature mysticism, they go much further in other directions. This is what really started the train of thought which culminated in the 'Son of Man' chapter.

The 'Propositions' arose out of certain thoughts in a sermon that came after the Easter one, but contain much other material as well. Part of this was developed when I was between the ages of sixteen and eighteen, both from listening to and talking with Dr. J.J. van der Leeuw, who was undoubtedly a genius, though cut off while hardly more than a youth. Further elements in the 'Propositions' appeared many years later, in the course of numerous discussions with the late Dr, A.R. Redfern. Which thoughts were my own, and which derived from these two friends, I cannot say.

The first part of the section entitled 'Interminable Dreaming' were not consciously influenced by Coleridge; nevertheless I have sometimes wondered whether he was their inspiration. The countryside described in the main part will be recognised by anybody who knows the setting of Peking.

I have set out such odd bits of thought as my magpie mind could seize on, and have included such asides, interjections and afterthoughts as have come to me. If all this got shaped up into looking like some new system of belief, I should feel constrained by it, and would seek to escape out of it. Indeed, I am very, very far from sure that I could accept the idea of any 'final picture'.

It is good to have thoughts in progress; and perhaps in sunny moments one may learn to follow the Tao. And perhaps, even better, when all is soured and broken, and one trudges along the same though now narrowing track, leading, one may fear, to an unknown morass . . . At least one moves on, and perhaps − who can say? − one may again, stumbling and guessing, happen on the Tao.

INTRODUCTION

I think that this book will be found valuable by many and by various people, for these essays all have a bearing on the old conflict between those who have confidently said that all is vanity, and those who have confidently said that all is well and even that this is 'the best of all possible worlds', and those who have confidently said that whether or no all is well it is not the case that all is vanity. And there are today, no less than in the past, those who ask themselves "Is it perhaps only too true that all is vanity?". And there are today also those who, whether or no they are "vitally concerned" with this question, are puzzled by the nature of the old, acute and yet seemingly chronic conflict which it generates.

The following remarks are not a summary of what Mr Köllerström says, but I think they draw attention to certain features of it which should not go unnoticed.

Mr Köllerström in his preface tells of his uneasy loneliness in early childhood, and says that at the age of ten he left home to take a course of training which took him to the priesthood in the Liberal Catholic Church. He tells us that what he learned in that period left him still with a sort of loneliness and still unable to help others as he wished. He tells us of how he found in Groddeck one who gave him a new view of the Gospels and of the faith of his childhood.

In the first three essays in his book he writes about those, or some of those, who have most profoundly influenced him. He writes about Groddeck and about Goethe. And he writes about Jesus Christ. Here let me remark that sometimes at least when Mr Köllerström refers to a belief important to some religion in the way in which the belief that Jesus of Nazareth rose from the dead is important to Christianity, in the way in which the belief that there is a life after death, an everlasting life after death, is important to many religions, he does so not because he wishes to say that that belief is true or false or a belief we cannot know or do not know to be true or to be false, but because he believes that reference to that belief will help him to present some thought, some surmise, which he wishes to present as deserving consideration.

Here, too, I should say something about a certain sort of procedure which Mr Köllerström follows at some important places in his essays. It is the procedure of one who gives to a form of words a modified meaning, a meaning still more or less akin to a meaning it has commonly had, but nevertheless different from any meaning it has commonly had. We are all familiar with this sort of procedure, but I think it worthwhile to call to mind a few examples, real or imaginary, of one who proceeds in this way. Imagine somebody who at a time when he and those around him are afflicted by a plague says "There is someone who is angry with us" and then adds "I don't mean someone we can see, I mean someone whom we can't see." He adds this explanation because he knows that otherwise his hearers will take him to mean that there is someone no less visible than themselves who is angry with them, because they have always taken the word 'someone' to imply that whoever is referred to by the person who uses it is visible. This person I describe is modifying the use of the word 'someone'. He may also be described as giving the word a meaning which does not imply all that its usual meaning implies.

When a child first hears such words as "There is someone, whom we call 'God' who watches over us all the time" it is, I guess, often necessary for the speaker to explain to the child that when he speaks of 'someone' and of 'God' he does not mean someone who can be seen. It may then be necessary for the speaker to answer some such question as "Then how do you know that there is someone who watches over us all the time?" And it may happen that the child though temporarily satisfied with the speaker's answer is later unsatisfied with it. He may turn to someone, Paley perhaps, who, even if his answer is on the same lines as the one that the child first received, gives a fuller answer. And of course it may happen that the person who is, for a time, satisfied by what Paley and others say about all that in nature which has seemed to many to support the hypothesis that the world was designed by and is controlled by someone with quite unparalleled power and knowledge, may later come to regard what Paley and others have said as a very unsatisfactory answer to his question "How do you know that there is someone who watches over us?" For example, he may become dissatisfied with Paley after reading Darwin. At such a juncture he may read William James's book *The Varieties of Religious Experience.* If he does, he will need to ask himself "Does William James mean by the word 'God' what Paley, Newton or St Paul mean?" And if he later reads Bultmann or some very modern theologian there will be still greater need for him to ask "Does this writer mean what for so long has been meant by the word 'God' and if not what meaning does he now give that word?"

Here it should be noticed that though it is true that sometimes, when a person gives to an old form of words a new meaning, he believes that, given its old meaning, it expressed what was in part false, or at least doubtful, this is not always so. A person who gives to the word 'wave' a meaning which does not imply that what he speaks of is visible, does not do so because this does not imply that he believes that when the word is given its old meaning by one who says "Today the waves are high", what is meant is false or doubtful. He takes the licence with language in order to have a way of drawing attention to and speaking about disturbances of a certain sort which, though invisible, are in certain respects akin to the movement of a visible wave. Spinoza gives to the words "We are eternal" a meaning which does not imply that there is a life after death. But this does not tell us that he regarded a belief in life after death as a belief for which we have no adequate grounds. And when Mr Köllerström gives to a form of words a meaning which does not imply some proposition which is implied by what they usually mean, it should not be inferred that he regards that proposition as false or as something we cannot or do not know to be true.

We know that the sort of procedure I have been talking about can be extremely valuable. For example the work of those who have given to the words "There are waves which are not visible" a meaning in which they express a truth has been extremely valuable. When Cantor gave to the words "A part may be equal to a whole of which it is a part" a meaning which is not self-contradictory but true, he opened up for us an arithmetic of infinite numbers. And we know that this sort of procedure, even when it is not valuable on this tremendous scale, may yet be valuable.

But we also know that when a person follows this sort of procedure his hearers or readers are sometimes left at a loss as to what he means, or with a mistaken idea as to what he means − a mistaken idea which sometimes leads to fruitless argument which goes on for a long time before things are cleared up, and sometimes threatens to be interminable. (Philosophy provides good examples of such unfortunate situations, but they can be found in other spheres.) Some of the dangers associated with this sort of procedure can be illustrated by reference to Spinoza.

Spinoza makes it quite clear that he gives to the words "We are eternal" a meaning which does not imply that we live everlastingly, nor that we live after death, nor anything as to life's duration. Although Spinoza makes this clear I think that one who reads him will do well to ask himself quite explicitly these questions. First, isn't Spinoza here taking licence with language and giving to the words "We are eternal" a meaning very considerably different from any meaning normally given to those words? Let us imagine a reader who does put to himself this question and answers it in the affirmative. He will do well to ask himself, then, "What new meaning is it that Spinoza gives to these words?" He may then, like

Professor C.D. Broad and other able men who have read Spinoza, be obliged to say that he is unable to make out what Spinoza means by these words. Let us imagine, however, that he thinks that he does now know what meaning Spinoza gives to these words. Imagine that he says something like this: "Spinoza gives to the words 'we are eternal' a meaning which has seldom or never been given them and certainly very different from what most people have meant and do mean by them. However, I think that from what Spinoza says, I can gather what the new or modified meaning is which he gives to the words 'We are eternal'. He means what we might express by saying 'We can come more and more to see things in the light of the eternal.' For Spinoza would say that a man is 'eternal' in so far as he can and does come more and more to know things with what Spinoza calls 'the second kind of knowledge', and especially in so far as he can and does come to know things with what Spinoza calls 'the third kind of knowledge'. Knowledge of the second kind is knowledge of truths, which are eternal in that they are truths about what happens at any time anywhere – laws of nature. A man comes more and more to know things with the third kind of knowledge the more he comes to see each individual thing, each individual incident, as he in life encounters it, in the light of the whole of nature, as a part of the totality of events. That totality can have no predecessor and no successor, and in this sense has no beginning and no end, and is in that sense 'eternal'. This totality, this whole without beginning and without end, the parts of which in conjunction manifest in infinite variety, its unchanging character, Spinoza called 'God', for it seemed to him of divine splendour. The more he saw things in the light of this whole, the less he saw things sadly, and the more he saw things with that love, that joy, of which he spoke."

Now I am not here concerned with whether or not this imaginary commentator is right about what Spinoza meant, and in particular about what Spinoza meant by the words "We are eternal". What I want to remark is that whether or not he is right about the meaning Spinoza gave to the words "We are eternal", he needs to ask himself a third question, namely : "If we give to the words 'We are eternal' this new meaning, do they then express a proposition which is true?" And after that he should ask a *fourth question,* namely: "If we give the words 'We are eternal' this new meaning, do they then express a proposition as capable of bringing consolation to those who accept it as that proposition which those words did express?" A man who believes that we can come more and more to see things in the light of the eternal may yet be one who distrusts the consoling power of this belief, because in his experience the seeing of things in the light of the eternal does little to diminish sadness and bring satisfaction of mind. He may agree that a part of a whole may look very different when looked at in the light of that whole. He may agree that a broken toy, a broken limb, even a life lost, *may* in certain circumstances be less distressing when seen in the light of those circumstances and of all that happens, and yet insist that sometimes this is not so, and even that sometimes the opposite is so. (Here we may think of one who sees his child dying, as does the father in Peter de Vries' *Blood of the Lamb.*)

Obviously whenever someone gives a new meaning to a form of words which given its old meaning expressed a belief which brought consolation to all who accepted it (and thus perhaps to thousands), then it is important to ask whether, when that form of words is given the new meaning he gives it, it expresses a belief which is not only as consoling to him, but also as consoling to others as that belief which that form of words expressed under its old meaning.

The position I think is this. Mr Köllerström at some important places in these essays gives to an old form of words a modified meaning. Sometimes this new meaning does not carry some of the implications carried by the old meaning. It should not then be assumed that he regards that implication as not true, or even as something we have at present no good right to believe. He is not offering an opinion as to whether that old implication is or is not something we have a right to believe. What he is concerned with is the truth of what is meant by a certain form of words when it is given that meaning which he is now giving it.

However, it is still true that at certain important places in his writing he follows the sort of procedure I have been talking about. Consequently, if one is to read him with an open mind and without prejudice against the sort of procedure which plays a considerable role in his thought, one does well to read him in the light of various occasions when the sort of procedure he follows has brought valuable results. It should also be said that because of this, and because he is concerned with matters related to human happiness, one should read him with a readiness to ask the following questions. Firstly, isn't he here giving these words a meaning very different from any meaning they are normally given? Secondly, what new meaning is it that he is giving these words? Thirdly, is it the case that when these words are given this new meaning they express something true? Lastly, is it the case that when these words are given this new meaning they express a belief with the consoling power of the belief they used to express?

I come now to a passage in which Mr Köllerström describes an experience, a dream, he once had and speaks of its great influence upon his apprehension of things, and thus upon his feelings towards things. I believe that this passage is very important because in it Mr Köllerström, by example rather by precept, combats certain habits of mind which have at times led badly astray both those who have made reply to the question 'Must we agree that all is vanity?' and those who have accepted, rejected, commented upon those replies.

Mr Köllerström had the dream he speaks of within the very few minutes between the time someone with him left the room he was in and the time when he returned and woke him. Of the first part of the dream Mr Köllerström says: 'I dreamed my whole life over again, but backwards, like reading a novel starting with the last chapter and working backwards chapter by chapter.' The experience was one of disturbing frustration. In the second part of his dream he lived a life starting from his position at the time he dreamed and ending in his committing a murder and dying of disease in a condemned cell tormented by guilt. In a third part of his dream he again experienced, 'in full detail' he says, another possible life which started from his age at that time and ended in lonely squalor and suicide. In the last part of his dream he lived a life of success and happiness and love, purged of guilt and bitterness – a life in which his deepest desires were fulfilled.

Speaking of his life after the dream, he says that it took him years to digest the experience, to discover himself and re-grow his being. He also says: 'But everything that is spiritually my own, everything of true worth that I have found for myself, derives from that great dream. Still it enriches and instructs me; without it my life would have been a husk. Though the gifts of the gods may blast or wither us, if we can at last bear them, they will transform us.'

I now remark upon certain features of this passage which I believe deserve careful attention, especially the one I mention last.

Mr Köllerström separates what he says about what his dream was like from what he says about its significance. Usually when a person speaks of an experience he has had, and of its significance, there is no need for him to separate what he says about what his experience was like from what he says about its significance. But sometimes there is need to do so, and sometimes that need is neglected – with unfortunate consequences.

In the first place when a person speaks of an experience he has had, and of its significance, it may be important to note that it may happen that the experience gives him an excellent right to say what he does about what his experience was like without giving his hearers, *or even himself,* any good right to believe what that experience inclined him to believe. If a man in a dream or a vision sees his brother who years ago vanished in the forests of the Amazon, then *unless he knows that on many occasions in the past when he had a vision, it was veridical and seldom or never deceptive,* he has little or no right to believe that his brother is alive in Brazil – or in any other world. Very unfortunately, William James overlooks this point at that very critical juncture in *Varieties of Religious Experience* when he faces the question whether mystical experience gives a warrant for the truth of what the mystic thinks. Dr R.M. Bucke, a mystic quoted by William James and referred to by Professor Stace in *Mysticism and Philosophy,* speaks of an unusual experience he had, without separating how he describes his experience from its significance. He writes:

"All at once, without warning of any kind, I found myself wrapped in a flame-coloured cloud. For an instant I thought of fire, an immense conflagration somewhere close by in that great city; the next, I knew that the fire was within myself. Directly afterward there came upon me a sense of exultation, of immense joyousness accompanied or immediately followed by an intellectual illumination impossible to describe. Among other things, I did not merely come to believe, but I saw that the universe is not composed of dead matter, but is, on the contrary, a living Presence; I became conscious in myself of eternal life. It was not a conviction that I would have eternal life, but a consciousness that I possessed eternal life then; I saw that all men are immortal; that the cosmic order is such that without any peradventure all things work together for the good of each and all; that the foundation principle of the world, of all the worlds, is what we call love, and that the happiness of each and all is in the long run absolutely certain. The vision lasted a few seconds and was gone but the memory of it and the sense of reality of what it taught have remained during the quarter of a century which has since elapsed. I knew that what the vision showed was true. I had attained to a point of view from which I saw that it must be true. That view, that conviction, I may say that consciousness, has never, even during periods of the deepest depression, been lost."*

Dr Bucke does not say why he regards his experience as providing a warrant for these tremendous claims. This is the more remarkable because Dr Bucke was a psychiatrist and had, I suppose, encountered many a person who believed that his experience justified his belief that evil people or evil spirits were trying to harm him or were accusing him of a crime.

In the second place, when a person speaks of an experience he has had, and of its significance, it is important to note that it is possible that the person's words are quite intelligible to himself and to his hearers as an indication of what his experience was like, though they may not be intelligible to them, or even to himself, as an indication of what he takes its significance to have been. For example, if someone says "Yesterday I had a strange experience, I took a certain drug and, soon after, time slowed down and even stopped," it may well be that his words are intelligible to him and to his hearers as an indication of what his experience was like, but they are not intelligible to his hearers, or even himself, as an indication of anything more.

This point has been overlooked by those who have said or come much too near to saying "When people don't understand what a mystic says about an experience he has had, and its significance, it is because they

---

*The quotation is the preliminary version of a passage in Dr R. M. Bucke's *Cosmic Consciousness,* which William James quotes in his *Varieties of Religious Experience* in the chapter entitled 'Mysticism'.

don't know what the mystic's experience was like, so that the mystic is in the position of one who speaks of his love of, or perhaps his 'oneness with' a certain woman, only to find that his hearer has never been in love and has hardly more idea of what that experience is like than has one born deaf of what it is like to hear music." It is not true that *whenever* and *in so far as* a person doesn't understand what a mystic says about what his experience was like, and about its significance, it is because that person doesn't know what that mystic's experience was like.

In the third place, Mr Köllerström in the passage I have quoted does not represent his experience as evidential. He represents it as the harbinger of a new view of things and a truer view of things. But that is a different matter. What has been called "an experiment of imagination" or "an experiment in thought" may, without being more evidential than a picture in the mind or on a screen of, for example, a perfect sphere moving on a windless plane of faultless ice with never-changing velocity, lead a person to formulate a new theory, which then, in the light of evidence later available or in the light of evidence already available, becomes a well-founded, and perhaps a vastly illuminating theory.

But now, in the fourth place, Mr Köllerström, in the passage I have quoted, does not represent his experience as having led him to form a theory, and so does not represent it as having led him to form a theory which he has later found to be true. He does indeed represent his experience as having occasioned a change in him which has not only changed his feelings towards things, but also his apprehension of things. He says of his experience, his dream, not only that without it his life "would have been a husk", but also that it "still instructs him". But he does not attempt to indicate the nature of the instruction, the enlightenment, his experience brought him by formulating one or more propositions and saying that his experience brought these to his mind. Consequently he does not mystify us by speaking of truths which are "ineffable", not merely in the sense that they cannot be expressed in any words at present available, but in the sense (*sic*) that they cannot be expressed in any conceivable words or symbols. No, in his account of his dream and in what he says about its significance in the passage I have quoted, he represents the change in his view of things which his dream initiated as having been *a pervasive and persistent change in his apprehension of individual things as and when he has encountered them in his life.* He thus combats any tendency we may have to think that enlightenment must be a matter of coming to know some truths or truths. He thus reminds us that it again and again happens that an experience or course of experiences quickly or slowly makes a more or less pervasive difference to the light in which a person thereafter sees things when they come before him. Such experience may be a dream or a vision or the reading of a book, perhaps Spinoza's *Ethics* or St John's *Gospel* or Wordsworth's "Intimations of Immortality", or a conversation with a Grand Inquisitor, or a psychoanalytic session, or seeing a child dying of leukaemia.

In practice we know this already. Nevertheless it too often happens that when we need this notion of a change in a man's view of things, which is not a matter of his coming to believe some proposition, but a matter of his coming to see in a different light individual things and happenings, we make no use of it. Too often when the change in a man is of this sort we either describe him as though the change in him were merely a matter of a change in his feelings towards things, or describe him as having come to believe some proposition, or as having come to believe some "ineffable truth". For example, William James in his chapter on conversion in *Varieties of Religious Experience* quotes the words of one who, in describing the change that came over him at his conversion, speaks not only of his new feeling towards things but also of the new way in which he thereafter daily saw everybody about him and even his horses and his hogs. But James neglects this when he writes about the "cognitive aspect" of the change brought about by mystical experience and speaks of the mystic as having come to some tremendous belief which, true or false, is ineffable. And too often mystics themselves talk this way. To take another example, for years I could not understand what Spinoza referred to when he spoke of his third kind of knowledge in spite of the fact that he says plainly enough that it is a knowledge of individual things. It was not until I had read Mr Köllerström's account of his dream and the difference it made to his apprehension thereafter that there occurred to me that surmise as to what Spinoza meant when he spoke of his third kind of knowledge, which I have put (above) into the mouth of an imaginary commentator.

Professor Fingerette in his good book *The Self in Transformation* reminds us that enlightenment need not be a matter of coming to know some truth or truths and begins to indicate how it may be a matter of change in the way in which a person sees things as an when they come before him. But more needs to be said about this. Here I make only a few remarks about the relation between this sort of change in a person's apprehension of things and enlightenment, and the relation between enlightenment and happiness.

When a person comes to be one who sees certain things, perhaps very many things, differently, the change is not always in the direction of seeing things more as they are. It may be. But it may be in the direction of seeing things less as they are, or partly in the one direction and partly in the other.* For example, after a certain experience a man may come to see a certain person, or almost everyone he meets, with appropriate suspicion. In such a case we do not, of course, speak of enlightenment any more than we do when someone comes to believe what is not true.

---

*Freud, *Collected Papers*, vol. II, XIX.

As we know, it is not true that change brings happiness to a man whenever he ceases to believe what is false, or comes to believe what is true, or comes to be one who sees things more as they are. A "truer" light is not always a happier light. On the contrary, enlightenment may bring a man nearer to despair than he has ever been.

This leaves it still conceivable that there is for everyone a point on a road of enlightenment which is a "point of salvation" in the sense that, if he reaches it, then he will have a new happiness, and no further step on the road of enlightenment will take that happiness from him. To put the same point in another way: the fact that increased knowledge and increased power to see things as they are may sadden a man, and even make him sadder than he ever was before, leaves it still conceivable that the nature of reality, including the nature of human beings, is such that if a man goes far enough in the direction of knowing what is so and seeing things as they are, he will see things with a happiness which is greater than any he has had before and so based on seeing things as they are that no further enlightenment will take it from him.

Many people have believed that this tremendous proposition about the universe and its relation to human happiness is in fact true. They have seldom formulated it but they have said what makes it plain that they believe it. Some have been led to believe it by a mystical experience. Some have believed it on the ground that the universe was made by a God who cares for us, or on some other religious ground. A few, for example, Spinoza and MacTaggart, have thought they could prove it by philosophical argument.

On the other hand those who have said that all is vanity appear confident that, on the contrary, if and in so far as a man sees reality for what it is he will see it sadly. Bertrand Russell in *A Freeman's Worship* does not say that all is vanity, but he is confident that science gives us very good reason to believe that "all the labours of the ages, all devotion, all the inspiration, all the noonday brightness of human genius, are destined to extinction in the vast death of the solar system."

Mr Köllerström does not here make any of these tremendous assertions about the universe and its relation to human desires. Scawen Blunt in the poem which begins with the words "He who has once been happy is for aye out of destruction's reach . . . Time is his conquest. Life, if it should fret, has paid him tribute. He can bear to die," reminds us that a person who has "once been happy" may then be one who, whether or no death is the end of him, now will never say "All is vanity." Mr Köllerström is not only reminding us of this. He is somewhat like a man who says to a friend "I used to dislike Jack. But now I know him better and see with greater understanding the things he does. I think that you too would like him if you knew him better." In these essays in which he speaks of those who have influenced him and of his own experience and his own thinking, he is indicating in outline a road which has brought him from an uneasy loneliness, through a depression near despair, to a happiness which, though there is still sadness in it, is a wide, deep happiness.

He believes that the road he has travelled has been like that he travelled in his dream, not only in that it has led him out of despair into a wide happiness, but also in that it has led him from a place in which he saw things in a light that distorted things, to a place where he sees things in a light which, imperfect still, is yet a light in which he sees things more as they are.

He hopes that by indicating the road he has travelled, he has done something which will help some others to come to see things in a happier light, which is also a truer light.

John Wisdom,
Trinity College, Cambridge
(written at Eugene, Oregon, 1973)

Part one

PREDISPOSITION

1

GRODDECK:
FIRST ENCOUNTER AND THE BACKGROUND
OF IT ALL

There was a loud, banging knock on my door, and simultaneously the door burst open. A split second after his tumultuous entry, Groddeck turned, and stood: immense, he filled the end of the room, lowering, with the whites of his eyes somehow much in evidence. It was not for nothing that he thought of himself as a troll. But before one could quail, he was with one, and with quiet informality had shaken hands, and was listening — for as by some inevitability, one at once opened one's heart to him. Whatever it was that had happened as he first managed to effect his entry was obliterated by his unaffected dignity and sincerity, by the overwhelming effect of his presence, Yet though indeed obliterated at the time, it had had its immediate effect of one, and the impression later became available to memory. In that split second before he had towered to survey one from the door, it had seemed almost as though he were about to glance back over his shoulder, and perhaps to bolt. Was he a hunted creature, or, as he had seemed an instant later, an immense, dark force. Years later he told me he had realised that his manner of seizing a door handle betrayed anxiety. Later, too, I realised he knew he sometimes seemed immense, and seemed to radiate a power. As we now sat talking he looked quite ordinary in size; he said nothing, but he listened with utmost gravity. I knew that he knew I could never deceive him nor withhold anything.

But I was there to learn and experience psychoanalysis, and for Groddeck there was no analysis without message — a brief but agonising form of nerve message. (Though I know it was later that he first massaged me, the memory of it telescopes into that of my first session with him.) For this Groddeck screwed an ancient, brass-bound monocle into his eye; and as he concentrated his gaze, his face creased into a score of wrinkles surrounding, and radiating from, his eye. His eyebrows swivelled to reach from the root of his nose to the upper limits of his forehead. I never saw such mobile brows. All his expressions engulfed every bit of his face and being. In a puckish sort of way, he now looked ferocious, as he set his jaw, breathed in a rather guttural way, and then went at one. He suddenly seemed like a small boy attacking his mud pie. One writhed and screamed with laughter, not merely because one could not contain oneself, but also because the very spirit of fun seemed to have taken over. We were a couple of children playing doctor and patient, and one understood how Groddeck's father had seen the boy's gift for medicine in the latter's childish games with his sister and her doll. Groddeck once remarked to me that patients revealed themselves when massaged. Certainly one "came off it", and he himself dissolved: I had made some sort of crack, and his whole laughing face seemed furrowed with horizontal fissures. But the moment it was finished he closed up, and abruptly took his leave. With very visible reluctance he turned back to consider a question I suddenly produced. But then, quietly, unhurried, and as uninvolved as though a mere witness of himself giving utterance, he gave me the counsel of a sage: and his face was expressionless.

Forever with me are the giant troll who towered at my door, the merry child who play-massaged me, and the wise eyes of the counsellor.

Any who would plumb the soul of Western man, or blaze his path out beyond himself, and any who would start again to build the everlasting City, must all alike begin with Groddeck. First he plumbed the same depths as Freud: he had a system of analysis before he had even heard of Freud; and Freud acknowledges his indebtedness to Groddeck's writings on the It for the Freudian notion of the Id, but fails to acknowledge the theory of the super ego as equally present in Groddeck's It, just as he fails to acknowledge the It as the source of his ill-conceived death instinct. Further Groddeck avoids Freud's terminology – felt by some to be monstrous – and avoids too, nearly all the associated theories that have led scientists to condemn psychoanalysis as superstition. Instead Groddeck wrote it all in the language in which it happened in the psyche, the language, almost, of a child, or at least the language in which you and I experience and think about our problems. It is, too, in such words that it will live on, as literature; and it will begin that immortality for us here as soon as we have felt able to afford to stomach our prudery; for it is stronger meat than Freud and than the writings of Freud's followers. (Not, of course, that I would belittle Freud. He took the lead, for he made the great public stand, became the acknowledged mouthpiece of the unconscious; and worked through every analytical theory to its ultimates; moreover his great book on dream interpretation gives him a unique position, which alone would establish him.)

Our second reason for taking Groddeck as our starting point is seen in the kindly spirit of personal understanding shown to his patients, which was never vitiated by regarding them through diagnostic spectacles.

Because he did not think in the terms of psychoanalysis, and very minimally in its theories, his patients always remained people to him before they were patients. If that does not seem a very great distinction to the reader, it must be pointed out that nearly all the complaints one has heard against doctors, especially since the introduction of National Health, are traceable to such 'objectivity' on the part of the doctors. Even when Groddeck did admit that a patient was neurotic, he would often point out that the neurotic condition existed for only small parts of the day or in certain situations, or phases — for otherwise the fellow would hardly be able to carry on his life. Further, he would add that we are all neurotic sometimes. But this was only one way in which he avoided judgement of others, including his patients. Moreover, what I have said is only the beginning, in the sense that it describes merely one of the crimes against the patient that he avoided committing, and therefore represents a negative virtue in him. On the plus side, we find his great reverence, not merely in the face of external nature, but also for human nature. His entire therapeutic endeavour was to re-discover anything of that that had been lost to the patient; for the natural in man was sacred. This did not mean that he condemned the rest: although he pointed out that the one psychic element present in all neurosis was the ego, and that therefore it was the ego that must always be the object of the treatment, he yet emphasised that, without the ego, we could not be human. Essentially, therefore, his attitude to people's neuroses was kindly, not to say indulgent. He was apt to feel towards the ego and its problems as a kindly parent toward childish pranks. There were no rules in his sanatorium; as he explained to me, he wanted people to do as they liked, for how otherwise would they be themselves?

Given such benignity and reverence, and given too that he was a poet, was he not bound to discover the Gospel story as the essential shape of every biography, to find and venerate Christ in all into whom he looked deeply? Alas! Judas too was there to be discovered. And so too Peter, who portrayed the tragedy of the good man: Peter whose attempted goodness, his pledged loyalty, was fated ere the cock. The heart of man is rich with all these — and, of course, Oedipus too.

But all these contraries were to be discovered in the same person. How could this have been possible without considerable empathy? Indeed the great warmth of his heart was apparent to all about him, and his patients became his friends. He was utterly removed from the image of the psychiatrist as a coldly detached and purely scientific observer. Actually he took a keen delight in shooting to pieces the 'science' of these wiseacres, and was never happier than in poking fun at their pomposity.

And this brings me to an anecdote that may, at first, seem an irrelevance. Groddeck hated new clothes, and not only that, he loved the most awful old rags. For many years he had the most horrible old suit, a truly dreadful-looking garb, which he insisted on wearing day in and day out, whatever the occasion. At last, however, his poor wife managed to get hold of it, and threw it away. But the wretched Groddeck somehow got it back, and with many a chuckle, reappeared in it as though it had never been lost to him. Here surely, we see the child in him, the boy! And this is the clue to his genius: his whole being was childlike. (This does not mean that he was soft or weak: a rebel from the first, he was as tough as a rebel who survives has to be.) The core of psychoanalysis is its elucidation of all that takes place in the child's mind before memory begins; and one in whom the child is still alive and awake has the best understanding of this.

But such insight is not the only gift to us of the child within. Every Christian will recall Christ's words on the need to become childlike if we would enter the Kingdom.

However, it would be incorrect to describe Groddeck as religious, or as subject to the 'oceanic' feelings of such people; and it would be dangerous to characterise some of his inspired writing about nature as nature mysticism; this would at once be attacked by psychiatrists. As all the world now knows, certain drugs produce visionary states of consciousness comparable to some of those experienced by schizophrenics. But even something like the mystic's consciousness may be thus induced. It has been suggested that the drugs inhibit areas of the brain which normally shut out such experiences or perceptions. Because the schizophrenic and the addict are sometimes open to experiences momentarily like those of the mystic, regardless of all those who are in no way like the mystics, and regardless too of the totally different lives of the afflicted from the lives of the mystics, psychiatrists have been happy to condemn mystics as suffering from pathological conditions. Even the greatest, St Paul, Moses and indeed Christ Himself, have been formally arraigned and pronounced on in the literature of psychiatry, and would accordingly have been certified if they had lived today, and had come into the power of these writers. This is no place to go into the question of the psychiatrist's mind, and in any case it must be obvious that many psychiatrists would disagree with this attitude. The apparent intent of some psychiatrists to outlaw casts of mind other than their own, and their potent, legal means of doing so, makes them uncomfortable-looking figures in our midst, even though we may greatly value psychiatric ministrations. However, all sensitive people have experienced something of the mystic's vision in contacts with nature. In his *The World of Man,** Groddeck writes of it:

> "Every man without exception is made to learn at some time that he is but the creature and instrument of nature, and if he forgets his lesson life itself will soon remind him of it. He will realise that his

---

*Page 47.

heart is beating without reference to his wishes, that his lungs expand and contract in obedience to natural law, not to that pitiful thing he calls his will. Sleep will subdue him, even though he may be the ruler over empires: hunger and thirst reduce the mighty as easily as men of low degree. To every one comes the hour when he is made to feel his utter helplessness, and it is from this feeling that all religions and superstitions have arisen, all temples and churches, all reverence for a Power above mankind, even God Himself. At the root of man's feeling and thinking, of all his creations and inventions, lies the hidden knowledge of his own frailty, and that anxious fear which is so fruitful of design.

"As deeply buried is the other source of his vitality and power, the consciousness that he is at one with nature, neither her slave nor her instrument, but absorbed in her, indissolubly united, powerful even as she is, divine, eternal. Think back over your own life. There have been moments when you felt a peace as calm and clear as the blue of the sky; moments when all that was about and within you was in accord, when you could for once believe you heard the music of the spheres. Such moments come in every life, and that is why we think of childhood as a paradise since little children still feel the world as one with themselves, and a dog, a rag doll, even a street-gutter, can seem to them a living friend, just as real and human as mother or playmate. This unquestioning unity with life comes again later: to woman, when she greets her newborn child with that strange smile one never sees but then; to man, when he forces deed or thought to his will, when he wins his wife or masters a spirited horse. Few people realise, however, the meaning of that utter calm which transcends both joys and pain, which does not shrink from death and is as indifferent to gold as to love, that opening of a heaven without fear and without desire. It is no other than a union with Infinite Nature, a being at one with the creative universe, a surrender and dissolution of the barriers of personality so that the part, the ego, becomes merged with the whole.

"And as one looks back over the years it comes upon one suddenly that these moments have not been so rare, after all, though truly they yield neither to demand nor entreaty, nor are they to be bought; they cannot even be ensured by the presence of those whom we desire or love. They steal upon us silently, unawares, it may be in the twilight, or with the cheep of sleepy birds at dawn, or sometimes as we lie among the wild flowers in a meadow with the grasshoppers springing all around, while in the silence of noonday heat the world begins to hum with life. Or again, we are transported as we stand before a birch tree showing its early green in a bare wood where hoar-frost lies thick on the branches, or by a window on which we see the delicate tracery of ice-pictures and fern-fronds. Or it may be merely a strange child's shout of joy, a girl's carriage or a man's strength, people we never saw before and shall certainly never see again. Or the sea! We look at it every day for weeks and months on end, we sail over it, admire it, rejoice in it, but do not know it; then suddenly we realise for a second only yes, that is the sea! Hail, friend! The sea drowns all our arrogance, and gives us peace. Out of its waters rose beauty, and the beating of its waves can be heard throughout the great epic of humanity, the Odyssey.

"Living again through these moments, we mournfully shake our heads. Life is so rich, but we did not know it; so beautiful, yet we showed it no reverence. Why, oh, why were we so blind? With hearts full of yearning we hasten to take up our lives once more and share with others the wealth and joy that Infinite Nature can bestow."

For all this the mind needs no tutoring, and Groddeck shows how naturally we thus start on the mystic's way. He would not have wished to take us further. But I believe him: in his last and, some have felt, his supreme pronouncement, *Seeing Without Eyes,* he spoke of ecstasy, in which space-time did not exist. Once set on a path towards that, there are many who would follow through and up to the peaks, but for their fidelity to the open mind of the twentieth century, and for their fear that mysticism is inimical to it.

What I seek is to show a way of experience rather than to present a case. It is possible to think of eternity in a new way, and thereby to liberate the mind to actual experience. A way is open to modern man, a way that does not involve the jettisoning of his hard-won freedoms of the mind. In spite of the levelling of our prosaic realism, and in spite of the destructiveness of such as the critics, the peaks still beckon the ardent spirit.

2

GRODDECK:
HIS CLINICAL AND THERAPEUTIC
WORK

I should like to begin by affirming that I regard Freud as the presiding genius of our epoch. This is a view which I am sure was also Groddeck's.

Groddeck demands a special manner of presentation, because, in his passionate loyalty to Freud, he sought to bury what was uniquely his own; and sometimes we can glean this only from what we may descry between the lines, or from his implications. To focus on these, and also to provide suitable extracts for any who may not be familiar with Groddeck's writings, I have chosen examples so simple and well known as to be beyond dispute. I hope thus to avoid red herrings. Also, since we are quite often involved in bringing out some individual version of Groddeck's of a well-known analytical doctrine, I have throughout been as explicit as if presenting the matter to beginners – to show that nothing individual to Groddeck is intended. I trust these procedures will not prove frustrating to the majority of my readers, who are probably thoroughly familiar with Groddeck's works. I must hope for their forgiveness for having often stated the obvious. At least I feel that what I say can neither be proved nor disproved. My hope, of course, is that it may be recognised as a portrayal of Groddeck.

Not long since I heard from a former patient of Groddeck's, now a very old lady, that she was ill with what was said to be a serious heart condition and that nobody seemed able to help. In response to a comment by me, in her next letter she wrote, 'No, what I need is to have Groddeck confront me with his question, Why are you ill?' In a third letter, she seemed to feel that the thought of his question to her had started something; and it was not long before a fourth letter told of her almost complete recovery. His old magic seemed to have echoed up the years.

There flash to mind stories of his 'miracle' cures, for which he was so widely famed. There are also the many references to his remarkable personality as the sole and sufficient explanation of his fame. I do not think these were merely the voices of envy, nor of incredulity: people needed to explain away his impact on them. It is well known that a London analyst — the late Dr Michael Balint — who 'remembered' Groddeck as getting on for a foot taller than he actually was, and who then wrote assigning Groddeck his 'correct' — and of course, lowly — degree of greatness, by measuring him against Freud. Groddeck thought that a doctor's mere presence could be healing: certainly he himself only had to be there to get under one's skin: and to those who had come seeking what he had to offer, the experience was a therapy, or, as Keyserling implied, an illumination. 'Charismatic' is a term that has been used to describe his appearance. I recall with special clarity the emphatic use of this adjective by the late Dr Winnicott, of blessed memory.

But merely by references to his personality, and even by characterisations of it, we do not give an actual account of the part it played in his work. And with such widespread acknowledgement of the magnitude of this effect, we clearly require the appropriate insights. Actually he is a superb example of the fulfilment of personality through dedication to vocation: with Groddeck at least, neither can be conceived without the other.

In any case, it would be inappropriate to concentrate on this discussion of mere personality in the case of Groddeck, for as he avowed, the word was to him as a red rag to a bull. Its cult was our great falsification.

Groddeck's father had greatness in his character, and its spell captivated his son, the young Groddeck. He was himself a doctor, and he offered his son the chance to be a doctor too. Thus the father created a hero-worshipper out of his son, who followed first himself, then Schweninger (Bismarck's doctor, and Bismarck's only master), and finally Freud. But it was his father who was his true model, and from whom he acquired a primary trait, his scepticism. It was this that enabled him to contend with a practice built of patients who were generally regarded as incurable. Soon after I had met him, he told me about a child who had been brought to him with a penny stuck in its throat. Another doctor had already tried to fish the penny up, but had only succeeded in making the child's throat very sore. So Groddeck pushed the penny down. That, he told me, illustrated the basis of his practice. His scepticism of all orthodox medicine drove his mind to seek new ways of treatment — whence the appeal of Schweninger's procedure, a form of 'natural' therapy. There was, however, another determinant at work here, a profound feeling for nature that was made meaningful by Goethe's illuminating term *Gottnatur.*

But his scepticism drove him still further afield. His thesis for his M.D. was devoted to proving the ineffectiveness of a popular drug for the treatment of skin diseases, and to demonstrating that the real therapeutic factor was the personal influence of the doctor on the patient. Already we see the budding psychotherapist.

Freud acknowledges Groddeck as the source of the theory of the It, which has been dubbed by English Freudians the 'Id'. But in his borrowing, Freud denatured the It; he made it a 'seething cauldron of excitement', impersonal, and as humourless as the unconscious itself. Groddeck's It was actually 'impish', and like all imps, was dual, ambivalent: over against the seething excitement, were the It's warning and disciplining tendencies. The essentials of what Freud later separated out and built up into the structure of the super ego were there already present in Groddeck's It, a simple concept which thus had great advantages from the point of view of the economy of the hypothesis. (No anti-Freudian bias is suggested. Groddeck was always the first to acclaim Freud, and agreed that his theoretical dispositions were necessary to his outlook.)

The term itself Groddeck acknowledges as coming from Nietzsche; but the idea originated in certain linguistic considerations of Groddeck's. Groddeck put it to me: "Sometimes we say, I have an attack of 'flu; at other times, I caught the 'flu; sometimes, that is to say, we speak in 'It' language, and sometimes in 'I' language". A child will speak of itself as Tommy, or as me; and we have all heard tell of the black man's, 'Give it (me) 'baccy boss.' The adult 'I' may be found striving towards some glorious goal, but is also as theatrical as the Pharisee; whereas the primitive self is determined by nature — it is natural, and is to itself, and to others, as to natural objects. Is there, in point of fact, any such entity as the 'I', anything separate from the whole? Is this conceivable? But

> "if this idea is false, then the word must have some other significance than the one usually accepted, and behind the word must lie hidden something which is powerful enough to allow us to think wrongly, without disturbing the course of events thereby. One may well believe that this mysterious power, this something, this 'It', has invented the word and the idea of 'I', that it pursues and attains definite ends by this means, that it blinds man, and gives him an Ego-feeling without which he cannot *be* man".*

A page or two later Groddeck points out that "the Ego is something cultural, thought out, not native". He shows how the It uses its invention, the 'I', to enable us to feel responsibility, and so to ascribe merit and guilt to our lives. Though he thinks this state of affairs so necessary that "it would be wicked to attempt to abolish it" he yet feels that "this sense of responsibility is an almost insuperable obstacle to an unprejudiced

---

*Groddeck, *The Unknown Self,* p. 37.

contemplation of human life".* For a moment he thinks it would be well if occasionally, we could put aside the idea of 'I', perhaps to put in its place 'the universe', or 'nature', or simplest of all, 'God'. Yet he thinks

> "such an attempt would not be successful; as men we can only think as men. The best thing we can do is to imitate what is done by life through the invention of the word 'I', and to consider the individual person apart from the universe, only this time with the conscious knowledge that we are thereby intentionally distorting the world-picture, and then give this individual thing the most indefinite and flexible name possible, a signification which should make clear from the start that every attempt at definition must come to grief. For this purpose, I have for many years been using the word 'It', and instead of the sentence 'I live', I have trained myself to think 'I am lived by the It' ".**

The attitude implied in the formulation "I am lived by the It" became the kernel of Groddeck's philosophy, and underlay all his psychoanalytical science. Throughout the pages of this book, I use the term 'egotism' to mean the denial, or opposite, of this essence of Groddeck's thought. There is, however, a difficulty about this term in that whereas the Freudians conceive the ego (later reinforced by the super ego) as the function that modifies and canalises the Id drives or instincts, the dictionary meaning of egotism is selfishness and self-conceit. His proposed usage, he asserts, is merely a matter of expedience, in order to facilitate a different way of thought. It was a way that furthered his therapeutic goal, which was "to make conscious the unconscious complexes of the 'I' — from which we may realise that he anticipated the more recent 'ego psychology'. 'I' "*** from which we may realise that he anticipated the more recent 'ego psychology'.

Of the Ego he says that "it is a mask used by the It to hide itself from the curiosity of mankind".**** And here at once he implies what is perhaps his primary dichotomy, between appearance and reality. Since Plato, philosophers have been vainly telling us that the world of the senses is unreal. Nobody really took them very seriously, until our modern scientists transmogrified our solid world into a rarefied world of atoms, and even — infinitely more rarefied — electrons. In our day, physicists, chemists and biologists each in their different ways, seem to present the reality of the universe as something so utterly different from, as to be almost unrelated to, its appearance; and with remarkable docility, most people seem to believe this in a general sort of way. That is to say, they believe it about everything in the world about them; but they are furious,

---

*The Unknown Self, pp. 38-9.   *** The Book of the It, p. 282.
**Ibid., p. 39.   ****The Unknown Self, p. 42.

as Freud so painfully discovered, if it is suggested that the same principle should apply to themselves — that there is a strange reality underlying the plausible 'I'. The It is Groddeck's name for this reality underlying the 'I'. His many attempts to study the It led him to the realisation that the reality is in itself unknowable, that we know it only via its effects, by its meaningful expressions. "We are fond of talking about the reality of some things, the unreality of others. Obviously the 'real' exists but never for one moment can we come into contact with it. Our organisms have their own limitations, and moreover they make a selection in the impressions they allow to become conscious. The It changes the unknown Real and produces for us the Actual, the workable. What we apprehend is not what may really be there, but what we can make of it, and this actual world is lost to us if we attempt to grasp Reality."*

Obviously Groddeck was dubious of our ordinary ego values, indeed of the importance of the ego, particularly when cultivated as personality; he seeks to revert to something simpler, more primitive. It is plain that he had no thought of creating any theoretical structure of the psyche, nor an associated terminology. He wrote in good plain German, and sought to avoid definitions, norm names, and this not only in the promulgation of his own ideas. He opposed the new terminology then being introduced into psychoanalysis, saying it would fix our ideas prematurely and impede research. Further, he felt that diagnostic names could not only impede therapy but actually poison the patient. Thus, of someone described as hysterical, he exclaimed: "That's a falsifying term that inevitably makes people feel the trouble is due to the womb (Greek, *hustera,* womb) which is quite innocent. Besides, at most, she is neurotic only for periods; and we all have some such moments." (Nowadays, existential psychotherapists have discovered this anew.) The term It itself, let us recall, is acceptable to him because it is so indefinite as to be beyond definition. We might perhaps regard the term as little more than a *façon de parler*; and we should be right in the sense that Groddeck at no point thought of the It as having an existence apart from that of our life itself. Certainly it is a linguistic device affording us a new and simpler — or at least less pretentious — view of ourselves, less determined and inhibited by rigid views of social norms, and warranting more forthright self-expression.

Groddeck's first insight into the working of the It came to him through accustoming himself to accepting the curious demands and roundabout expressions of a certain patient.** Various quite ordinary articles had to be banished from the sick-room, and the patient would not tolerate certain movements, such as plucking at the lip, or playing with the chair tassle. "Her vocabulary was extremely limited, and she used circumlocutions for

---

The World of Man, p. 91.
**The account that follows has been slightly curtailed.

quite ordinary objects; she would refer to the wardrobe as the thing for the clothes, or the stove pipe as the arrangement for the smoke, and so on. Certain objects were thus intolerable, and the real names of others unmentionable because they are symbols representing situations or actions charged with overwhelming or horrific emotion." Groddeck gradually realised "that human thought and action are the inevitable consequence of unconscious symbolisation, that mankind is animated by the symbol."*

Shortly after my first long stay with Groddeck, he produced an article that was published in the *International Journal* in 1926, under the title 'Dreamwork and the Work of Organic Symptoms'. He compared the relationship between the manifest content of a dream, and its latent contact (the dream's significance, or the 'message' obtained by interpreting it) with the relationship between symptoms and their underlying reality in the pysche: "the symptom is not the event itself, but only that which occurs simultaneously with the event. In the organic event there are relationships between the manifest symptom and the latent processes." The parallel goes further, for just as in dreams we encounter symbols, so also in the manifestation of the underlying reality in the symptom: thus for example, the heat of fever will symbolise hot emotions. As with dreams, so throughout the whole range of the human organism's activities, including even its production of the symptoms of organic disease, we are concerned with problems in language. Alfred Adler in coining his term 'organ jargon' acknowledged this principle in the sphere of the organic, but did not, like Groddeck, press forward to the treatment of organic disease by psychotherapy. At this point a case history will perhaps clarify much of what I have been saying** The patient suffered from athritis deformens.

> "Fingers, hands, and elbows could hardly be moved, so that she had to be fed; the thighs could be moved only slightly apart, and both legs were perfectly stiff; she could not turn nor bend her head, one could not get a finger between her teeth, and she was unable to raise her arms above shoulder level. She said with wry humour, that if the Kaiser came riding by, she could not wave to him and call Hurrah! as she had done as a child. As a result of treatment by psychoanalysis, the patient was able to walk again, to feed herself, to dig in her garden, go upstairs and bend her legs, turn and bend her head as she wished, and spread out her legs as far as she liked; if the Kaiser was actually to come by, she could raise her arm and shout Hurrah! She still walks, however, with her buttocks pushed out behind, as though she wanted them smacked."***

The whole thing came about, says Groddeck, because her father was called Friedrich Wilhelm, and because she had been told jokingly that she was

---

*The Book of the It, p. 58.
**Here again I have somewhat curtailed a case history.
***The Book of the It, pp. 157-8.

not her mother's child but was found behind a hedge. Groddeck goes on to give an account of 'the family romance', the fantasy that one is nobly born, and stolen away to be given to the people who are nominally one's parents. In the case of this patient, there was the fantasy that she was the child of Kaiser Wilhelm, a boy child she thought, and therefore true heir to the throne. She had been stolen away, castrated, and hidden behind a hedge, with the sole sign of her position being her name, Augusta, the lofty one. All this fantasy was created before the child was four years old. In her fantasy she was more father than the father, a rightful Kaiser in fact. "The wearer of a crown looks neither to right nor left, he judges without side glances, he bows his head before no earthly power. She carried her head firmly to hold a crown. Her jaws were tight closed so that she could not shout Hurrah! as she had once done when, in her childhood, the usurper had passed. Her shoulders were to be lamed so that never again with upraised arm could she do homage to that false Kaiser. Her legs were stiffened so that never again should she, a mighty Kaiser, kneel before anyone. Her thighs had to be held tight together so that no man could ever lie between them, thereby proving that she had been robbed of her native maleness. She had to hold herself with the lower part of the body drawn backward so that no man might ever find the entrance. And she had all the time to prove to herself that perhaps some day her manhood could come back. With all her limbs she had to prove it was possible to make lax members stiff; in symbol she was male."* It will be clear that the symptoms of arthritis were viewed as language; indeed they were cured by treating them as the mere external manifestation of a childish fantasy and its associated emotions; the symptoms were frozen gestures as meaningful as any gesturing. The case is of value in that it illustrates a further vital point, namely that the reality, the essence of the human being, has little to do with the approved values of our adult world. The ego, with all its adult self-importance, is show, and for show; the reality, the It, is an unself-conscious child. To Groddeck the reality in man's heart is the child in him. All illness is, in some sort, an attempt to return to childhood; and "the task of the physician is to teach the man to be childlike without being childish".

His manner of setting about this may be indicated by the following examples of some of his technical procedures. To a patient who told him that, after struggling with insomnia half the night, he finally had to get up and take a sleeping pill, Groddeck retorted, 'Why did you have to go to the trouble of being sleepless half the night purely to have an excuse for taking the pill?' In the same vein, and re-phrasing his question a hundred ways to fit the case, Groddeck would again and again ask what purpose could this symptom serve. If the patient could put words to his

---

*The Book of the It, p. 160.

purpose, he was better. Nevertheless psychiatrists often object that symptoms that are caused by emotional conditions cannot be got at by conscious influence. Doubtless many such have proved themselves right by trying it; some may even have asked one or two of Groddeck's actual questions, and getting no results, feel they have proved him wrong. Of course we must agree with them: a literalistic use of his verbal formulae today might sometimes be as inappropriate as one finds yesterday's colloquialisms. Besides – as is generally recognised – the unconscious is as elusive as a trout in a well-fished stream.

But there is a further and decisive consideration here that I can best present by the following story. I once knew a very learned psychologist, whose manner proclaimed him a mass of learning – and perhaps little else besides – who started asking small children the question, What do you think about God? or some such form of words. After a bit he laid off, because even he could see that he was not getting much forrader. A young girl who loved playing with children was rather amused by it all, and started asking the children the same question in her own way – with most interesting results. Groddeck lived by his principle: he had long schooled himself to look at things through the eyes of a child, and had become truly childlike; the personality that he presented to his royal patients was exactly what he presented to others, and it was the same Groddeck as with children.

He spoke direct to the child in man, of those matters that concern the child, and in the language of the child. At the outset, as soon as he had realised the significance to us of the child, he took steps to view the world from the child's point of view. For example, he once went down on hands and knees, and came up with the realisation that the child often had its head at the level of adults' genitals, where from some of its reactions, he concluded – in its unconscious at least – that it had an animal awareness of smells and their significance. There were other ways too, by which he sought to capture the child's world. Profiting by his many insights, he quickly developed the child's forthrightness; he spoke his mind. But if one thus draws a bow at a venture one may be wrong, and there is sure to be someone who will enjoy checking the forthright spirit by proving one wrong. If one is a man, it will not uncommonly be a woman – a professional of some sort – who does it to one, proving the sexual motivation. (Not that I decry professional women: on the contrary, although they have a particular problem in the present world, many of them have a special fascination.)

Groddeck was sometimes wrong, though rarely. His worst error, which was activated by misapprehension, was that he had once written attacking Freud. Yet he never abandoned his forthrightness, nor any recaptured attribute of the child. It was the child in him, and his freedom from jargon, that made for his therapeutic success: he thought in the same terms as those in which the patient experienced his condition. This is a key to his technique. On all fours with the child in his patient, he talked its own language with it. Lived by his own It, without intermediary, he moved his patient's It.

Direct and childlike, he was really happier lecturing to workmen about the It — which he regularly did — than to learned societies. The extent to which he took the whole problem of illness or health as based on a child's evaluations, is illustrated by two routine questions that were asked of any patient who got worse while under his treatment: What have I done against you? or, What have you done against me?

He had a number of such set procedures which together constituted an important aspect of the form of psychoanalysis that he had developed before he learned Freud's technique. By such means he often succeeded in springing the relevant material into awareness. Because of these dynamic pro- cedures — and because also of his personality, and of the new 'philosophy' of life he brought them, "People have described him as a physician who burst like a storm into the souls of men, penetrating into the depths where all life is one, all boundaries are broken down, and body and mind are fused together. There as a true creator in the dark realm of the It, he shaped new life and new Forms."* But though of very great therapeutic value, Groddeck's activist procedures did not by any means comprise the entirety of his method: they were one of the languages in which he might approach patients. Primarily he was the understanding listener who knew how, with the minimum of encouragement, to elicit just what the patient most needed to avow. He did not think he could or should try to reduce it all to prime elements. Indeed a vital clue to his procedure is found in a remark he made to me: 'The name "psychoanalysis" gives a wrong impression; it is not like chemical analysis.' This remark was partly an example of his reiterated confession of our ignorance, of the inadequacy of reason as a means of penetrating life's mysteries, and, therefore, of the patchwork nature of our science. Here he did not feel himself to be on the side of the adults. It was not a case of the analyst restraining himself from asserting a conviction of his own superior knowledge, but of Groddeck's sense of mental humility before the mystery of another's self. He was the would-be learner, whose patience invited the relevant confidence. Graf Hermann Keyserling wrote of him as "one of the most remarkable men I have ever met. He is indeed the only man I have known who continually reminded me of Lao Tse; his non-action had just the same magical effect. He took the view that the doctor really knows nothing, and of himself can do nothing, that he should therefore interfere as little as possible, for his very presence can provoke to action the patient's own powers of

*Dr Boss, in the posthumous preface to Groddeck's *The World of Man*.

healing."* As an analyst I would say it was this seemingly passive part of his work that was hardest to learn.

In Groddeck it was part of his total attitude, one which he took to such a point that he would commonly avoid correcting even gross mistakes in others. This tendency was all of a piece with his exceptional power of communication: it appeared as evidence of an understanding that was obviously content to accept a man as he was. He positively radiated this acceptance, as by some form of telepathic force, which proclaimed how deeply felt it was. His absolute scepticism regarding norms amounted almost to a reverence for individuality. Completely individual himself, alike in his very being and in all his ways, he was an exemplar of his own medicine, of what he cured his patients by: he released them into being more themselves. However, before I get too remote from the activist aspect of his technique, I will describe a case that illustrates this well.

The patient was a woman whom he cured in a short talk of an inconsolable grief that had possessed her since the death of her child years before. Seeing her depression, Groddeck at once said to her, "You must have wished the child dead," a statement which she hotly denied. He cut her short and commanded, "Mention a date at random," which she did. He than said, "Mention a place-name at random," which also she did, the name of a fashionable resort. Groddeck then asked her, "What happened in that place on that date?" This question she replied to with negatives, but then went pale and fainted. On coming round she told him the following story. "You were right," she said, "I was at that resort on that date before my child died. He was with me, but my husband was at home. I met a fellow guest there, a man with whom I fell in love. Sitting on the balcony of my hotel, on the date I gave you, I was thinking of my lover, when I looked up and saw my small boy on the balcony balustrade. Before rushing to save him, I had the infamous thought, if he falls, he will die; then I could be free of this marriage and go off with my new lover." That was all the treatment she had.

In this last case we saw the It punishing, but there is also its warning function. A person about to take what he feels to be a wrong step may have some minor accident; in some cases it can be that he will catch his foot — so literal is the It at times. If he ignores the warning, he may get a second more serious warning, and then, if he still persists in this course, he may receive an injury that will prevent him fulfilling his design.

To show that I speak of what is familiar, I will recall, but will not describe, the case of a woman who wished her sister dead, and got a paralysed arm so that she could not stab her.

We have had examples of trouble with three of the four sectors of the human individuum as it is portrayed by Groddeck. The one I have just

---

*Preface to *The World of Man*.

described is that of a woman whose problem was conscience, an ego function. The first case I mentioned, the one from which Groddeck learned the nature of symbols, and our unconscious use of them — the case of the woman who had such clumsy circumlocutions — was that of a person whose problem was with the child in herself: this child within — her It — had overwhelmed her adult faculties. The case of the woman who could not raise her arm to say Hurrah! to the Kaiser was of a woman who from childhood had had a fantasy of being male. Finally, an example of a man who found himself, and became creative through realising the female in himself, was Groddeck himself. Groddeck cured himself of a large wen on his neck by understanding it as a displaced pregnancy: In the period before he wrote a book, his stomach would enlarge, to get thinner again as he brought forth his literary creation. What made it possible for the woman with the circumlocutions to trust him was an admission of, and an expression of, his own female nature, which she elicited from him by treating him as a mother. The child in her conquered the fierce father doctor that he had always been before. We are all double-sexed, and must learn to give expression to the opposite sex in ourselves in ways that are not a nuisance — as, for example, by a wen — but are of value, as in the good bedside manner of a good doctor.

It is to be noted that Groddeck's sceptical view of norms enabled him to accept the female in himself with no difficulty at all, just as he had accepted his wen. In this, his attitude was the same towards himself as it was towards others. Symptoms, foibles, 'abnormalities', whether in himself or in another, were merely subject matter for his tireless and ever-fascinated powers of observation.

For Groddeck everything about a human being, from his illnesses to his artistic creations, was language giving expression to the hidden reality of man's nature; as we have seen, this nature was fourfold, child, adult, male and female. This fourfold individuum, he saw set in its background of nature, *Gottnatur*. His portrayal of all this shows him a poet, or again, one might almost say, something of a mystic. Though the most practical of physicians, often earthy, or alight with Rabelaisian wit, yet angered by smut: though very much the humanist, this more than life-sized character could be filled with a tender reverence; indeed no other humanist can ever have written with such depths of reverence about Christ.

In my own remarks in the posthumous preface to *The World of Man* I said:

> "Much of the apparent difficulty in following his meaning is due to people's reactions to his personality. Some are offended and hurry away lest he should reveal to them their own hidden sores; some look upon him as an angel from heaven, delivering them from the pangs of hell, while others see him as the devil in person; to others again he is merely a physician of extraordinary skill, or a poet, and

to many he is no more than a thought-provoking writer, or even only
an obstinate heretic. It seems that he must have been Proteus himself,
now a flame, then a dragon, and suddenly a waterfall."

A great deal of what is central to Groddeck's psychoanalytical thinking is
rooted in his earlier work as a writer on literary themes. He once told me
that, having set out in life in a direction of his own choosing, he had been
diverted by Freud's influence on him, but that he was again finding his
own original path. His last book, though it suffers so much from the
urgency of his need to finish it while he yet had time, nevertheless perhaps
shows us something of this return, if only because it is largely a book
about words. Yet it would be untrue to claim that the author in him
sought to oust the healer; rather his insight into language opened new
vistas for the therapist. The nature of these is not, I think, adequately
understood.

I have heard Professor John Wisdom discuss a very rare form of
modification in word usage which is always associated with a changed
outlook of great cultural significance. He gave three examples. The first
was Christ's stretching the meaning of the term adultery, as in the text:
"Whosoever looketh on a woman to lust after her hath already committed
adultery with her in his heart." A spiritual dimension was added to what
had been a legalistic morality: mercy and love could breathe between the
rasping tones of judgement, and law's spirit was given a lasting precedence
over its letter. Professor Wisdom's second example was Newton's
stretching the meaning of falling, and expanding it into his concept of
gravity. By this, we were given the assurance and freedom of a cosmos
ruled by a law, the workings of which were, in essence, apprehended by
all. His third example was Freud's stretching of the meaning of thinking to
include the unconscious mental process. By this great change, man has
been accorded the freedom of the psyche: for the first time, he has a
means to awareness of his own motivations.

I would suggest to you that, in his own way, Groddeck had done
something analogous in conceiving his 'I' as more than self-consciousness,
and not only a function of self importance; and as having an unlost
existence in the mere awareness of an abstracted moment – even in sleep.
When vanity and shame no longer measure us against our fellows, and
when we therefore no longer feel a need to match our thought with the
fruits of their experience, nor to limit our demands by theirs, pleasure
supersedes the 'I', yet does not extinguish it; indeed, does not the 'I' seem
to expand as it is lost in the sense of pleasure, whether being achieved or
experienced. Further, such a Moloch is the 'I' that, once so far gone, its
omnivorous lust is sufficiently beyond reason to forget consistency: a 'no'
– like a coquette's – means 'yes'; and pain, given or received, is swallowed

up in its pleasure. Individual differences are so transcended that in the lover's absence, another will do as well; and as with a sado-masochist who will as well lash another as himself, the 'I' becomes so grandiose in its participation in the pleasure processes as to go beyond the bounds between thee and me; it may be carried away by an identification, even to its own detriment. That I speak of nothing recondite will be plain when I remind the reader that, from the beginning, men have been so transported by their delight in the prowess of a leader as to throw away their own lives for his ideal. Thus do we see the 'I's' impersonality, its 'It'-like nature rampant. Yet we must follow it one stage further. So wild and remote does it become, that the growing of a cancer is as much an achievement as the composition of a masterpiece of music (Groddeck); and the same self-abandonment that is required for the composition is passionately given − we can no longer use the term 'I', and are therefore driven to say by the 'It' − to the processes of the alien and inimical growth. The distinction between self and cosmos is thus overleaped. Groddeck tells us it is the It that finally brings about a man's death, and points out that, in the very processes of the body's dying, by withdrawal to even deeper levels, the It seeks pleasure to the very end; and that the goal is then the womb again, the grave, unity with the mother, with mother earth. And there is no stop here; all goes on, in a Heraclitean sense, and Groddeck speaks of this in terms of wonder, with a poet's reverence.

I have sought to cram into the foregoing paragraph the essence of it all, to show Groddeck's unitary hypothesis, and the graduations whereby the notion of the 'I' is stretched to include first this, then that attribute of the Id, till at last, the It itself bestrides the whole page. I would not however suggest that Groddeck's intuition ever needed to plod the sequence of all these steps.

Groddeck told me he could not follow Freud beyond the pleasure principle; yet, as I have indicated, he had a sense of what later Freud was to call the death instinct. As his concept developed, he widened the meaning he gave to the word 'pleasure' to a point at which I myself would have preferred the term 'ecstasy'. But whatever we call it, tracing its paths was what led Groddeck to expand the notion of the 'I', and thus to creat the 'It'. And it is the same whether motivating a man or a cell: it is thus that our existence is in *Gottnatur.*

Perhaps we might further clarify the picture by a glance at other formulations, even if our purpose is not so much to trace similarities with them as to differentiate from them. In Vedanta philosophy, we may recall, atman and Brahm are one. The Christian distinction between creature and creator, it is often pointed out, is here absent; the spirit of a man and the supreme are one, not two (*advaita*). And in a state of *samadhi* this oneness is in some sense realised; yet *samadhi* has been characterised as indistinguishable from deep sleep. A vital condition, of which one is unconscious. Perhaps we here have parallels to some of the concepts we have been considering.

The Buddhist heaven, nirvana, has been translated 'snuffed out', like a candle, and is thus comparable to the state of *samadhi*. The attaining of nirvana has been described by Sir Edwin Arnold in the words 'The dewdrop slips into the shining sea', as though atman were obliterated by Brahm. A literal translation of nirvana, I understand, is without a vehicle, or body. And perhaps this gives an important clue: Buddhism is very non-carnal; it wants to escape from the wheel of life, to stop incarnation, its bliss is sexless.

Like nature, Groddeck's world picture was sexual throughout, everywhere it was dual, at times passive, at times active, and always with at least the potentiality of the product of these. Where the Buddhist would stop living, Groddeck proclaimed the joy of life; indeed, as we have seen, there was no desire towards anything beyond the quest for this. Further Groddeck was not interested in the oriental, and his sphere was utterly remote from that of bodiless bliss. Baron von Roeder, who knew him very well indeed, once referred to the title of one of his pre-analytical works, *Ein Kind der Erde,* saying it characterised its author. And we may here recall that Groddeck's image of his spirit was that of those impish nuisances, the trolls. Indeed, except perhaps for his profound sense of reverence, Groddeck was in everything of this our earth. And he was bounded by its bounds; thus he was thoroughly European, and proud to be a German. It is to Goethe's thought we should turn for help in understanding Groddeck rather than to oriental concepts. That trollish, earthy child felt at home in Goethe's *Gottnatur,* and like Goethe, could merge himself in it. In Goethe he saw an exemplar who had the ability to feel "at the same time a whole, and yet a part of something far greater".*

The Pharisee in us – ever separating from, being more important than, the rest – was the root of our troubles; and it was as an antidote to this that Groddeck momentarily considered the possibility of putting nature, or God, in the place of the 'I'. We may indeed note certain similarities between all this and the oriental position we touched on – but perhaps there is an even greater similarity to the medieval view of man, in all his parts, and in most particular ways, utterly bonded with nature, while yet having his identity heightened by the role and personal individuality conferred on him by the relationship. This intimate symbiosis was, of course, conceived in the terms of the wide notion of astrology that underlay all medieval culture – a subject that in no way concerned one whose whole being was of this earth. Perhaps we should mention the Stoic view that every actual existence has its ground in the great God-pervaded whole, and is endowed with reason, which ought to guide us to follow

---

*The World of Man, p. 51.

nature. But this excludes personal ends, especially pleasure. Alas! We meet limitations to any attempt to find a parallel with Groddeck's thought. Lao Tse's Tao is perhaps nearest to the It in its workings as a guiding function. Await the voice of the It, Groddeck would counsel. And, as we have already heard, it is not that I live, but that I am lived, by the It.

This was because he had truly followed this guidance, he had become childlike, he was free from all compulsion to conform, and could respond with any of the four aspects of being — with the male in him, or with the female, with his 'I', or with his It pure and simple. His personality was thus like Jurgen's description of the best part of the universe as being "The place where almost anything is more than likely to happen". No wonder his personality was said to be charismatic. As he saw the It, it was our great fount of goodness — of worth, creativity, healing — and he could sometimes mediate this, because in a sense he had become the It.

Be it noted I have not used the word 'spontaneous' to characterise him, for he did not abandon the 'I': *'Schiess Klug',* warns *das Kind der Erde.*

Yet he would not, as 'I', force a change on himself. When he was ill, his wife asked him why he would not give up smoking. "That's not my way", he retorted. Similarly, when he was warning all his friends about the coming inflation, he himself would do nothing about his money; he endured, and watched it melt. "I am a German and this is happening to Germany," was his attitude. Again, similarly, when mortally ill, he refused an anodyne. He gave the reason that he wanted to observe the processes taking place in him. From this, you will perhaps see more of what I mean when I say that while yet keeping his 'I' whole he had in a certain sense so merged with as to become the It, and was therefore enabled to speak to the It of a patient. We may here note that he would make patients get up from their death-beds to go out for walks with him. His pursuit of the pleasure principle seemed to mean participation in life whatever life brought.

I was not with him at the end, but one who knew him very well said to me, "All the pain he endured sent him dotty". Conscious to the end of his critical attitude to psychiatric terms, he remarked of his own condition: "They would call this manic depression". It was only a week or two before his death that he gave his supreme lecture. Though he spoke of his favourite subject, he seemed to give it new meaning: his learned audience was dazzled; people were affected unaccountably. He looked out from a body that was almost disintegrating, and he towered and was like a god.

It was very soon after this that Dr Boss observed "On his dead face there rested nothing but kindliness and a great calm."*

---

*The World of Man, p. 23.

3

GRODDECK: ON REALITY AND SHOW

Whereas Groddeck's interest in medicine was aroused by his father being a doctor, his mother's family had produced distinguished literary figures, and from the first, Groddeck had shown a literary gift. In other ways too he was dual, for instance, he was both rebel and hero-worshipper. To a considerable extent he could harmonise these opposites by following rebel leaders, though this was to the detriment of the individuality of his own vision. He is best known as a sort of follower of Freud, through whose study of the unconscious he sought the natural in man. But his first love in medicine was Schwenniger, Bismarck's doctor, reputedly the only person who' could control the Iron Chancellor, who was the originator of a system of natural therapeutics, which Groddeck adopted. In both cases what he sought was touch with the natural substratum of our being, which to him as a doctor was the embodiment of the sacred. To thwart it, as by abortion, was horrifying; to deride it, as by smut, was near blasphemous; but worst of all was seeking to go one better than it, as by Pharisaism. It was the very principle of life and joy, and of dying and creating. All this he found portrayed in Goethe's conception of *Gottnatur*. In everything, throughout all phases of his career, his involvement with *Gottnatur* remained constant, underlying and linking all other interests; and always his reverence for *Gottnatur* remained paramount.

Yet no one could for an instant have taken him for other-worldly; throughout all his sensibilities, and in his method of thought and being, he was of this, our good, our very good earth, and was always practical and particularistic in his medicine. Thus, to provide a few random samples: to an analyst who was theorising about anal sadism, Groddeck all but cried, Have you ever looked at an anus? One reason for his massage was to gain a tactile impression of the patient in movement, another to note the varying smells the person gave off, for these told Groddeck their story, not only of the body, but especially about the emotional life of the patient. A medical psychologist returning from a visit to Baden-Baden told me that, in future, he was going to pay more attention to the sort of noise people made than to what they said — though he did not actually attribute the idea to Groddeck. Certainly Groddeck took special note of the actual words patients used, and perhaps of their roots; and he often thought the symbols by which they expressed themselves told him more than all their fine-drawn, intended meaning. He also read their symptoms as plain symbols, without the medium of medical theory. He would put his ear to a chest in preference to using a stethoscope.

Thus in everything, he went direct to the most relevant matter, always with his own unmatched form of objectivity, whereby he sought, as he put it, to "treat people as natural objects . . ." But this objectivity had a special quality, a warmth, for people were objects in living *Gottnatur.* The cult of personality was, to him, the great falsification; we should seek ever to descry the human individuum, i.e., nature as it appears in human form. Instead of the 'I' quality in a man, we should seek his 'It-like' nature, that in him which is childlike, primitive without pretention, that which he manifests when he is without consciousness of 'I'. Each It, as Groddeck called this, expresses a man's individuality as his way of being human, so that all Its are as basically similar as are our bodies, and like our bodies, each It is a particular instance of the universal shape we recognise as man's. As an It, therefore man is whole, and whole with the universal; as 'I', he is part; and setting himself above what is natural to him, he boasts, Thank God I am not as other men are. This striving 'I' is — though I do not think Groddeck ever said this — modelled on the potency that makes a father, and on a father's controlling power. Thus the part comes into being, the great whole is sectioned, by sex (*secare,* to cut). In his *The World of Man** Groddeck writes: "Since Adam and Eve did eat of the apple together, yet each for himself, every son of man has felt himself to be as God, has irretrievably separated his ego from the universe, the All, and has then become ashamed of his nakedness and denied his manhood." And later in the same book, he speaks of "man's destiny to be at the same time individuum and sexus, an indivisible whole and a section of the great circle which is the universe".

But although in this spiritual-chronological sense the prime split is thus between the whole and the part, for us, speaking existentially, the truth of experience is that the split between appearance and reality is basic. Learning to be guided by the It gives us a sense of reality; and in such moments we know how much the 'I' is show. Yet the It we know only in its effects, never in its nature. How well we know that actions tell strange tales, and seem to disavow most treasured motives. And even if there are times when both agree, their agreement may plainly vary from the spirit

*Page 217.

and total intent of their host. Though introspection may disclose what we truly willed, by then the It has perhaps moved on to new willing. The 'I' and its world are indeed always derivative. Yet only by means of the 'I' can man *be* man; for the It is his nature, not his humanness; and it is by virtue of his 'I-ness', and not his naturalness, that man assumes responsibility, or if you like, becomes responsible – and thence able to assess, to reason. Though Groddeck thinks it would be wicked to attempt to destroy the human sense of responsibility, yet we may wonder whether this does not sometimes better fit the requirements of our personalities' internal economy than of their relationships to the outer world. Whether responsibly or otherwise, it is with our own will that we seek to work on this outer world. And all too often the assumption of responsibility, however genuine, masks deeper motives; and perhaps this is the heart of the matter, that the 'I' is a mask, a check to the vision of others – and is thus shut into its own world of darkness. The truly responsible power is, happily, beyond the 'I's' confines. Indeed, we might say that reality is what the eye of ordinary consciousness misses, what alone the man of vision sometimes may glimpse. Thus, beyond the symptoms, which are only the appearance, Groddeck saw the symbol, whereby he could apprehend the malady in the terms required for its cure.

Similarly, Goethe saw the idea of a plant beyond its outer shape. Schiller told him this was impossible, that an idea could not be seen. But Goethe could see, in his mind's eye, the entire growth of a plant, from seed to blossoming; and this would evince to him an impression of the principle which gave the whole its special character. And this archetypal plant was so clear to his imagination that from it he could imaginatively evolve, in all details, new varieties and types of plants.

Goethe is at pains to show us how, by virtue of imaginative vision, the artist, by his portrayals, completes nature's handiwork. We might put it that such portrayal gives that handiwork its point, as, perhaps to the ancients, the concept of the *genius loci* was the essence, character and living focus of its entire glade. Really it is only through culture that we get back to nature; it is only by being taught by art that we love her, that we have turned in our course to seek and contemplate her. Thus we are obliged to experience her as mutated by art. Further as Owen Barfield has shown in his *Saving the Appearances,** the love of nature was bound to be a late product of culture. Indeed, so far from its being natural to poetise about nature, it is often attempted only as an expression of a form of mysticism. Whether to the ancients or to the romantics, nature is something more than the living larder and the shelter of the primitive. To one whose vision penetrates appearances, she is *Gottnatur*.

In comparable fashion, Groddeck – like Freud – looked beyond human appearance, personality, to its motivating reality: the individual

*Page 245.

was understood in terms of all human nature, as portrayed in myth. In studying the gospel story Groddeck went further, and in differentiating between our concept of a historical Jesus, and the divine figure of Christ, he called the latter true, as distinct from real. In *Exploring the Unconscious,* he writes: "It is easy to remember but hard to grasp that all we see is but an image, that truth lies not in fact, but in the heart of man." In his short essay in *The Unknown Self* on 'The It and The Gospels', though he never deserts his humanist position, he is perhaps at his most moving; he writes with a simple reverence that brings to light a new semblance of Christ, the while, by the manner of his conception, he exemplifies how wide his non-literal view can open our horizons.

From Christ's 'Why callest thou me good?' Groddeck goes on to reveal a Christ who, in spite of His many stern words, is yet so much Himself as to be beyond all striving to be good, or making any such recommendation to others. In his 'Render unto Caesar', He puts morality on a level with the state. But morality has nothing to do with entering the Kingdom – for that we must become like little children. "Who has ever yet seen a little child to whom the word 'good' could be applied? A child is a child, neither good nor evil . . ." And from this, he moves easily to "morality in the usual sense had nothing in the very least to do with Him", and to "no kind of life has any value except the childlike". Christ's new commandment is love, and "it is to children we must go if we would make that *agapé* part of our nature." His "whole being was one protest against self justification by righteousness . . ." Far from being a moralist, He asserts, "I am come not to judge the world but to save it". The child, whom Christ holds up to us, "shows something of that true righteousness which allows the sun to shine upon the unjust as well as the just . . ." Judge not; herein perhaps is the essence of His message. "He pays no heed to sin; it is not there if the belief is there that the Kingdom of Heaven is within us." To the thief who believes, He promises, 'Today shalt thou be with me in Paradise.' "That one moment . . . is sufficient to obliterate all sins . . ." And then, "Perhaps the main thing is that we should believe something, but that we should just have faith, should keep the attitude of mind of faith, should have confidence in what we hope for, and not doubt everything we cannot see; that would be the condition of the unborn child." Because Groddeck rather turned his back on orientalism, it is much to be doubted that he knew how the Taoists, having sought the ideal in the child, then turned to the unborn child. To him, this idea was as original as was his total vision of Christ.

"Before Abraham was, I am, He said of Himself. If we put this together with the expression the Son of Man we understand that He takes Himself as essentially man. The point is then that He is Man, that He is with us, or as it must be translated, *in* us . . ." Thus Groddeck sets out, through his portrayal of Christ, to show us our human selves in a new dimension.

"Christ said of Himself: Before Abraham was, I am. He was not, neither will He be; He is. He is not real. He is true. It is not within my power to put all this into words; indeed, I believe it is impossible for anyone to express truth of this sort in words, for it is imagery, symbol, and the symbol cannot be spoken. It lives and we are lived by it . . . Christ is mystery, and only mystically can we approach Him; His essence is in being, not in doing, and what He does He does by means of what He is."

It is actual vision Groddeck here presents us with. It was as though Groddeck truly 'saw' the realities of which he spoke, almost as Goethe had seen his archetypal plants. Groddeck had this gift, and perhaps on this account, vision, both physical and imaginative, was his favourite topic. It was the subject of his first psychoanalytical talk at the Hague Congress, and of his astonishing last lecture, to the Swiss Psychoanalytical Society, twenty-four years later. Though in the last stages of a desperate illness, involving both mind and body, he yet entranced his audience, and before those many eyes, he towered, and stood immense* and radiant before them all. It was perhaps as though he looked out from a vantage point, and as though the brighter world he thus beheld had filled his being with its effulgence.

Groddeck's writings present us with a variety of scenes from his childhood: some are as bitter as the problems he was later to investigate in his patients; some are a little hilarious, almost in the vein of his uproarious novel, *Der Seelensucher,* which so delighted Freud — though they lack the novel's Rabelaisian wit. What they all share is Groddeck's naturalness, even those in which he characterises himself as a little actor: in all of them, one feels the genuine quality of childlikeness, which indeed was the core and explanation of everything that was most characteristic in Groddeck. In truth, he was a child, or should we rather put it, he personified the It. As he tells us, childlike people are ambivalent, dual in their attitudes, and have the gift of irony, the ability to see many sides of life. In his dedicated study of nature he found the moment all-claimant: his entire being focused on the particular that was presented, whether the symptom before his eyes, a curious symbol, or a new face. His gaze could thus penetrate beyond the superficial appearance, to the point where nature revealed herself to him as divine. But because it was a child that thus discovered this source of a life-time's delight, she was to him a cause of fun as well as an object of wonderment — or reverence.

Because we are human we can see the world only in our own shape: on every hand there is only the trinity of male, female and child. And of these

---

*Many have reported such impressions of him, e.g. Dr Michael Balint, already mentioned. Groddeck himself knew he could sometimes seem a giant.

man's imagination, working unconsciously, produces an unending proliferation of symbols. These are the very stuff of art, and of culture generally; by his imaginative use of them man does indeed complete, give point to, external nature. We have already spoken of the ancients erecting an image to portray the *genius loci,* and thereby expressing the atmosphere, character, or spirit of a glade, giving to the prospect a fuller visual significance. Similarly by our art's expression of the *Zeitgeist,* we bring to light and complete the meaning of our epoch. So too, Groddeck, by his therapeutic interpretations, evoked health and the talent for living, even in those suffering from organic diseases. Unique among psychoanalysts for his understanding of the symbol as multivalent, he was able to portray anew to us our sacred symbols, revealing their meaning in both a personal sense, and cosmically — showing them both as mystically true, and valid as universal symbols. This we have glimpsed in my quotations, from what he wrote about the Gospel story; the psychological approach became inadequate and it came to him that "only mystically can we approach Him. . ." Perhaps the way in which, by expanding the symbol's scope, he made it speak may be more evident if I now quote the end of his interpretation of Raphael's 'Sistine Madonna':

"Every man is of both sexes and both ages, but this truth is known only to his unconscious mind. In everyday life it remains a mystery, and its world, the world of eternity, is cut off from our consciousness by that curtain of error without which man would not find it possible to live. It is only the image of this truth before which the curtains may draw apart to show the Madonna stepping towards us with the Christ Child, the trinity of female, male and child. In unending circles, as the swinging drapery shows us, this trinity, eternal male, eternal female, eternal child, sweeps through the measureless infinite, a symbol of God in man, of man in God. The heads of countless angels crowd the space behind the curtain, eternal childhood, and forever through the circles of the spheres the woman carries her son, the man-child with that profound and God-like gaze."*

*Exploring the Unconscious, pp. 126-7

The Tale of any Prophet

The singing of his presence
    Poured trouble on their lives
Like a spray of whitening water
    Leaping from a rock
And whipping to white movement
    The stillness of a pool.

The perfection geometric
    The curving grace from which it fell
The people did not see.
    They saw instead
The streaks of shadow between its tumbling drops
    And the broken stillness of the pool.

They did not hear its music
    Hidden by the fierceness of its crashing fall
They were deafened by its roar
    And could not hear its songs of pity woe or splendour.
Someone blasted out the rock over which this
    Waterfall of dawn was leaping.

1926

Part two

AMBIENCE

4

THE SON OF MAN AND EVERY SON OF MAN

From Adam's day till this day, man's existence has been in and through knowledge. It is through knowledge that all our achievements have been reached, and through the knowledge we have won that we have lost all knowledge of the gods.

That great man, the late Dimitrije Mitrinović,* once said to me, "It is the nature of man to be for ever finding the way out," implying that our nature exists in and by means of having a problem. Every achievement that is worthwhile is so because it has involved finding the way out of a prior position, state, or difficulty. The high valuation we put on achievement is far more due to the effort of finding a way out, to the quality of that effort, than the arrival at the position of having achieved. Whist was a good game, but we have to complicate the rules to make it better, to make it into bridge, then auction bridge, contract bridge, each involving progressively more calculation, suspense, sense of hazard and feeling for the psychology of others. Alas, however, life is not a game in which we can control the cards. As though our complications were not enough, life produces its own, produces them in the heart of our solutions; for in the very moment of achievement, we deepen or widen our problem, or discover a new problem. Already as you reach your skyline, enlarged horizons spread before you. To cope with such unexpected embarrassments, man has for long made the effort to stand apart from, and survey, and get proper objective knowledge of, the problems that keep growing in front of him. This very effort, however, has itself still further deepened our problems, for by assuming this objectivity, man has denied the subjectivity in his nature, making it unconscious, and has thus split himself

---

*Mitrinovic had a morphological view of mankind's development and culture, on which he based a prophetic insight into our present problems. He influenced an astonishingly wide circle in London, and has left his mark in many minds.

into two. There are now two of him to be dealt with, one of which is invisible. And, in fact, no problem that is personal, no problem that touches any human tissue, can be resolved in a mood of mere objectivity.

Our subjectivity must play its part in any personal judgement; no man can remain purely objective in the choice of his wife, his vocation, his gods; his whole mind, his whole being, is involved in such choice. His principles of reasoning, all his objectivity, and his very self — all may be flooded over, lost, in the process of such choosing. The invisible self may take over, in spite of him. Or is he able both to retain the awareness born of objectivity, and to avoid denial of his urgent subjectivity? By itself, objectivity may indeed acquaint him with the situation to be dealt with, and the steps to be taken in the course of finding the way out of a predicament. Yet though these be taken, he may find his heart still back in his old mood of doubt; or the new position he has brought himself to may prove a mere emptiness. On the other hand if subjectivity has completely taken over, the ideal of its mood may effect a loosening from our inner struggles such that gusts of feeling sweep us through decision to a new position where, for lack of awareness, we at once repeat our old, and now inappropriate, patterns of action. If, however, both these attitudes of his being can operate in a man, we have insight, the knowledge of motivations and purposes in relation to the totality of a situation.

This knowledge establishes a principle of action, whereby a man will act true to himself, and true to the nature of his situation; at least for that moment, he will have realised his destiny. He achieves personality by thus making possible the unfolding of his destiny. Insight is a particular kind of knowledge involving a fusion of aware purposiveness with consciousness of the nature of reality factors, an imbuing of the observing mind with the knowing will; given insight, a man takes a definitive stand, for once admitted, subjectivity is endlessly clamant. And his stand is meaningful, a declaration of personality, a commitment to and affirmation of his line of destiny. Thus man's style of life, his development, and therefore his very personality, are indeed dependent on, and an expression of, his knowledge, his kind of knowledge of the path that he takes, of the process of arriving at a choice that will prove valid to him, the process of knowing. And in such a moment of awareness his very being exists over and above, beyond, the sphere of blind nature, by virtue of his relationship to the problem of knowledge.

Yet personality, though thus achieved, is at once lost if he becomes what he knows: thus for example, I have an ideal, in the name of which I make my choice, for the sake of which I make my choice; in the moment that I have made it, my tendency, at once, is to identify with the ideal; I seem to become an expression of it; and in that moment I am lost. In that moment my individuality, my power of instantly choosing again, is gone because sold out to, or if you like to put it that way, dedicated to — at all events lost to — the ideal, to that which I chose. In short, in the moment of making our choice, we identify ourselves with the role we have chosen and become lost to it; the choosing or knowing human being — the unknown knower in each of us — is lost.

We must relinquish the pleasure of the former identification before we find again the growing-point of choice, the point of awareness, the point of actual knowledge; we must relinquish, and for ever be relinquishing, our choices, our past fulfilments. Yet here we at once encounter a contradiction. For over against this is a contrary need, the need to be faithful to the processes in us that have resulted in our establishing a position, a loyalty to the stand we have taken, without which, it would seem, we might well lose ourselves down zigzags of inconsistency. I would most certainly not deny this need, and in any study of the Son of Man we must always be mindful of the eternal verities of which His life was an incarnation. Yet, as a clue to action, fidelity to a 'good' that we have established has grave dangers. Blood-vengeance and torture were once moral duties. And the 'hard sayings' in the Gospels are largely sayings that are hard on pre-established 'goods'. And so long as we can avoid arbitrariness, and so be faithful to our insights, the new 'goods' established — though seemingly opposite to the old — will retain a subjective thread of consistency with the old; it will seem to us that they are a development from the older positions. But count it good if that thread is discovered later; meantime, if a new choice is to be of the spirit, let the ego cling to nothing. For, deep in our hearts, we know that if ever we are to be born again by a new insight and a new choice, our individuality must die in an agony of doubt; we must die into the totality, merge again with nature, achieve knowledge of our nothingness.

To remain, however, in a state of spiritual death, a state of unknowingness, uncertainty, a state of doubt, is as bad as — though perhaps no worse than — to remain in the state of conviction, of dedication to, of identification with, the ideal. And again and always, "die and become";* only so is there veritable life, personality realised in the achievement of individual destiny. Stay the unending becoming, and at once you are the pawn of any Caesar, or the mere mouthpiece of a god; and in either case your life is arbitrary and impotent, and without awareness of that subjective quality we call freedom. And, indeed, such is commonly our life. Life that promised to be an interesting game has involved us in cosmic processes and spiritual mysteries that have made our knowledge nonsense, for life's demands on our insight are incessant, and sometimes we must sleep. With his whole being, therefore, man cries out for the principle of a fixed 'good', and loyalty to a stand once taken seems the only tolerable ethic. For who can live continually, his whole life

---

*Goethe.

through, in the agony of constant choice? Which of us has the strength?

I once met a Jewish theologian who accounted for Jacob's struggle with the angel — his wrestling with the messenger of God — as symbolising the whole Jewish race wrestling with God, wrestling with Him to get a good covenant for man. This suggests that man was claiming the right to a way out of the impossible state he found himself in, that state in which he had to live on a razor's edge of awareness and choice, or else be lost, be a nothing. It seemed beyond man's power to remain human in such a plight. Therefore man wanted to know: If I do this, and live by these rules, shall I then be safe, have salvation? What terms can we come to in this matter? And the Jewish people's struggle, as he put it to me, the whole history of the Jewish people, is a wrestling with God to establish a good covenant for man, to get terms whereby man will know that, if he does live by the rules, all will be well. And a good Jew, he told me, believes it is possible for him to follow the law, and that, by keeping specified commandments and rules, he has done all that is required. Without such a struggle for a good covenant for man, I do not believe that the best in man could have arisen. Our whole existence is dependent on that covenant. The early Church — a fact which is very notable — was concerned vitally with these same problems, of precisely how much was in the sphere of man's will, and how much was to be relegated to God. And the whole problem was dramatically enacted in the struggles over the great heresies, in the Councils which defined basic points of doctrine — about Christ indeed. And yet these points of doctrine are also for every man himself; in that the figure thus defined has the personal meaning of an archetype for every man.

There was Arianism, in which Christ was represented as on the side of the creatures, and Apollinarianism, in which there was no human will or reason in Christ's human nature; Nestorianism seemed to affirm unduly the human nature of Christ, and Eutychianism was almost a claim that Christ's manhood is swallowed up in the Godhead "like a drop of vinegar in the ocean". In spite of the heresies, in spite of the disgraceful ambitions, both personal and political, of the contestants, through it all there came certain basic and everlasting enunciations in which Christ was declared to be perfect God and perfect man, as opposed respectively to the doctrines of Arianism and Apollinarianism; and one person with two natures, as opposed to the doctrines of Nestorianism and Eutychianism. Here we have a basic picture of the human position as it might be if man could become perfect. It is a clue to the kind of individuality that is conceivable: neither lost in nature, and, therefore, tending to fall back to the primitive, towards animality, nor absorbed and outshone to the point of extinction by an 'over-godded' and inhuman heaven. Henceforth, every man might find status on earth, and yet enjoy something of the freedom of the world of the spirit.

The meaning of Christianity is that Christ carried forward the covenant struggle of the Jews with God, and carried it further; He obtained the right for individuals to become persons, to have a destiny, as the Jews had obtained this for the race. He stood up to Caesar's judge on the question of His own individual right to see and proclaim and act on truth. (The crucual question, you will remember, was: *What is Truth?*) I will put this the other way round. Has Caesar, has the state, a right to define what is truth, what shall be the goal, and, therefore, the manner of action, of an individual human being? More important, just as the Jews struggled with God for their covenant for man, Christ stood up to God for individual man, as every man must do. Whereas animals are inevitably obedient, man's freedom makes him an explorer, constitutes him an experimenter, a seeker after knowledge; therefore, he creates problems, and with them is forever harming his own nature, contradicting the nature that he has from animal and biological sources. Thus he sins against life, digs his own grave, opposes the will of those sources that give him beingness, opposes the Life-Giver. Equally, if he seeks the safety of a system, he denies his freedom and individuality and, therefore, sins against his nature as spirit — sins against spirit. And, thus, man is born in the state known as original sin, born with tendencies with which, if he expresses them with the freedom with which any animal expresses its nature, he will involve himself in sin. He is at loggerheads with the Life-Source, with the Life-Giver, and at loggerheads with spirit, by virtue of his very expression of himself as an individual human person who has risen up over against nature and yet does not exist as one of an angelic species.

In his self-chosen status as Son of Man, the title He preferred for Himself, the Son of Man, every man, Christ, stood up for man against nature, the natural state of affairs, and its expression through Caesar, and stood up also, it would seem, against spirit and God. And here, for a moment, we must trace His course through a strange-seeming pattern of actions, and face the inference of conclusions that, for the moment, will seem even stranger. For He would not play the game of community, nor that of the spokesman of God, of the religion of the best men of His time, the Pharisees. And these were good men, very good men. Was not St Paul glad to acclaim himself one of them? We would all of us instinctively feel today that we aim to lead the life of a good Pharisee: we are good citizens, we should have good consciences. He went about sowing doubt. He sowed doubt in such goodness, and disrupted the community. He disrupted the pattern of His own family life: He would not earn His livelihood, He broke from His family, He went away and lived the life of a vagabond, an outcast, disowned His own mother and brothers, and when they sought Him He disowned them publicly. And He went about breaking up other families; He would call His apostles, working men, from their work, from looking after their own families, call them to leave immediately: 'Forsake all and follow me.' He went about neglecting His health. Dr Binet-Sanglé,* in analysing the whole story and all the traditions, concludes that it is hard to avoid the view that He developed a tubercular condition of the chest. He went about so outraging all the current standards of decency, these everlasting human values, that He was, in fact, beyond the pale and the law. He even urged His own disciple, Judas, on to a deed that was the man's undoing: 'That thou doest, do it quickly.' And He provoked a situation in which even his best-loved followers could not but doubt Him, as they did. He played away His every card, so that there was nothing left but the 'impossibility' of retreat or capitulation, or alternatively, death, and desertion — desertion, remember the word, — by the spirit.

And all this was foreknown to Him: "Jesus, therefore knowing all things that were to befall Him." The only way through the impasse of original sin, the intolerable state into which each man was born, was to challenge the entire system, the entire universe, to go through with the challenge to the logical conclusion of pointlessness. By doing this, He demonstrated full knowledge of the human predicament for the individual, and He would not have life on such terms. He saw through them. He showed them up. He let Caesar take His life, and God His spirit — for there came that moment, which He had also foreknown, when the universe was narrowed just to dustbins, to the charnel hill and the broken body, and there was no longer a purpose nor the possibility of a goal before Him, a moment, surely when His spirit was gone. Yet still, somehow, out of the guts of His manhood (we can hardly say from His animal or corporeal nature, for that was all but tortured out of existence, nor yet from His spirit since His spirit was gone), the quality of manhood He then and thereby created out of Himself, He produced the spirit to upbraid God: "My God, My God, why hast Thou forsaken me?" Ultimately there was nothing left but the naked obstinancy, the courage unsupported by hope, the courage of a desperate and isolated human will. Yes, purely human, because abandoned by God. Thus the doubt and dissolution that must follow the vision of faith, the moment when we have chosen our road. The doubt in His case followed clear through, followed full; and this made possible the emergence of a newness: die to become.

And what was the newness? And how had all this availed to save man? What was His message? It was spoken to simple people, very simple people, in very simple language, the spiritual directness of which is so naked in the Gospel According to St John, though some of our better known translations of the Gospels perhaps obscure its simplicity. In this, perhaps the greatest of all the Gospels, the message is simple to the point of harshness. Yes, harsh, bitter. It seems almost as if He said: Don't play either game, the game of Caesar or the game of the gods. C.J.Cadoux in his *Life of Jesus*,

---

*Professor Binet-Sanglé, *La Folie de Jésus* (Albin Michel, Paris) 1929.

excellent from the point of view of an unbeliever, says that He was giving a political message, saying to His fellows, the Jews: If you go on provoking the Romans like this, you will be overwhelmed. It was almost as if He had foreseen the sack of Jerusalem. He was urging them to come to human terms with the Romans, saying: Do not do this, this is an impossible way of life. He certainly spoke in very practical terms, very practical indeed. There is almost a worldly wisdom here:

> "If thou bring thy gift to the altar, and there rememberest that thy brother hath aught against thee, leave there thy gift before the altar, and go thy way; first be reconciled to thy brother, and then come and offer thy gift. Agree with thine adversary quickly whilst thou art in the way with him, lest at any time the adversary deliver thee to the judge, and the judge deliver thee to the officer and thou be cast into prison. Verily I say unto thee, thou shalt by no means come out thence, till thou hast paid the uttermost farthing."

A very practical, a very worldly wisdom, we might say. And again: "If any man sue thee at law, and take away thy coat, let him have thy cloak also." He knew the dangers of the law. Practical, worldly counsel, almost. There was the time when they were going to stone Him in the temple: "Then they took up stones to cast at him; but Jesus hid himself, and went out of the temple, going through the midst of them, and so passed by." His hour had not yet come. There were no heroics about His life. He would strike only when His time was ready.

Again: "Let your communications be 'Yea, yea, nay, nay,' for whatsoever is more that these cometh of evil." We are sometimes trapped by friendly frankness, and need craft; hence this simple, practical, and utterly wise counsel. And what shall we make of the parable of the unjust steward, so little spoken of? A strange parable about a man who, having swindled his master, quite cleverly, in order to preserve his own status in the business world, is commended. And thereafter the position is summed up in the words: "Make to yourselves friends of the mammon of unrighteousness." And the meaning in the original is, by means of, through, the mammon of unrighteousness. Strange advice. And what of the expensive ointment, about which Judas remonstrated, saying it might be sold and the money given to the poor? "The poor always ye have with you . . ." And the story of the camel through the eye of the needle? For the rich men of today, who are good men in many cases, just as the Pharisees were often good men, this would have seemed indeed a harsh statement. Then there was the curt word to his mother when, though only twelve, He had been away in the temple: was that a proper attitude to His parents, when He had been away for three days? What would any good Pharisee of today make of a child who gave that answer to his mother? And of His violation of the Sabbath, and the answers He gave on these matters? Clever, casuistical, one might say.

In short, He preached a religion which, to the good man of His day, must have seemed an absolute individualism, something like the philosophy of Stirner — and for that matter, with a similarly individual view of responsibility. Further, He seemed to preach an avoidance of committing oneself either way to this or that situation, an avoidance of the traps of the community system. It was a kind of ju-jitsu: love your enemies; avoid their traps, but love them. And over and beyond this avoidance of traps was an avoidance of becoming a pawn in their systems. Yet that does it less than justice. *Agapé,* the pure, creative love He taught, does not bind; it grants the conditions of free development. It exists in freedom, and, therefore, not only the beloved, but the lover himself, is free; it may not be bound, and avoids the conditions of bondage. It was this purified love that was the essence of His whole message. I do not mean by this statement to wipe out everything else that the Church has found in the Gospels; for indeed they embody the warrant for all its ritual and formulations. They exist as expressions of, and means to, His love. He showed love as the way, a love in which we might preserve the awareness, the choosing point, or that razor edge of free will, of the really knowledgeable will which chooses. It is possible to have a degree of human freedom by changing the relationship of man to man, the practice of this doctrine of higher love. When there is no freedom there is, of course, no choice. One obeys or disobeys. but neither of these is an actual choice. A choice is an outgoing freedom of the heart; there is no love, no morality, therefore, without the awareness of that basic freedom.

And His disciples, what did they preach, the eleven disciples? A simple account of what happened, and His directions about how to make such things happen in the lives of all — of what He did, in short, and of what it is possible for human beings to do.

It was His action that was preached about. For the rest, the early Christians, those early followers of His, must have seemed an odd assortment to the contemporary world. The Romans were not only unable to tolerate their religious views, but — one has heard it claimed — even found the Christians intolerable personally. We may, indeed, think such an account biased in suggesting that there was anything actively unpleasant about the Christians, or that they were unendurable to the nice people among the Romans. Yet to the Romans, they must have seemed no better than sceptics, misfits in the then known 'good' world — for bad though it was, it was not all bad. They were constantly being put into jail, not, I believe, merely because of the wickedness of the Romans, but because they were intolerable to the moral forces of that epoch. In this moment, however, they achieved something unique in all history, fulfilling His new commandment, they realised that love which is described as *agapé,* and through this a genuine theolepsy. Did you receive the spirit? they would ask one another, a question, as has been said,* which refers to something as tangible as the question: Have you had influenza? It was an experience as real, as bodily even, as this, and something that was a regular occurrence to them, so fully did they live in this new world of love of God and of their neighbours, so completely had they broken through the fetters of their 'good' world. They were actively inspirited, in their joy experiencing the full release of healing powers, the powers to achieve miracles. The gifts of the spirit were all on hand, so that they could go even to martyrdom with joy, and prefer it to the 'good' life proposed by the wise men of the contemporary community.

Indeed He had opened the way to us, He had brought a new becoming, a new gift, due to His piercing through the armour of the old-established 'good' world. Mankind was born anew as never before, or renewed by the fires of Pentecost. People experienced each other as human persons, and each was, as in Ibsen's words, in some sense "cradled in the heart" of his brother. The individual, who is for ever severed, a partial and lonely entity, somehow achieved wholeness in the eye, understanding and heart of his brother. Here was a new thing in the human world.

Yet in bringing this utter newness, more precious than anything the old world had known, He was yet dependent on what had gone before, on the tremendous struggle of the Jewish people. It was built on, and existed by means of, and through, acknowledging their achievement. For the first time in history, they had formulated the notion of the perfect super ego; they had created their own spiritual unity through their principle of utter consistency, their ideal of one way, of one right thing to do. We find ourselves by means of doing the one thing that must be done at any given moment. The Jews had perfectly formulated the sense of unity and consistency in the face of all the Gods in the neighbouring tribes, each of whom represented a wanton tendency of the inconsistent human heart. They had perfectly formulated the sense of human integrity.

Christianity faced terrible problems, yet had this behind it. But somehow the Christians could not hold to all that was given to them. They faced the dualism of Manicheistic worship. And this might, one feels, have been a value to the early Christian world — not its dualism, but the gnostic strivings toward spiritual experience and a cosmic consciousness that best bloomed in India, and which, surely, were part of mankind's inspiration. Christians, too, might have enriched themselves from the mystical practices of Hinduism, that great sphere of the human spirit in which everything that could never happen in history happened. Here we find an ecstatic dream in which the human spirit transcends its own very nature and becomes one with the universal spirit. We might well have drawn on these tremendous sources or reservoirs of human experiences of spirit, conceived, known, or created by the Hindus. We might — yes. And,

---

*See Gordon Taylor's account in his *Sex in History*, (Thames & Hudson) p. 260.

indeed, there is much of that orientalism in early Christianity. For example, the concept of reincarnation is well known and established; we can see it implicit in the Gospel question: "Who did sin, this man, or his parents, that he was born blind?" The answer was, of course, one that did not take into account this problem of causation in the past. Our Lord is here interested, not in causation from the past, nor in the ultimates of the human spirit; the answer is given in terms of making known, making manifest, the glory of God then and there. In that historic situation suffering in darkness was being replaced by light – vision and faith. For many, the doctrine of reincarnation gives reason, sense and explanation; gives a sense of comfort. I do not undervalue this. But in that moment – for the Christian soul being born in that moment – comfort was the last thing that was wanted. This was a moment when the misery of man had reached a point such that the human spirit was utterly trapped; a turn had to be made in the direction of human affairs. And as the Jews had struggled for a good covenant for the race, so our Lord was creating a good covenant for the individual. It was an action of the spirit in the alteration of history that was taking place. Everything had to be crowded into that point or moment of existence, into that moment that culminated on the cross.

The very possibility of a Christian future for man hung on the action of an individual in that moment. He defied the then universe, the then nature of things. His agony had to be conceived of and felt, experienced, as the potential in the heart of each one of us, as something beyond hope or comfort or explanation. Otherwise it would have been dramatically false, false to His meaning, His purpose with regard to history – the purpose of emancipating the human spirit, and of thereby giving a new meaning to history. The Kingdom of Heaven had to be within, not explained in terms of the cosmology of the current religion and its community values. The worth of these I should be the last to undervalue, but here, one admits, they had to be brushed aside.

The world, Groddeck pointed out, swings between the poles of Ptolemaic and Copernican views of the cosmos; for before Ptolemy there was already something of the nature of the Copernican view.* And spiritually, too, we swing between our moments of inwardness, or death, and then of renewal, the expansive phases of our becoming, between the moments when we are concerned entirely with the process of introjection, and then others when we project. The crystallographer of today finds it most convenient to describe the inner nature of his crystal by projecting it, and by describing it in terms of an imaginary sphere that surrounds the crystal; there he can best evaluate and express its inner nature, the mathematical relationships of its constituent parts. And in many cases it is

---

*Of course, early heliocentric theories were purely speculative, and not widespread.

best for us to know our universe in terms of its circumference. But in this moment, in this moment when a world change had to be produced, the source of the change could only appear within, not from the system we have always so carefully externalised. To all there now should have come something of the experience of the moment when the limited and spiritually deserted human being produces out of his self something new. This experience constitutes the centre, the key-point, of every son of man; in each life there is this moment when the external is gone, when, if a veritable personal existence is to develop, the external must be further excluded by our forgetting it, when there can be only that point, moment, when we ourselves make a choice to be — to become again, in a sense. For that, a point of light must appear in the heart.

Why, when this had been achieved and a new world of spirit was launched, did the Church lose the theolepsy, why did it lose the gifts of the spirit, why did it lose the divine ambience of *agapé?* And why, when this was going, did not the Church draw on the oriental spiritual sources?

For truth to be human there has to be battle, there has to be struggle. History, it has been said, is an unfolding tragedy; we live in an expanding universe, a universe in which, more and more, we see perfection, in which more and more insights come, more and more power over nature — and worse and worse wars, worse and worse criminality. We live in an expanding universe, which opens like a black and white flower, and expresses . . . what? Human nature. We live in this greatest of all the world's centuries, this century which more than any is true to . . . to what? To man. More than ever like man. This most human of all centuries. This most incredibly wicked and diabolical of centuries. This century, in which we have most extensively increased our knowledge, have built the best welfare states, and have taken cognisance of all the finest insights that the whole flower of humanity can produce; how like a man it is: split to its heart by conflict, divided and ambivalent to its roots! Only by battle is an outline gained* — battle within each individual, ultimately. The battle may be projected out into external forms, but ultimately it is a battle in each individual. Strife, strife in the full Heraclitean sense of the word, is the process whereby this becoming and dying, and again becoming and dying, continues to take place. History is, indeed an unfolding tragedy; and as the grand and heavenly moments appear, so inevitably, to be true to human nature, to be true to those who enact and produce and manufacture history — its human sources — there must come, after the glorious moments, the moments of degradation. Indeed, these have been repeated so often that we are apt to forget the other side of the story, and its triumphant success as a leaven in a difficult world.

---

*See Alan Upward's development of the theme, 'Outline is gained only in battle', in his *The New Word* (A. C. Fifield).

We have the picture in broad terms before us, and the picture corresponds with that which each of us knows, or must come to know, about the opposition in himself. Such beginnings of self-knowledge constitute the first fruits of knowledge to which man's long, blind strivings destine him. Through this is gnosis. In this sense man knows himself, and may, therefore, come to know his universe, as Adam knew his Eve. "Man, know thyself," it is written. But we often forget the rest of the inscription: "and thou shalt know the world." And as Adam's knowing was creative, so will such gnosis re-create the world it discovers anew.

It is in the nature of all of us, as in the nature of the sperm that is our begetting, to struggle, to sacrifice and to move towards our own destruction, as did the Son of Man. We must, willy-nilly, produce the destruction of our own values; we must produce these horrors in our individual histories. It is in our nature to sacrifice ourselves. As Groddeck put it, what man loves best is the torment of the task. The most ordinary and stupid little man chooses a way of life in which he wears out his pride and ambitions for the sake of tying himself, for no apparently good reason, to a family, wears himself out, in a sense, in establishing that family in life. Almost, we might say, we cannot help it being our nature so to live that we shall undo and destroy ourselves. From the moment of our conception our nature tends to be invaded by spirit and made untrue to actual nature, — which, biologically speaking, is supposed to seek survival. But human living is a move towards death, towards destruction; the creative element in us leads us in that direction, as the sperm in its great race for its own destruction and death. But why? So that it may explode, touch off, a new existence into beingness — a new life. Goethe spoke of life as a continual process of renunciation, of dying: yes, but to be reborn. And Goethe, after all, was a paramount example of constantly resurgent life. It is to resurrect, it is to explode a new life into being, that the sperm destroys itself. It was to bring a new epoch, a new possibility, into human history that our Lord sacrificed Himself — and set Himself against, set Himself as though to destroy, the 'good' values of the then 'good' men. It is that man might become again, that the human spirit might resurrect, that He always comes, as our fuller life; it is that we may exist as free human beings, as persons and individuals, not merged, as a mob, by the state. Christ was the first to stand up for the notion of human individuality on all planes, and so fully and effectively and meaningfully that He has, in fact, turned, not only outer history, but the history of each individual human spirit and its striving. He stood alone against all; He sacrificed as, in our lesser, and different, ways, we must sacrifice. Yet if we seek to model ourselves on Him in any merely external sense, we shall have denied Him. His message surely was that He denied the possibility of modelling a personality on anything. He denied the ordinary human standards. And if we are to discover the Christ in the heart, do you think that we shall discover it comfortably, say by moralising at ourselves, or merely through some inner feeling, some inner sweetness, as of something good? We shall discover it only as His life existed, we shall discover it only by dire and effective action — and then by noticing the results we have produced, often with their terrible indictment of the complacency founded on meaning well; "by their fruits ye shall know them."

And what did He come to bring? "I came not to send peace, but a sword." If we are to discover the Christ in the heart, it can only be after action; then we may know that the Christ *was* in the heart, provided we acted with that sort of effectiveness with which He acted, but in a new situation, made new by His action. To copy Him, in a merely external sense, is impious — as though He had not fulfilled the task, not achieved. To try to live in terms of His life is to live in a self-centred and egotistically sacrificial picture that we have inherited through our culture. To do this would be to deny the spirit that He preached. This would be to deny the possibility of again changing history, and of making a new pattern in the history of an individual existence. His great act was a fulcrum, a point on which spirit so moved that history was lifted on to a higher spiral. There are those who think in terms of a second coming. And this is a concept of immense value, to think of our Lord as here and now. What would He be like? For the reasons I have been mentioning, if He were like what He was like in those days, He would not be Christ. Existing in a new situation, made new by his former incarnation, and by our present reaction to His reappearance, He would have to be different, utterly different. I do not, of course, mean to deny those everlasting norms in the growth and figure of every saviour that arise in the very beginning of mythology, nor the special qualities — if that is the appropriate word — of godliness that are intrinsic to our Lord's being. But such spiritual attributes are not readily apparent to most of us, and being of the spirit, need not be experienced in accordance with the mores of any particular culture pattern. Therefore, should we think we could recognise Him by the signs of our devotion and spiritual feelings have taught us — by what we have learnt and trained ourselves to feel about His memory — then we would almost certainly deny Him. His nature then was to be effective, to destroy something in order to build again. And how else can a new thing be created? The good Pharisees that we all are — or seek to be, or hope to be made into — the 'good' Pharisee in all of us, even, and especially, in the 'good' man — (the attempt to be human and decent that we all make) would have to be outraged, would have to be outraged anew.

If another world war is to be avoided, and a reappearance of His *agapé* is effectively to lift us on to some higher spiral, then again we shall be outraged. Again there will be agony and suffering; but this would mean that there would be the possibility of true change. Since the spirit is unique, as against nature that tends towards repetitiveness, the manifestation of spirit may be expected to create a new form. Therefore, its coming must be, in the words of His promise, 'like a thief in the night', unrecognisable, at least by the old standards of 'good'.

There is only one way in which we can know: "where two or three are gathered together in my name, there am I in the midst of them." What is in the midst of them? An insight into the meaning, the potential outcome, of their gathering: logos, a knowledge of the logic of the events concerning their appearance together in its relation to God. When two or three are together in the name of an action that might conceivably change the tenor of history, in however minute a degree, then I would say, yes, He might conceivably be present in their action. An artist who is to produce something more than derivative must have been schooled to obliterate himself sufficiently to feel for the inherent form of what he is to paint, and to open himself to a new expression of this. For the new to appear there must, of course, have been a prior obliteration.

If we meet as two or three with a known objective, we shall dedicate ourselves in terms of a known something, something that has already been conceived, and is, therefore, *déjà-vu,* and of no vital interest to the world. If we know what we are there for, our knowledge will be a misknowledge, a misperception. The old knowledge, the old knower, must die if the knowledge and the knower are to become. I do not advocate revolution; we cannot abolish what knowledge has so long cultivated. Besides, the new grows from the old — provided we relinquish the old. If we can meditate deeply enough on the old then we may, in discovering its truest intent, be graced with insight into a new way of fulfilling this, or of carrying it further, and be moved to do so. Then, if out of such spontaneity we create something which is new, then, perhaps, it will be said that the spirit was present. It was either 'good' spirit, Christ or bad spirit, the devil. It was spirit at least. Spirit in itself is that which is unknowable; "No man hath seen God at any time." But if a meaningful, spirited action gives reorientation to the sense and trend of history, aids destiny to a providential fulfilment, or even points a feasible way to this, then we may say Christ was in the heart of the doer; his reading of the logic of events was by a living knowledge. This is gnosis, that sure insight in action that drives a way out through history's dilemmas; it is this clue that every Adam still seeks, though his quest has lured him to ivory towers, and Faustian pacts, and Woomera or Nevada. Such gnosis might descry the new-come Christ in the heart, *before* He was in the hand of the doer.

The doctrine of the second coming is the affirmation of the potentiality of every son of man, and the hope of his self-realisation in his heart. Without this, history increasingly appears as the course of our predestined degradation, through regimentation to enslavement or extermination. But despair is a sin, not only in a theological, but in the psychological sense, that to deny hope inhibits our life. We cannot do other than look to the finding of a new way out of the ever-recurrent human state of dilemma, a way to a new integrity, a new style of personality, a new incarnation. As neurosis yields to the underlying love that, in spite of us, still keeps our world turning, may we, perhaps, hope for a new glimpse of His *agapé,* in the glow of which even science might discover warmth for us before death, and its knowledge become the gnosis of wisdom?

5

AN EXISTENTIAL MOMENT

Existentialism began with Soren Kierkegaard, an intensely devout, though rebellious Christian, and has continued into the hands of the atheistic Sartre. However there seems no reason why it should be left so largely abandoned to him; it can do much to make the realisation of spirit more immediate.

Existentialism is concerned with the experiential rather than with the merely conceptual. In a sense it is nearer to psychotherapy than to philosophy, for its sphere is the person and his actual predicament in life: his problem of how to be, to exist, in the world, that is his experience of living, of being the Guest that only a human life is. Therefore, to the existentialist, philosophy proper, as also theology, and for that matter perhaps even psychology, are apt to seem remote from the arena of our world; they may seem abstract, or merely theoretical. Theirs are the endless logical delays of proof and disproof, the inductions and postulates constituting reason's empty being, with psychology overtopping all by measurements that come ever closer to giving soul a girth, weight to our emptiest thought, and shape to the non-existent 'I'. Although of course my need for reason in general and objective matters is absolute, the vital decisions on which my being hangs:- Should I change my faith? What shall be my vocation? Whom shall I marry? — and a host of lesser ones throughout daily life alike leave reason in its frozen detachment, while the beat of my pulse commits me. My reality proceeds from my inwardness, whereas what has been generalised, defined, or codified is at one or two removes from the burning issue — or the unending hesitation — that results in the principle thereafter formulated. "Truth," said Kierkegaard, "is subjectivity." And falsification and degradation he saw as from the crowd. What then is the subject? Who, or what, am I? The root of all anxiety lies here: to prove and know that I do indeed exist, and then to be enabled to know the nature of my existence.

In his *Existentialism and Humanism* Sartre,* speaking of an article of manufacture, says "that its essence — that is to say the sum of the formulae and the qualities which made its production and definition possible — precedes its existence." He then says that similarly, according to pre-existentialist philosophies, "each man is a particular example of an universal conception, the conception of man." In contradistinction to such ways of thought, he speaks of the existentialist point of view, that man "exists before [he] can be defined by any conception of" his existence. By saying that "existence precedes essence" we mean that man first of all exists, encounters himself, surges up in the world — and defines himself afterwards." If as first seen man "is not definable, it is because to begin with he is nothing. He will not be anything until later, and then he will be what he makes of himself. Thus there is no human nature, because there is no God to have a conception of it. Man simply is. Not that he is simply what he conceives himself to be, but he is what he wills. "Man is nothing else but what he makes of himself." And again, "Man is, indeed, a project which possesses a subjective life, instead of being a kind of a moss, or a fungus or a cauliflower."

Through such considerations we glimpse the importance to Sartre of subjectivity, and here we should recall Kierkegaard's feeling that only the individual is valid, even real, while the crowd is ever the source and cause of deception and error. It is the individual realising himself in purpose that makes a man's career, and it is this that is the prime requisite in the fulfilment of his destiny. But man's supreme purpose is found only in the mystic's quest; and if the steps and direction of this have external form, one would speak of vocation rather than of career. But the way of spirit, whether lightning-like or never-ending, is without justice, for attainment may still be denied him who trudges all that endless length, while yet it may be granted instanter to an unknown who has not raised a foot. Someday, in some moment, a spark of God must flame behind your eyes, till your glance flash meaning and command. It may be said that you are a visionary; but you will no longer be a mere cipher: your work will prosper, for it is now for more than you, your voice be heard, no longer to cry your wares, but to preach the true path, for "in choosing for himself, he (man) chooses for all men" (Sartre). Such is the existential moment, the moment when I am myself — for my self's sake, and for all. Therefore by such a choosing, I choose myself into existence. By my individuation I participate in the human communion.

We may here recall a striking explanation: if as first seen, man "is not definable, it is because to begin with he is nothing." It will now be plain that the world in which man may, or may not, exist is the world of significance, and not of mere nature (being). We may therefore be said to

---

*Tr. Philip Mairet, Methuen.

exist (as something more than mere moss, fungus, or cauliflowers) in terms of, and by virtue of our meaning, of which our purpose is derivative, or an expression. By the creative act of making a decision that is fully characteristic of me, i.e. that is genuine, I become significant, and do thus bring myself into existence. By such an act I show my colours, declare myself, make myself responsible for myself. And in this I produce an image of myself which, as Sartre put it, is an image of man such as I believe man ought to be. What I do is what I believe to be the right thing for a man to do: in fact, in thus making myself responsible for myself, I make myself responsible for all men. In getting married, joining the Society for the Prevention of Cruelty to Animals, or in having a cup of coffee instead of a brandy, I do what I think is in the circumstances the proper thing to do; and thus, "In fashioning myself, I fashion man." Although one may have reservations about how far this argument can be taken, at least it shows us the means whereby Sartre makes the individual's subjectivity human-wide. Of perhaps cardinal interest here is that the universality herein achieved is by means of an assertion of individuality; for it is I who decide on the appropriateness of my act; and indeed, it is only by deciding in the way that *I* feel to be the proper way *for me,* that my act is sufficiently genuine for me to feel its universal validity. In short my universality begins with, and grows out of, an act of significant individuality. To exist is to stand out.

To exist is to stand out. Any existentialism could be said to be essentially concerned with the standing out of persons from nature, and most truly concerned with those who stand out from the innumerable counterfeit personalities. Existentialism should thus be thought of as concerned with actual living existence, instead of with living lies – faking, or even living in one's rationalisations – for all this involves being cut off from any real participation in the life-giving communion of society. What with their predictable motives and their scheming, those resorting to such ways become derivative creatures, little more than echoes, without claim to any valid existence of their own other than as organisms with birth certificates.

The dreary lack of originality of many of the evil figures of history likewise excludes them from our present purview. Diseases, whether we apply the term to the body or to the psyche, are everywhere the same (plague is everywhere plague, and paranoia always paranoia): it is health that may be conducive to originality and interesting performance. That history can, however, produce malign existential figures is amply demonstrated by the mere mention of Stalin and Hitler. Speaking generally, all those who are evil – here meaning wilfully cannibalistic – can exist only by a denial or abolition of the reverence for personality, whether human or divine. And bereft of reverence, human existence is only half human. Consideration of such malign cases must, therefore, be here omitted, to be dealt with in a consideration of the pathology of existentialism. It would however be wrong to conclude from the foregoing that existentialism favours goodness as such. Although we here adopt the position of excluding derivative or falsifying personalities together with the malign, it must be said that an approach via the categories of good and evil is not a fruitful one for the understanding of our subject.

The existential moment is that moment in which I am so completely engaged that I am in no state to theorise about, or to make definitions of what engages me (unless it is theorising that is engaging me). When I sit back to indulge in such theorising, I have 'stopped to think'. Stopped what? In some degree or in some manner I have stopped existing to become the onlooker.

This is not intended to be an unfavourable comparison between the thinker and those who never stop to think. Indeed, inaction is as blessed as action. God laboured six days, and on the seventh He rested and meditated on what He had done. The Sabbath is better than the six days together, but though on all but the fateful second day, He was able to say that it was good, on the seventh, He was able to feel that it was all very good. And on all Sabbaths, or rather, in his every Sundayish moment, the existential person must feel very good, and his very good feeling will then include even his second-day feelings. One can understand God not feeling good on the second day, because He was then busy dividing off heaven from earth, and perhaps He wept a tear for the vale of tears He was creating. For here we have rather few wholly good moments, and it is hard to feel Sundayish all the week. And yet we have to keep on existing through each of the unheavenly days.

What is of primary importance is to be able to exist unequivocally with a whole heart, and abandoned in faith, for an instant, for any instant, for this instant. Of course these moments must be recollected in the tranquillity of meditation if they are to result in fruitful living. But at once there is the danger of neutralising the reality, as with someone who might seek to view a documentary film of his own life rather than live it, or like one who would become a mere item in his own construct of reality. There is too the old-style philosopher, the thinker whose life is sacrificed to his thought. Such an onlooker is often needed by society. And while he remains quietly observing, from within his heavenly yet ivory tower we can only honour him; obviously however, difficulties might arise if he used his tower as a fortress against 'actual' existence. But although his intelligence would probably save him from this, a would-be disciple might withdraw from life into some such mental position, and thence seek to explain the life thundering against his gates — explain it instead of living it. All such explanation, ultimately, is self-explanation, indeed self-justification. Most of us spend our lives justifying our lives instead of living them. We are sick with guilt, and dare not exist as we are: instead, we exist as justifications of ourselves. And all the different views we take of life are simply scenes we project, the nature of which are such as — we hope — to enable us to conduct our lives in spite of our guilt. We take these or those views, project our selected and carefully coloured pictures of living, instead of giving ourselves to a full existence. Our viewpoints, or observer posts, are truly defence posts against undue encroachments by the reality of life. We carry this policy to such extremes as to warrant the seemingly extravagant assertion that, in an emotional sense, we are actually solipsistic; and by this I mean that the springs of each man's actions make sound sense on the assumption that he is the only person in the world, or that others exist only as figments or mechanisms (robots) for the fulfilment of his wishes. Basically we remain as when we were born.

Having come down to the mad absurdity of solipsism, I may perhaps restore our psychological health by a hair of the same mad dog. Bertrand Russell told me what he characterised as the classical story about solipsism, perhaps the neatest bit of philosophical absurdity: a student coming out after a lecture on solipsism was so thoroughly converted to it that he "couldn't understand why there were not more solipsists".

Perhaps the reader will agree that this is a suitable place from which to digress — to consider a controversial position we have stumbled on. Mr Barfield comments: 'Incidentally there is the old, but to me unanswerable, objection to this page (which seems rather a central point on the whole) that, if "*all* the different views we take of life are simply scenes we project . . . to enable us to conduct our lives in spite of our guilt . . .", then so is *that* view!' He goes on to question whether I am making "an objectively valid observation . . . or just dispersing (my) own guilt."

My point is almost covered by Leonardo da Vinci's 'we must see to know, but be blind to act'. (In effect, I almost say, not that we blind ourselves, but take biased, partial, or falsified views in order to act.) But, of course, as Mr Barfield would point out, even Leonardo, as he perceived this fact, was inhibiting his own action. Yet would he pronounce Leonardo's observation any the less true because it itself was an example of the truth it formulated? One is sure he would agree that a preposition is a bad word to end a sentence with, to give the schoolboy example of this type of formulation.

However I must acknowledge that Mr Barfield is fully justified in his criticism of my 'all', indicated by his putting the word into italics. Surely the truth is that though we do project a great deal, yet we may also take perfectly valid views at other times.

To return from our digression, existentialists may show us existing in the experience that we ourselves create; or the existential moment may be seen as a realisation of our isolation and lack of goal, or perhaps best, of our individual uniqueness, and even, perhaps, as a re-discovery of the wholeness of all. But whatever else it is, an existential moment is an experience of intensified reality that occurs when a rupture occurs in one's relationship with the rationalised world, or as a result of such a rupture. Theorising about life commonly results in the invention of norms and standards. We all have such norms to give ourselves a false sense of security. By means of them we hope to prevent the intrusion of an existential moment, to dull the sharp edges of any new and vital perception, to make an average lie out of a unique truth, or even make God Himself into a nothing, just a part of religion.

Detachment might be a good slogan for those in an opposite camp to me. If, they might cry, nobody is going to stand back and observe and establish norms of conduct, and what might be called social truth or validity, then we might as well turn the world into a lunatic asylum, and all become voluntary inmates. Of course, some would need to be keepers. It is, however, a great question whether this is not more or less what has already happened in spite of all our norms, and of the keepers who make them. Indeed it may be that these norm keepers are the cause of the trouble. Would there be the same allure in crime if there were no police? It would appear that certain primitive peoples have managed without scrutineering and disciplinary forces. Not that we could suddenly abolish the police: indeed, as we now are, we need more of them.

Detachment today is most signally evident in the position taken up by the scientist. And surely the adoption of no other attitude has ever proved itself by such a show of results? It is not that one wishes to claim that no other attitude to life ever worked. The black tracker shows a power of observation of, and intelligent interaction with, his environment that is lost to us. The Africans' immediate, distant knowledge of Gordon's death is the classical instance of an awareness that we lack. An eminent anthropologist has told us that if Cro-Magnon men could appear in modern clothes in our fashionable streets they would attract no special attention; and that their intelligence must have been somewhat above ours. Surely this intelligence brought the kind of knowledge that it sought? Yet no one could for a moment pretend that anyone before has ever attained a knowledge and power in any sense comparable with the scientist's; he does not have to argue the advantage of his detached, impartial attitude.

But what are we to say of an age when the most generally respected figure is that of the scientist rather than the sage? Consider him in comparison with Buddha, supreme example of the sage, and the priest of detachment. We may speak of the scientist — within the limits of his detachment — as impassioned with sincerity, splendidly ruthless (sometimes), alive, and of unsurpassed keenness and devotion. But what does his wife say if he is wooden enough to try to live his daily life with her as a scientist? Or what more will she say if he tries to shape their joint existence according to scientific rules? Perhaps the most significant criticism of him in this context is that the very considerable extent to which he is bound to rely on reason must surely make him prominent among those responsible for the general failure to see or understand symbols, which, Groddeck observes, so characterises our epoch. Women, often both more sensitively aware and more intuitive than men, are apt to be less blind about this. They may be aware of the defect in their men as an obtuseness and as a lack of poetry.

Some will have it that what irks the women is merely that science claims what they feel to be an undue proportion of their men's attention, and that in this, the priest may find himself in the same predicament as the scientist: Yashodara, Buddha's wife, could not have been very pleased when Buddha went off on the long trek that was to lead to the Bo tree. Yet it is noteworthy that, once he had attained enlightenment, Yashodara was his first initiate.

Complementing the scientist's detachment is a particular form of attachment. Bacon, for example, pleaded constantly for a way of working that would produce the fruits of knowledge. And we all want to get something out of a machine that we have put our pennies into. The scientist can make nature deliver the goods; obviously, therefore, he will want to make her do so increasingly, and to employ, and dispose of, more and more of us to this end. And where have fiction writers and Utopians got the picture of a future ruled by science if this is not implicit in what the scientist does? And however much he might disapprove of anything of this sort, may we not nevertheless ascribe to the scientist − even if its implications are unthought out − a desire for the indefinite extension of his empire as strong as that of former dominant classes of priests and kings? Has he not already often been held implicated in the dread results of his weapons? Indeed it is his vision that has transformed the earth, and filled it with every device to tempt and seduce us into transposing our faith in the heavenly to faith in the earthly heaven. He above all stands for, and now stands to gain by, attachment. His detachment − a superb *tour de force* of his priest-craft, which is thereby princely and magnificent, but not heavenly − is thus bought at the cost of repressing his desire for attachment. But there is always the elastic return of the repressed.

In spite of his detachment, he too, like the rest of us, is ambivalent; but with the high value his reasoning mind places on consistency, he might find it hard to acknowledge his dual nature. Caught off guard might he, perhaps, be goaded to exclaim with the late and ineffable Sir Boyle Roche in the old Dublin Parliament: "Am I a bird that I can be in two places at once?" Loftily, if ruefully, meditating the frailties of our human kind, might we, perchance, wonder if the onlooker exists at all, or is he only some fabulous bird of schoolboy imaginings?

But if the high seriousness of our subject results in our breaking down momentarily into flippancy, this is in no sense intended as derogatory to the scientist's great role. Our question is, does this onerous role in any degree depersonalise the man, and perhaps thereby colour, or even direct him in his work? Further, although he exists on the grand scale as conceiver, not only of a new world, but of new truth, a truth that bids to embrace, or rather surround, the world with its intended wholeness, does he have much of an existence apart from his role? Imagine him stripped of all his knowledge and status, then ask how much of a real person this is. Or is he simply the mouthpiece of the *Zeitgeist,* without spirit of his own to sound through the mask? Is he merely a type, lacking the existential uniqueness of personality, a product of our age and circumstance, whereby the world spirit breaks into its own dream? Always apparent is the fact that we are able to speak of 'him' as the representative of his class, the scientist class. To what extent can we speak of him in his role as a scientist and at the same time feel we know him as a person, as we can with the priest, Buddha?

Here I might quote from a letter written to me by my friend Mr Christopher Gillie, in which he brings us, if I may say so, to a very precise conclusion on the matter, and shows it in an interesting light.

"One point about the scientist-onlooker. Aren't you conceptualising the scientist? It seems to me that scientists don't exist, though scientific method does, and don't we all use it every day? . . . My point in saying that scientists 'don't exist' is that as such they are mainly creations of the popular mind. People who rely on scientific method exist, but not scientist-onlookers. What needs to be destroyed seems to me to be the scientist-*concept*. It seems to me that you adopt it, though, perhaps you say just this on this page . . . you may be describing a popular concept, or you may be describing a phenomenon. I feel that in so far as the scientist is a phenomenon, he is one only in a Pirandellesque sense − people say he is 'that', and so he has come to think that he is 'that'."

Exactly; he is a bit too much an expression of the *Zeitgeist.* Quite a bit.

I recently came across Rudolf Steiner's view that from about the time of Bacon, the whole of our Culture has been in a phase characterised as that of the 'onlooker, or consciousness soul'. Steiner regards the scientist as the typical representative of this phase.

It was as necessary to discuss the scientist as it would have been necessary in the Middle Ages to discuss the theologian, or in Greece, the philosopher. And so elevated and representative is the scientist's position, that he alone need be mentioned; he alone rivals the everlasting claim of the priest in his utterly dedicated ways. Yet has his form of reality been damaged or undermined by Buddha's healing?

To avoid distracting attention from my main purpose, I have not attempted to justify the role here accorded to the priest or sage; he has therefore appeared in these pages as little more than a foil to the scientist, and I must now add one word about his great exemplar.

In a curious sense, Buddha's detachment seems to merge into attachment, a love for all, just as the scientist's attitude merges into its opposite. But in the case of the scientist, unlike that of Buddha, this is far indeed from being a spiritual gain. It is the bitter price he pays for the tremendous — and wholly admirable — development of his mental faculties without a corresponding development of his human or spiritual self. For Buddha, of course, it was the other way about: the spiritual came first, and out of this he was able to formulate his wisdom.

Consider Sir Edwin Arnold's simile of the dewdrop slipping into the shining sea. *From Lama Anagarika Govinda:

> "The Buddhist does not therefore endeavour to 'dissolve his being in the infinite', to fuse his finite consciousness with the consciousness of the all, or to unite his soul with the all-soul; his aim is to become conscious of his ever existing, indivisible and undivided completeness. To this completeness nothing can be added and nothing taken away ... The Perfectly Enlightened Ones are those who have been awakened to the perfect consciousness of completeness ... Edwin Arnold's Light of Asia ends with the words 'The dewdrop slips into the shining sea'. If this beautiful simile is reversed it would probably come nearer the Buddhist conception of ultimate realisation: it is not the drop that slips into the sea, but *the sea that slips into the drop*..." (my italics)

The perfected soul merging with nirvana. Here we are presented with an inconceivable, because self-contradictory, concept; for the dew drop personality does not lose itself as it slips into the shining sea. Such a doxastic existence would be the most truly existential state — or should I say, act? — for in it personal existence would no longer be dependent on the contingencies of any subject-object relationship. We might continue, but shall we get any nearer to understanding existence?

I recall, when a boy, watching a young man fall in love. He had seemed a pleasant, sensible young fellow, more reasonable than most of those mad, incomprehensible and wayward creatures called adults. One could understand him, count on him to behave sanely, and so get on with him. But suddenly he too had gone mad. He was valuing himself, his own feeling, more than anything else, and so had lost all sense of proportion. This was bad enough, yet he made it worse by also, and at the same time, valuing his beloved and the relationship with her more than anything else. He was doing something that was inconceivable.

Is existence, like love, contradictory, and beyond the reach of reason?

Our difficulty lay in the fact that the dewdrop slipped, without losing its identity, into the shining sea. But supposing we put the accent on *shining*. Perhaps it slips into the sea of shining, into *doxa*, into

---

*In *Foundations of Tibetan Mysticism* (Rider & Co.).

glorification, and as a beacon exists significantly only by its shining, so now the dewdrop exists only as its glory — as an actual drop might exist to a child's gaze. But the glory is not comparative. It is not glorying above anything else, but only glorying in glory, like a beacon shining in a world of only beacons. Did not the whole world light up with the understanding brought by Buddha?

Could I have written this little essay without using the word *existential?* Could I have used *experiental?* Would *factual* (i.e. what we make) have done? Or, perhaps better, *actual?* In considering such words we may bear in mind that knowing is by no means such a passive form of observation as was once thought. In, for example, the act of seeing there is an enormous amount of perception (and memory of perception) of our own muscle sensations, for an eye originally saw flat; and it was only in 'stretching' our eyes, or in walking, or reaching round, or most importantly, into, an object that we introduced perspective. Perception is factive or creative; knowledge is motor as well as sensory, as Adam found when he experienced Eve.

Our existence is no mere passive being; our lives are more than 'phases of biology'. Each of us, in his own way and on his own plane, must make the superb Buddha-like act of standing out; otherwise we remain in mere being, karma-ridden, negative, forever merely reacting to the senseless forces of chance, utterly without spirit. People do rise up out of this, and find themselves in a life of spiritual freedom. And we all recognise these valid personalities. There is however no willed — designed — act that will suffice for this; yet without willed and sustained action, a personality does not achieve significant existence. Reflection on these considerations will perhaps justify the choice of our term.

Words are very important in existentialism. It is truistic that it is in language that man, most of his time, most exists as man: his 'humanness' is founded in the word; and its full, existential development may be reflected in language. The prophets, who of all mortals have spoken most existentially, have used spirited, non-literal, indeed poetic language; it is only science that really demands the prosaic. Science is the nth degree of reason. As philosophy approximates to that rationality that finally congeals into science, it loses its grand manner. In similar regress does law lose its imperiousness, till the laws of Manu are watered down into departmental edicts, Religion too descends into a social asset for the butcher, the baker, the candlestick maker; it becomes a more or less rational code of social hygiene, whereby a moribund society is enabled to keep on breeding, to keep on living. All is prosaic. Thus religion too often tends to become a sort of reinforcement of society's policing services. At all events, it descends down into a state of being safe against the intrusion of the prophets. Communion services may be held, but mass is less often sung. The moralising preacher may be lauded, but the mystics remain unread. Yet the records of the life that died for the sake of valid existence are written in the most unprosaic and most hard-wrought words that poetry commands. The Gospel According to St John is like a core of all poetic achievement.

The tale of the man who was utterly man and yet wholly God could not be told in prose. He does not exist at all to the rational – even His historicity is doubted; and His significance is sought on the prosaic plane on which finally He scorned to exist. To the world, His existence is crossed and irrational and irrelevant, not truly to be known at all; and the most that all could do would be to agree that He existed. And the most that any one of us can know is that, in his own sphere also, He exists; but by that awareness, the very nature of personal being is transformed: man may – mystically – experience the divine, and God's being takes on meaning for man. The mystic's experience is the fully existential moment.

A note on 'An Existential Moment'

As purpose develops, however secretly, ego is being matched, measured, against ego, and mastery is measured in terms of time. How much has each done by the hour. Is all that was scheduled complete? Such is the nature of work; and it is work that makes our week, till the blessed aimlessness of the seventh day releases us from the bonds of time. And looking back on the week's work from the vantage point of the sense of having achieved, from that still point of effortlessness, the downs as well as the ups of our week seem good; for both now have place in the mind's quiet, are alike experienced as consistuent of the Sabbath's stillness. The truth of this is in part because the second day, like the errors of the well-intentioned, when viewed *sub specie aeternitatis* is understood. We see how it came about as an incident in sound purpose, and even that it was not only necessary, but in its own way beneficial: and further, in supernal light, the very divisiveness of the second day is only the principle of polarisation, whereby we are enabled to contrast and differentiate the true and the false. Even that originating error, idolatry or literalism, as seen in the manufacture of time by the destruction of eternity, or in our indulgence in egotism by the abolition of the divine – even all that becomes but a metaphor whereby the poet in every human heart may be granted a glimpse of eternity. In such light is indeed no error, and One Who radiated it, even though He seemed to preach a kingdom of this world, a resurrection of the body and its unending life, had already, by His constant use of parable, metaphor – and irony – yes, and humour – had already proved Himself that greatest of poets, whose sole and constant burden was that eternity He called the Kingdom of Heaven. "Before Abraham was, I am," He said of Himself. If we put this together with the expression 'the Son of Man' we understand that He takes Himself as essentially Man.* Perhaps we might say that He is the very spirit of man, which speaks to us out of that place where only the childlike live. As a denizen of that Kingdom He could speak only as a child, and could address Himself only to the childlike, or to those willing to listen as children. To such the distinction that we intellectuals of today make between eternity and everlasting life is non-existent; both simply mean, that is, convey to the hearer, a reassuring sense of peace of mind.

In distinguishing the world of the real from the merely actual, Groddeck characterises the former as the sphere of all that really moves us, and in which we are truly ourselves; it is the site of mankind's great dreams, of symbols, and of our fantasies – all out of childhood. In this is the latent content of all that is manifest in the external forms of His metaphors. In this, the semantic kernel of our living. Christ makes no mistakes. Here is the plane of a consciousness ever untrammelled, eternity: His coming, and His passing, are to make, to show, the way to this, to life beyond error, open to all of spirit free enough to be like the untaught child, which does not strive for rightness, and for whom no second day is wrong. However often we may fall back into the world of the literal, where we again bear the guilt of our always renewed error, the memory of one instant's knowledge of the real will remain as an indelible command that will at last send us back to our true home. Yes, one instant's knowledge: or perhaps we might tolerate that overwhelming peace for another instant, perhaps an instant repeated from time to time. It is not required of us that we should so renounce our strife and sweat as to be constant or faithful children of the kingdom, though something of it must pervade the being of all who yield to it in their moments, either more or less as they prize their own efforts. Yet its peace is ever at hand when we call.

'The moment' or 'the instant', I wrote. Yet in moving from the existential moment to an instant in His Kingdom, have I not perhaps, while retaining the terms, totally changed the subject? From a passing moment in an individual life, to a glimpsing of the eternity of the heavens? In vedantist terms, almost from the world of 'the little self' to the infinity of Atman, the great self, which is one with Brahman? In one sense,

---

*Groddeck, 'The It and the Gospel' in *The Unknown Self.* The question of whether He is also more – much more – than this is not here disputed, and my use of the quotation is not meant to indicate any attitude to the matter.

according to the Christian view, the gulf seen by the oriental between the little and the great selves is not so wide, for man is made in the image of God: therefore while the Hindu and the Buddhist must kill desire, the life of the little self, indeed must even kill the little self, its Christian equivalent can be saved by forgiveness. Hence the great emphasis on love in the Christian view, as the prime healer of the rent between the lesser and the supernal. We are to have faith in salvation because the humanly meaningful moment is consonant with what we may glimpse of the heavenly. Indeed their respective spheres are so close as to make it possible to have a man who, though fully man, is at the same time so wholly God that He will end up reigning on the right hand of the Father. What doctrine could better portray the contrast between the second and the seventh days, while at the time displaying that the nature of their difference is such that it is bound to be swallowed up by the consummation? Almost we are confronted with the thought that forgiveness is inevitable, that to fulfil ourselves we must learn to forgive, thus mending the break made by the offender in the human communion, which latter, in its perfection, we must conceive as what is meant by the coming, or the manifestation, of the Holy Spirit.

6

PROPOSITIONS

I got up early, and all day I went alone, avoiding even footpaths where I could; my body vibrated with an intensity of awareness of all the life about me; I was in an ecstasy. And a few days later, it was Easter 1919, and I preached my first sermon, and again the ecstasy shook me. My voice seemed loud, and I spoke with a torrent of words; and half the congregation was in tears. And next Sunday, because I said there was more to come, I was put on to preach again. And there was even a third time, but I could barely stammer the message of the third. It was not till twenty years later that I could put something of its essence into the following propositions; but the reader will see that its reaching articulation was at the cost of its soul and its sap, and their substitution by much that is very different.

Nevertheless something was articulated; the propositions do say something that had to be said. Although certain sorts of philosophers would criticise my form of statement, yet what I have written does reflect experience. The development of its significance is the culmination of this book, though I trust that something of my Easter message is in that culmination too. In any case, before the reader gets so far, he will encounter much that arises from that day's ecstasy. Without that the meaning of the whole would not be evident. My meaning must be felt if the book is to be significant.

I

That consciousness is the one reality regarding the existence of which universal agreement can be obtained, but that, since its ultimate nature is neither measurable nor demonstrable, it seems impossible for us to reach general agreement regarding what we mean by it: that it is the 'first word' in terms of which all other words or definitions are made, for nothing exists except it exist in consciousness: that we ourselves are both participators in, and creators of, consciousness: that we have the power of limiting it by the process of communal agreement known as definition: that in as much as it is defined, what was immeasurable may be said to have become measurable, though it must be remembered that to every definition there is an objection: that the ego itself is only a product of such communal agreement, or, in other words, that self-consciousness arises only in association with consciousness of the not-self, and vice versa: that each form of consciousness may therefore be 'explained' in terms of its complement, so that though man is made in the image of God (the totality or universe) the universe itself is seen in the shape of a man (for instance, the universal anthropomorphism disclosed by the study of psychoanalysis). In short, all 'knowledge' or definitions (language) exist ultimately in terms of plurality, number.

II

That since we have no experience of the cessation of consciousness, its cessation is not a meaningful assumption, is made on groundless inferential assumptions regarding the experience of others: that since consciousness is the basis of all 'reality' or experience, it is inconceivable (i.e., the mind cannot, in any actual or existential sense, conceive) that anything could have existed prior to consciousness. No one can, except arbitrarily, fix any point and say, "At this point consciousness began." The notion of a beginning of, and therefore of any time limit to, consciousness is untenable. As regards pure time, we are conscious only of repetition (identity), yet this is inconceivable without the complementary notion of variation.

III

That awareness of form implies the idea not only of form (identity), but also of forms, of variations in the repetitions (difference, or plurality). Thus the notions of the one and the many – in short, the notion of number – are implicit in the notions of time and space to the extent that neither of these latter is conceivable except in terms of unitary and pluristic concepts, in terms, that is, of number. Put otherwise, time and space are both coordinates of measurement, which is a process that is inconceivable except in terms of number. But measurement is a process, an act of comparison, of setting one thing against another; in short, it is movement. We might say that movement is incarnated or sensorily perceivable number, the application of the principle of number to the creation of a common world.

IV

Values are unitary states of consciousness, our interpretations of the feeling of duration, emotional attempts to produce identities out of a number of time phenomena. The ego is the prototype of all such. The relating of the self to extension is attempted by the invocation of meaning (number classification), but just as the notion of the ego is not a valid one (i.e., is not demonstrable), because the ego cannot be located in time and space, so the notion of meaning itself is only a system of inter-reference, without any external reference to any demonstrable basis of reality. Thus the notions of value, ego and meaning are in some measure comparable to the notion of matter as revealed in our concept of the electron. The electron cannot be located in both time and space at the same time, and is conceivable only as movement pattern – not the movement of anything, but simply as movement, which movement is, however, describable in terms of number.

Thus, in consciousness, there are unitary or subjective phrases on the one hand, and on the other, numerical concepts, or definitions, which are known as objective, or communal, concepts. There is experience of unity and plurality, the ego and the not-self, time and space; we attempt to compound the experiences of unity and plurality into what we call reality (a term with no demonstrable reference, whether it be equated with God, nature, truth, or what you will); we next attempt to compound the experiences of the ego and the not-self by the notion of meaning (a word which is again seen to be non-referential); finally we attempt to compound the experiences of time and space by what we admit to be an inference, namely, movement (in its more complicated forms this last concept is generally referred to as 'life').

The elements of these compounds are alike in that they are only phases of experience: though less limited than the compounds, the elements themselves are like the compounds in that they are only limitations of consciousness.

In passing, attention may be drawn to the necessity that arose in referring to the electron, to reintroduce the coordinate of time in the words 'at the same time'. It is indeed impossible to define without the use of the two primary coordinates, and the use of the one tends to be at the expense of the other. Thus the above-mentioned statement about the electron, which emphasised time, tended to cast doubt on its spatial existence. The more we are precise in the use or definition of the one coordinate, the more the other tends to be diffused, expanded; the more the one can be calculated, the more the other appears incalculable. It might be hazarded that the more the one has definition, the more one has the indefinable.

V

The notion of the present has no reference to the clock or any feeling of duration, has nothing to do with any sort of measurement, whether exact measurement, in the sense of measurement in terms of numbers, or measurement in the emotional terms of comparative achievement. The present is timeless and exists without reference to space; in short, it is indefinable, is consciousness.

VI

Time and space are to be apprehended only conjointly, their conjoint being movement. But since movement is an inference and not a fact of observation, actual belief in its reality must be regarded as faith, that is to say, we must resign ourselves to a non-objective apprehension of movement. This faith in movement is the basis of all illusion, limitation, definition, phenomenal existence, or 'reality'. That is to say, it is necessary to believe in movement if one wants to move, or, in other words, if one wants to live, or, in still other words, if one wants to exchange full consciousness for communal consciousness, or, to vary the statement still more, if one wants to believe in or deal with, number, the measurable, the demonstrable, substance.

To expand and bring out the implications of this: everything that exists does so pragmatically, by virtue of the human agreement — an intra-subjective agreement — that it exists, by virtue of that logos that is present wherever two (or two related in a form of relationship that could endure the presence of others, that is to say, a 'reasoning' relationship, or more accurately, a relationship in which there is concrete awareness of plurality, distinctiveness, i.e., in which there is consciousness) come together for its sake, for the sake of communication.

Now communication may be said to exist when agreement has been reached, in the same sense that a glass might be said to respond to a singer when it reproduces a note sung into it. But this communication, or agreement, takes place not only by the movement of sound vibrations (words), but also by all the gestures and rituals of life usually grouped under the term 'action' (movement) — our own, that of others, and that of 'nature'. The agreement is therefore an agreement regarding what is to be taken as logos, as the logic of events, or phenomena, by which the non-self-willed (that is to say those who are number conscious, or aware) will live.

Others insist on limiting themselves to two-relationships, which are disguised forms of unitary consciousness, in which there is pretended awareness of only one other (as though awareness could exist on a non-comparative basis), a form of narcisism in which that other is only a mirror or foil, a technique therefore for exploiting personality by the continuous enactment of roles, living by wilful blindness, hypocrisy, instead of by observations, i.e., instead of by agreement (since observation is only possible by agreement regarding interpretation, which interpretation is operative even in the reception of sense data, i.e., in the creation of percepts).

Such behaviour has been described as neurotic, or unconsciously motivated. Still further from the behaviour of the number conscious is the completely unitary state of the man who cannot agree at all. This is called madness. At times, as when in love, we all disregard the rest of the world. But observations made in dreams or when in love are recognised as apt to be in disaccord with 'reality'. It is clear that we are driven to agree on what experiences (phenomena, events, movements) we are to have faith in.

VII

The wise man is he who has abandoned the search for reality or meaning, either within or without. He observes the communally agreed conventions of movement (behaviour), is apart from them in that he is aware of himself observing them, is incorporated in them in that he himself, his own movement or behaviour, becomes a new example of them. In short, he ceases from either looking for a reality other than consciousness, or from trying to free himself from limitations to consciousness, i.e., from trying to get more consciousness. In brief, he considers the lilies of the field.

7

THE MASS, ITS SIGNIFICANCE FOR TODAY

Was man, from earliest times, made religious by a sense of wonder in the presence of the mysterious, somewhat as suggested last century by J.H.King, in his *The Supernatural: its Origin, Nature, and Evolution*? Did man from the first feel himself the child of some high god (not an ancestor), as suggested by Andrew Lang, and for many years now, by the great accumulation of evidence collected by Fr.W.Schmidt of Vienna? Was this high god as remote from man's vital concerns as we are taught? Or was he the recipient of man's wonder? Or was this focused on that inscrutable force whose nature and workings under the name of animatism (a pre-animistic conception), R.R.Marett described just before the turn of the century? This terrifying and potent force may animate a stone, a waterfall, the lightning, or be manifested by conditions of the sexual life, eclipses, blood, the elderly, a bull-roarer, and so forth.

The adjective 'numinous' was used by Dr.R.Otto in *The Idea of the Holy* (1917) to describe non-moral sacredness. It is something like numinousness that is behind the concept *mana* (*waken, orenda,* etc.), the luck or unluck that emanates from certain persons, which is inherent in certain objects, or is passed on by a priest, for want of which nothing will work well, or which will make a thousand and one things taboo. Freud in his *Totem and Taboo* cites Wundt's description of taboo as the oldest of man's unwritten rules.

Was it at a later stage that man's experience of the spirit of a place was focused in the *genius loci,* and every place or function that had its god? Animism as originally conceived by E.B.Tylor, three-quarters of the way through last century, supposes that primitives ascribe our own sense of personality to inanimate objects, thereby peopling nature with spirits. Various aspects of Tylor's view have been criticised for attributing to the primitive man's recently acquired sophistication. Owen Barfield, in his *Saving the Appearances* (Faber), has attacked Tylor's account of the projection of what is human on to the face of nature. Boldly taking us back to Levy-Bruhl's 'pre-logical mentality', by means of which the primitive relates himself to nature in a *'participation mystique'*, Barfield – though unhappy about the word *'mystique'* – has the primitive actually experiencing a living nature. One must feel that a poet would support him in this. The wonder, if not worship, in man's heart surely had its communion with the gods of the glades and streams.*

Barfield has other good things for us. In his *Worlds Apart* (Faber), he writes

> "a whole generation was quite satisfied that the Greek myths, for example, were simply statements about external nature – 'highly figurative conversation about the weather', as Farnell puts it. Another generation interprets them as mainly statements about the unconscious mind. Obviously they were both and neither. Go a little way farther back: dip into the *Vedas* and you often no longer know whether you are reading about birth and death, summer and winter, or breathing in and out. Why? Because symbolic language – and all language is symbolic in origin – can signify all these rhythms at the same time."

One is reminded of Groddeck's observation that poetry is constantly concerned with the relationship between the microcosm and the macrocosm, and, more importantly, between the mundane or symbolic and the heart's realities. (*Faust's* last verse begins: "All things transitory are but symbols.") Barfield's quotation continues: "Why on earth should language ever have come to be like that, unless it started like that?" And if such was the primitive's language, such was his experience. Aided by poetry, we can perhaps understand how his sense of wonder was released, not merely by the magical world surrounding him, nor merely by the point, or meaning of it all, his high god, by both its multiplicity and its unity; but also by what, in primitive eyes, must have appeared as the mysterious behaviour of many externals (animatism and *mana*), and by that which made, for example, a whole area such that he could experience a *thou* relationship with it, that is, with its indwelling spirit. His sense of wonder perceived all these as facets of the same gem.

Groddeck tells us that from the first, man has understood by means of the symbol. "But," he writes, "however carefully one may study a symbol, it can never be known. Symbols have a manifold existence; rightly understood, indeed they are all-significant." Like our many-faceted gem. Leading into the above-quoted passage from Barfield, we find: "The essence of a true symbol is its multivalence, its quality of meaning a

---

*Though grateful to Barfield for releasing us from Tylor's pan-projectionism, we need not follow him in his apparent total denial of projection.

number of different things at the same time. You even get a coincidence of *opposite* meanings."

Freud's limited and literalistic concept of the symbol, perhaps his greatest weakness, has served us ill. As some of Groddeck's examples show so well, a symbol suggests far more than it says; its meaning goes on reverberating through many layers of significance, indeed indefinitely. And therefore, however correctly we may interpret a symbol, there remains the harsh fact that, as Groddeck tells us, "the symbol may not be spoken." Indeed who would proffer a formula, a set of words, in lieu of a piece of music, or a painting? What we can put into prose we do not need to paint or put into music; and if we seek to make a symbol of it, all we get is a token, or counter. The symbol is poetry; its nature is wonder; and however much we would de-code it, we shall be brought up against Groddeck's "to disclose the mystery is not to resolve it".

Gradually, in the interests of repression, we have sought to limit the sphere of the symbolic to rites and creeds, and to emblems. The nordic warrior's ring was such a symbolic emblem; this and his sword were all that he really valued. From earliest times men have worn or carried emblems. Today psychiatrists have remarked that subjects with a deficient family resort to them. (See the discussion of a paper by Dr Ernest Hamburger, 'Tattooing'.)* Psychiatrists should recall that arms are borne by what are commonly considered the best families. Actually we should suppose the psychiatrists have confused symbols with badges, and that the reference cited should mention badges or tokens rather than true symbols — emblems with a specific intent, or a single meaning, such as the badge of office. Such an emblem's function is almost tool-like; it has a use to secure admission, or to label authority. The coat of arms, on the other hand, has all the multivalence of the totem, and is therefore a true symbol. Underlying the high valuation we give to the purposeless is the child in us that still treasures what, in their superior wisdom, adults designate worthless objects. Somewhere in his writings Groddeck mentions his habit of playing with his watch chain, and gives us the symbolic significance of this. Almost anyone in analytical circles today, having realised the unconscious meaning of such an action, would at once give it up. Not so Groddeck; a little skull hung from the chain, and he constantly played with it as he talked. Freud, genius that he was, is nevertheless described as never tiring of looking at or touching an antique seal he had had set in a ring which he always wore. He gave similar jewels to each of six intimate disciples, who with himself as seventh, formed what was almost a secret society at the core of the analytical movement. What could be more childlike, or cabbalistic! Alas, many of the brethren's thinking is, nowadays, adult, tool-like, and therefore blind. A highly esteemed analyst,

---

*In the *International Journal of Social Psychiatry,* vol. XII, no. 1.

who is also a charming man, said to my wife, who happened to be wearing a cross, "Why do you wear that thing? It's only a symbol of suffering." After that let us be sure to wear our emblems.

Anthropologists often characterise man as a tool-making animal, yet what an epoch it took him to think of hafting his flints! Meantime, from the very earliest graves, we have evidence of the rich variety of his attempts to cope with another world (manner and position of burial, type of tomb, the red colouring matter, shells, etc.); and all through every part of his life he is concerned with religion, as shown paramountly by his emblems. From the point of view of the actual evidence, it would be far truer to designate man as a worshipping creature. And surely the child's treasured objects are sacred, or at least talismanic, rather than tool-like. Our every concept of man today is of a functional entity, yet psychoanalytical insight reveals our entire world and mode of existence as symbolic, though even analysts need to study Groddeck to realise just how true this is.

The creed is described as the symbol of the faith, but unquestionably our outstanding symbol today is the mass. Like poetry, the mass is a construct that tends to elicit emotion, in this case the emotion of reverence, indeed worship. In *The Unknown Self,* Groddeck writes: "for me, as for all men, it is an absolute necessity of life to pay homage to the great; without this sense of reverence, one is not human."* And later, "we should accustom ourselves to regarding a blade of grass, a sparrow, or a fungus with equal reverence"** Given reverence, we need only be able to forget the precious ego in order to release the self on the flood waters of worship, where the ecstasy of the mystics may await us. Just as in music we may experience something that we do not otherwise experience, so also in worship we may have a unique experience of something, or someone, we call God. Worship is thus that form of the mind's activity whereby we may know God. By God, therefore, we mean the fulfilment and content of worship. We may thus say that worship is our organ of knowledge of God. The question then arises whether worship is our sole organ of knowledge of God. Groddeck, avowing his humanism, reached what many have considered the peak of his literary output in a profoundly reverential interpretation of Christ. He began by asserting that he regarded religion as a product of humanity, a view he elsewhere maintained about God. We might perhaps paraphrase — or should we say, transvaluate — this by saying Groddeck was unable to write about, think about, Christ and God in the terms in which we ordinarily think about this and that, and was only able to apprehend them in reverential terms.

---

*See 'Note' following this chapter.
**It is not long since an American psychiatrist called Schweitzer neurotic for his reverence for life.

Of course people do discuss them in terms that are not, in themselves, reverential: hence theology. Theology, however, seems so unexistential that one cannot imagine a living writer like Groddeck being content to remain long in its frame of reference. This is not meant to decry theology: the relevant parts of it are to the mystical experience as is prosody to poetry, or perhaps grammar to speech. We need theology in the same sense that we need grammar and prosody; but they come after the living event, and are not of its nature. Far from being a means for knowing the content of the experience, at most they can but be means of helping us to describe it, of analysing, sorting the various experiences.

Lord Herbert (1583-1648) is generally regarded as the first in this country to study comparative religion. Like his contemporary, Descartes, he began by looking into his own process of knowing; but he arrived at conclusion on a very different plane, that religion is the chief criterion of humanness. Thus he came to the position that there are no atheists. The statements of those who call themselves atheists are really objections to false accounts of God, which ascribe foolish attributes to Him. Atheists are thus those who would rather do without God than have one unworthy of belief. Groddeck, at the opening of his essay, 'The It and the Gospels', writes

> "some people trust to having all the knowledge and power they need, and try to persuade themselves and others that they can get on without a deity. Such people little imagine that they are thereby advertising their own fundamental insincerity, due to their repressions, for mankind is imbued with a belief in causation, and must always hold fast to faith in the Unknowable, no matter how much individuals may desire the capacity for atheism."

Elsewhere he relates our belief in an ultimate cause to our knowledge that we have fathers. Yet thus to explain it is to quit the plane of experience, and drop down to one comparable to that of prosody or theology. However, if we return to the position that it is part of human nature to revere and to worship, and that the ultimate content of worship is an experience of what we call God, we may yet, on a purely experiental plane, ask for proof – in the sense of the eating of the pudding. And on this plane we may indeed say that we have proof: after worship we are different, for all other experience is now different; moreover, since our human relationships are different, a veritable communion now exists for us. In a degree we are changed in the same sort of way as a man may be changed by conversion, whereby a life is oriented towards the ideal. We have only to read the lives of the mystics to be aware of the tremendous changes that are possible. Perhaps there are voices whispering that we may sometimes observe comparable changes in the lives of some who are not called religious. However, theologians would doubtless assure us that this was an effect of what is called the 'diffused Christianity' in our culture. (When maintained by an intelligent theologian, this argument is found to be a very difficult one to counter.) One fact stands clear, if worship produces changes. then, since Christ came "to bring life more abundant", the changes produced are of God if they are such as to lead towards fulfilment, in the sense of a freedom of the spirit. If, however, the changes inhibit the man's development, or merely constrict him, then it is not God, but perhaps a mere idol, that has been petitioned. "Try the spirits whether they are of God: because many false prophets are gone out into the world." And "By their fruits ye shall know them." Certainly there is much 'anti-abundance' released by what purports to be worship. We may wonder just how it got a footing; was there some original flaw in our form of worship; and, for that matter, what was the real nature and origin of our particular mode of worship?

As the ancient Greeks sowed the seed of our mind culture, and the Romans made the shapes of material organisation, the Jews, with a matching ardour and drive, were forging a religion that would intensify and sharpen the white man's spirit, and would eventually make its claim for the whole world. By the mysticism implicit in it, man would be lifted above nature to an existential awareness of his sphere and being as human and societal and spiritual, in contradistinction to the natural, and to the lack of status of the pagan as person. Judaism developed the notion of one-pointedness, integrity, and orientation of the spirit, the essence of vocationalism, and hence of the spiritual goal of living. It therefore eliminated the heart's claim to waywardness (multiplicity of gods) as a right. It at once marked the distinction between vocation and career by making the goal of man's spirit unknowable in material terms: God could not be portrayed. In a word, integrity of man's spirit was made possible by taking God out of nature, which of course involved taking Him out of the loins. Thus did man individuate and know his own strength. Standing above nature, he could then wrestle even with the divine, to win freedom from the arbitrariness of heaven still suffered by the pagan − to win, in short, a good covenant.

If it is thought preferable to exclude heaven from the picture, it could be put, though much less adequately, that man learned that he could come to terms with his Id and his super ego. As a result, he could orient his major purposes towards worthwhile fulfilments without anxiety. But there are further chapters to this story.

From earliest childhood I was taught that Christ received training from the Essenes. This was an esoteric tradition that in our times was publicly promulgated in the Liberal Catholic Church. Esoteric teaching further has it that Christ was the last of a series of trainees, His predecessors having all failed. And little wonder they failed: according to the teaching, the trainee had to live a life in which he would pass through various phases and ordeals traditionally associated with saviour figures, and would so act as to get himself crucified.

Something of this, apparently, has been detected by Dr Hugh J.Schonfield, and is expounded in his *The Passover Plot*. Many will already be familiar with Dr Schonfield's name as the translator of a version of the New Testament which brings Christ very close to the reader. It has been generally noted that Dr Schonfield's present work is, at least, a blow in the face to the 'advanced' scholars' anti-messianic views of Christ's origins. The book, born of the loftiest motivations, seeks to portray to us a noble design whereby Jesus engineered his own crucifixion and apparent resurrection in order to prove that he was the Messiah.

Naturally the esoteric teaching was not intended to deny the divine in Christ. The point was that if heaven was to descend, man must first work and strive upwards. If one man could be found who would enact and live the symbolic life-form, that lived symbol would save the whole world. Mitrinović was interested in this teaching, and said the Essenes were to be understood as attacking the old belief in blood. Most Essenes were celibate, and if an Essene married, and his wife became pregnant, he put her away. Increase, for the Essenes, was by affiliation. This was incidental to their striving to transcend nature. By conscious will, and by communal dedication, they sought to give deliberate guidance to human destiny.

Of course, Christ did not share the Essene strictness. On the contrary, His whole preaching was against such a literalist interpretation of the divine intent in man's aspirations. One might well go even further than the sense of 'literalist', and use the term 'idolatrous'. For the veneration of such ordinances and practices, in lieu of seeking the spirit of love and freedom, is surely an obeisance to mere brass. Indeed, so far did He move away from such obsessionalism that His means for the fulfilment of the law was only love, and healing through the forgiveness of sin. It was this insistence on love as a truer guide than mere law that made the individual person Christianity's centre of concern, instead of, as for Judaism, the race (a concept based on blood). Yet, though Christ's human conditioning could indeed be effected by the Essenes, His spirit was universal, and therefore beyond anything that could have been moulded or contained by a sect. Although He incorporated all the intensity of their spirit and meaning, the way He opened was a way for all.

An inability to live in the light of the new commandment involves an unacknowledged slipping back to the old; and thus we suffer a lack of the ability so amply to forgive as to heal, a lack of the spirit's ardour to fire with fuller life, a loss of the childlike transcendence of the literalistic. And having slipped so far, we find ourselves telling others what to do, and, especially, what not to do. Instead of in the first place remaining consciously on the plane of law, where we might have minded our own business, now that we are indeed back there, we may behave as though we were above it; and telling ourselves it is love that moves us, we may concern ourselves with the other's problems; but this we now do in terms of an unconsciously re-adopted legalism which makes us, if not punitive, at least superior. In a word, we moralise; the Pharisee, Christ's real devil, is reborn. And with this rebirth of what Christ lived to destroy, we lose Christ, are unable to know Him. Although orthodox doctrine does indeed constantly remind us that Christ was both God and man, yet, in emphasising the perfection of His human nature, churchmen are so swayed by moralising tendencies that they lose sight of the essence of humanness — that we err, that we are born divided, from the first are in raging conflict, that humanness exists in the sphere of the becoming, nor the become. The attempt to attain the static perfection of a god or an animal results in, respectively, hypocrisy and criminality: it is because man can fail that he has the saving grace of humanness — a truth that is acknowledged by all but the commissar and the executive. And it is because Christ failed that the world loved Him: because He was not the expected Messiah, and did not overcome Caesar, and could not — like our scientists — produce bread from desert stones, and above all, because He could not save Himself — because, in spite of the divinity of His spirit and its love for us, because of His inherent fallibility, that we are ever conscious of His warm and suffering and simple humanness.

Thus there was indeed a flaw at the very root of our form of worship. And anyhow, like everything that is truly human, our faith is as flawed as is our most divine core, our very heart. Inevitably, therefore, Christ's bride, after the seraphic honeymoon that brought back paradisal love, was soon indeed to be besmirched with every sort of wickedness. We all know the dreary tale of treachery, cruelty and ruthless ambition. Even bishops waged war for personal ends; love itself, the very principle of Christianity, was everywhere betrayed; religion became a clever trick. Christendom perhaps needed Joyeuse (the name Charlemagne gave to his battle axe) and forever Christ's whip and His invective were needed to defend the faith, to cleanse the temple, and to bring down the Pharisaical enemies of the little child. But instead, as a 'reaction formation', oriental asceticism and monasticism (originally more or less heretical) were quickly adopted by many devotees; and a good deal later came the celibacy of the clergy, on account of which Photius attacked Pope Nicholas I, claiming that it was ruining the morals of the Church. Meantime emphasis was placed on that fear of God and everlasting hell which it has been a major concern of the Liberal Catholic Church to expunge from the liturgy. In all the circumstances, it was perhaps natural that the Church as a whole should eventually have reached a position of 'safe' conservatism and literalism that, to active minds, has tended to seem remote from reality. Like God, the Church is dead, they report. Everything human begets its own opposite, and to ensure that it does so, we appear to be ready even to assist

Satan to usurp Christ and to glory in the death of Christ's bride. But whether suborned from herself, or dead to her love, she yet always retains the form of the divine impress; her sacraments are intact, the creeds and other formulations remain, and a majority of her sons truly revere: she is forever an undying symbol; and meaning will yet again flash from her every facet.

But stop. Are we not on the way to making the mistake that has been the undoing of that very sense of reverence we would promote – indeed, the mistake that has brought down religion itself? If the Church were all one would say of her in the above vein, how could she be dead? There is a vital distinction between a symbol that is purely meaningful, and on the other hand, a functional or practical institution that has also acquired spiritual symbolic significance, for example, the monarchy – and equally, the Church. (How instantly – from its very inception – the functional is found to have, or seems to have taken on, the shape of the symbolic!) Except that it is significant, the true symbol is as useless as a work of art, or at least far less useful than the ordinary single-significators (compare the Christian cross with the arithmetical symbol for plus). Thus it leads away from the mundane, via perhaps, the poetic, into the sphere of eternity – of all that is eternally significant. It is as a symbol that the Church is a spiritual reality; the incarnate fact is a functional institution composed of human beings, and which therefore fails and errs and is marred like everything human. To proclaim it as near to perfect is idolatry, a literalism that is the opposite of what is meant by the symbolic. And because the falsity of the claim must become plain as soon as the idol is tested in action, inevitably men will feel cheated in having been invited to revere, and will turn in rage.

We had indeed almost provided a further example of the root of our difficulties. To be quite sure that we understand the detail of that, let us resume the original position. By denying the fallible, human element in Christ's life, we brought ourselves to feel corporately that, as churchmen, we were the heirs of a God-like perfection; and by identification with the corporate ideal we were imbued with sufficient perfection to become thoroughly Pharisaical. Thus we become inhuman by denying what ensured Christ His humanness, arrive at a malignant fallibility by denying His natural fallibility.

When we plan to condemn others, it is understandable that we should first place ourselves in a strong position; this we can best do by identifying ourselves with what is commonly accepted as the right. This of course was the move made by the Church at the time of Charlemagne, and it marked the culmination of that tremendous reversal, in which the Church's original life-giving activity gave place to moralising, chiefly telling others what not to do. Dealing with situations by veto and prohibition is so much less trouble than by creative means. To permit in a way that will be generally acceptable may require wisdom: any fool can deny and condemn. The Pharisee is stupefied by his enormous draughts of self-adulation. Over against his constant condemnation of the sins of others stands Christ's healing principle of forgiveness — the price of love.

Clearly one makes no attempt to decry morals and law. It is, rather, as Groddeck points out, that Christ "puts morality on the same footing as the state, 'Render unto Caesar' ", and points to childlikeness as the way to the Kingdom.

Dostoievsky speaks convincingly of the adequacy of the Church's liturgies to convey her message: and the whole essence of that is in the mass. It is this greatest of prayers, this aspiration, and not any organisation or object, that is our supreme symbol. The enthusiasm for the Church as an organisation that we checked in ourselves a page or two back finds its truer outlet in the mass. All that Christ is and does is, essentially, in the mass. It leads us on a way of life, His way. It reflects the nature and structure alike of personality, divine and human, and of the cosmos, such is its scope and multivalence. Perfectly formed by its initial inspiration, by tradition and by the accretions of its history of devotion, it is the perfect evocation of our worship, our valid aid, therefore, to the knowledge that worship alone vouchsafes us. Today Rome presents a vernacular mass, and faces it about, the better to include, and to make it real to, the congregation. Yesterday, when the Liberal Catholic Church decided on the vernacular, it sought to emphasise the reality of the living Christ, and of His cosmic being. In my version I have tried to show His humanness, to convey His psychological meaning for each of us.

If one new version can be produced, I thought, why not others? And so I wrote mine. It is much too long for actual use (though easily cut); but being an individual version, it could, I hoped, set an example that would be followed by our poets, who might perhaps provide us with a growing variety of versions that could actually be used in our churches.* And what an opportunity for our musicians! By a variety of attempts to find an ideal modern idiom for the mass, indeed by making it into a theme for current literature, we might hope to awaken a widespread understanding of it, and to witness its magic stir to worship many who have hitherto known better. If the mass thus became the substance of a literary movement, Churches liberal enough to make use, from time to time, of the various new versions for actual worship would draw people who would never otherwise even consider attending. A symbol that is made into an art form acquires universal acceptability, like other works of art. And this remains true even though the symbol conserves its meaningfulness. We have only to recall the example provided by the totem pole for this to be self-evident.

---

*I experienced two great disappointments when first, T. S. Eliot went, and later Auden. I had hoped that one or the other of these might have taken up this idea.

Should it be objected that we do not want to attract merely by an aesthetic appeal. I would contend that it would not be like that. If we are at pains to find the best new idioms for our ancient rite, people will be interested to hear the message cast in the best current forms of their own language. And the more versions we present, the more will people's thoughts be sharpened, and their insight deepened. I believe we should soon be astonished to find how many there are with worship in their hearts, many who, if not believers in any literal sense, would be welcome to the altars of any truly liberal Church. To be co-worshippers is a thousand times more than being co-believers. In the act of worship, the soul is alone till the moment of union, which all the mystics describe in the terms of intimacy. Through, and by means of this, a qualitatively new relationship is established with the other worshippers, a form of intimacy with a public. This love is the *agapé* of the Gospels, and the relationship it creates is what we call communion. Though today we do not receive all those gifts of the spirit recorded as bestowed on the Apostles, nor even the blessedness and meaningfulness sometimes known in the first-century congregations, yet in a veritable communion we may still find a glad and ample experience of the life more abundant. Thus we may know that in our worship it was God that we knew.

Some day I shall write of the various new possibilities of psychological and spiritual experience with which man has provided himself. Again and again, by his creative imagination, man has lifted himself by his own bootstraps, raised himself to new levels of awareness and life. Among the more notable of these developments are romantic love and mysticism, both very new in humanity's saga, and both demonstrably products of literature. Whither might we be led by a eucharistic literature, especially if its products were actually used for worship? Might we, perhaps, hope for some development of the potentiality of communion, perhaps a new realisation of intimacy when corporately experienced, such as to produce a societal consciousness to match the great challenge of social change? The magnitude of our spiritual crisis must be my excuse for a statement of the obvious: the life of the spirit is threatened and could be overwhelmed; we could find ourselves whirled away into an existence composed of nothing but social-economic mechanisms, in which men and women would become male and female citizens, with no interiority beyond what was in newspapers, broadcasts and psychiatric textbooks. What is then to match the threat of these forces? And let us boldly ask, what is there that could even turn them to spiritual account? We all know well that the minimal answer is a feeling for the sacredness of life, death and eternity.

The esoteric story of the Essenes and Christ is one of a long-prepared, dire and utterly dedicated iniative that succeeded: by it history was lifted to a new plane. Since that day, there has been little for the faithful to do other than to spread the good news. Thus have we in small degrees continued in that initiative. What I propose is one more way of doing this. Oh yes; but if it worked as we have just hoped, would it not stand the world on its head?

A note on Psychiatric Classification

By viewing human deviations as exaggerations, or caricatures, of ordinary personality, psychiatrists are able to use the diagnostic entities then formed — paranoid, hysteric, obsessional, and so forth — as categories in terms of which even ordinary people can be classified. But of course the great are also included. It is then only one more step to the familiar view, long attributed to psychiatry, that genius is mad, or psychopathic. Obviously, however useful psychiatric classifications, the method involved has its limits, and we are in very real need of a further principle.

In describing his principle of intensification, Goethe has shown us that in nature's most perfect products, the idea of many lowlier growths is revealed. The development of this way of viewing nature brings rewarding insights into spirit's presence in nature. Once we have allowed the poet to open our eyes to this, it would be impossible to invert our view and again claim knowledge of the crude as a grasp of the developed. But to go still further in a negative direction, and to seek to understand the more perfect, or the great, merely by means of the categories of disease, would then seem perverse. Thus, although the analyst must indeed diagnose his patient, for example, must identify the form of the Oedipus complex from which the man suffers, yet he will never so understand his patient as to ensure his release till, Pygmalion-wise, he descries something of the potential man behind the imprisoning armour of neurosis. And just as the prime model of all our disorders is Oedipus, so the Christ in the heart is what gives shape and meaning to the new Adam. The significance of Oedipus is in the bonds and urges of the blood, and his fate is merely the extrapolation of these factors to their logical extremes: the blood's passions and loyalties can only result in conflict, in the grip of which man can never find his freedom. Christ is what Oedipus is not. His entire soul is given to harmony with the inner, heavenly Father, the while His attack is wholly against the bastions of an earthly father's world, the very fortress of all that is anti-heavenly. In consonance with His alienation of Caesar's world is that He is without connection with Joseph from the very start. And so much is He about His divine Father's business that He must repeatedly disavow His Mother's and brothers' claim on Him. He had thus transcended the temptation and motive of Oedipus, and could claim in kinship the world beyond the blood bonds of family, tribe, and race. He had stood alone — and had found mankind for everyman. He was the first free Man; and since only in freedom can the self realise itself, He is the model in the heart of every man who, above all, would to his own self be true.

If you would help a man, you must not only know his neurosis, you must understand him in terms of his own incarnation of spirit. Any help short of this is a form of spiritual mummification, or a deadening of the pangs of Oedipus.

8

DEATH

"Before Abraham was, I am", He said of Himself. If we put this together with the expression "the Son of Man" we understand that he takes Himself as essentially man (Groddeck).

Although I shall here seek to develop the significance for spiritual growth of the oddly named death instinct, I am far indeed from any wish to detract from the emphasis analysts so rightly give to liberation of and expression of the life instincts. A warm and happy love life is vital for the fulfilment of every personality.

In following a life purpose, and in our dedication to it, do we most profoundly differentiate ourselves from animals; yet without adequate expression of the life instincts, we do not best exhibit our human quality. Nevertheless, purposiveness so fires us that we love best the torment of the task, to use a phrase of Groddeck's. And certainly what we admire is the man whose vocation is more to him that his pleasures, or even, as with the hero, than his life. It is the death instinct* that gives man his significance to another, and indeed to himself; and man's quest is not essentially for pleasure: rather, he seeks ecstasy, and even, apotheosis.

In war, more than at any other time, the death instinct gains not only its direct requital, but is also, at the same time, overtly turned outward against others. Very plainly the unconscious meaning of war is man's need to know death: man's spirit, the spirit of both martyr and hero, flames into life, and now actively seeks confrontation with death! Clearly such mass activity blinds the individual's capacity for awareness of the springs of his being; yet all know something of the will to break out of sanity. Later, our strangled, conflicting urges drive us to deeper thought, and with death at large, some may feel that it is not only Freud's Oedipus myth, but

---

*See 'Note' at the end of this chapter.

also the Gospel story to which they should look for the true portrait of everyman. Perhaps in some sort of acceptance of death, of its timelessness, they might be free from anxious urgency. They feel that they should be able to remake their lives, for out of so much desolation, there may come a sense of rebirth, or more, rightly, of resurrection.

What is the Gospel story, but a story of increasing isolation, spiritual, societal, and finally, physical? It is the story of an individual, unique, not understood; through His singleness Christ achieves significant death. And then there is the Resurrection, after which He is an even stranger stranger. In a patriarchal civilisation He is early about His Father's business, but will not work His father's trade. Indeed we never see Him earning his living, and He calls His disciples from earning theirs. Perhaps, like Aristotle, He regards work as degrading. But what a crime (in the voice of the literal or non-spiritual moralist) in a pastoral society! Some work because they must, whether to wrest their bread from nature, or by the will of Caesar, or of those who enjoy his favour. Others work with passion, perhaps to spend and prove themselves, or because they have made their work an art. But whereas in the Orient the sannyasi wanders free, with only begging bowl in lieu of trade, how can we today, we who feel it a duty not only to support our families, but to send aid (which we must produce) to disaster areas, or to undeveloped countries — how can we take as our examplar one who will neither work, nor tolerate work by His disciples? Nor does He continue the family line. Indeed, He makes hatred of the family (see Moffat's translation) a *sine qua non* of the spiritual life, a condition which, in His refusal to acknowledge His mother and brothers, He himself would seem to have fulfilled. The individualist's failing! But worse still, He appears to be against religion, disputes with the priests, and goes about calling people vipers and whited sepulchres. His first miracle makes water into wine; He likes publicans and loose women, and chooses a school of minnows in which to whale. In the magical phrases of His Sermon on the Mount He captivates all; yet on a cool re-reading, one sees the magic is sometimes shot with the glint of irony. Thus one might almost continue with the Beatitudes indefinitely, for example: Blessed are the dying, for they shall be loved; and so forth. However, even if this is too crude, the Beatitudes do embody a sufficient trace of something like this for us to feel them as expressing a lofty realism of the spirit, whereby He would lead us out to a serenity beyond hope and despair. Yet He has attitudes it is hard to account for in such terms: for example, He praises the unjust steward, and recommends us to make friends with the mammon of unrighteousness. Like the author of the *Odyssey,* He would seem to regard guile as a virtue, for He advises us to agree with any sort of statement rather than risk jail, and explains that smoothing down a potential enemy is much more important than worship. And so on and on, till in the end,

He urges Judas to a deed that will be the man's undoing, so intent is He on the course that will bring Him to his own death.

Are we to find the spirit of communality in all this?

And what is the story of the ego and its growth toward good, what but a story of isolation? Man begins his life as pivot of the household; the baby commands by its inability to understand. Alas! In seeking to overcome this disability it often seems a man learns only that there is little real understanding in life, nor any certainty, except only that he must grow more and more individual till he achieves life's one certain goal – death. Will it be the hero's, the saint's, the great man's death, a death that will create a greater glory? Will he die to rise and live forever on the right hand of honour? If so his memory will be twisted to suit the ends of politicians, and history will use his name to embellish a cause to which he was a stranger.

Is it wrong to here recall Shri Krishna's "I am the gambling of the cheat", and our Lord's Why callest thou me good? Only God is good?"

Once we have stood up in our manhood, and have learnt to say, Thank God I am not as other men are, then out of our pride, grow all the civic virtues, honour, courage, justice, magnanimity, generosity, nobility and even something in the nature of forbearance, mercy, compassion, humility, should these suit our chosen stance.

We soon learn that honour is devotion to the cause of what others think of us; that courage is a display for these others, or for the compressed idea of these others' judgement that we carry about under the name of a social conscience; that though justice may hold the scales, her bandaged eyes can never see which way they tip – for who can tell at any moment what the majority of those others will think to be right? Whether thus disillusioned, or ripe with communal virtues, we may yet find no prospect of meaningful death, but simply that we are utterly alone in our wealthy or meagre old age.

If a man dies believing in the value of faking his ego. . . Or shall we, rather, speak of a man who adds to a more theoretical belief, such as a determinist view of human development? Then surely, in this latter case, if in any sense his existence continues across the grave, he must fulfil his determinist faith by taking the next logical step. What other course, then, has he but to know the other side of the picture, to learn to un-make money, in short to be reborn as the young rebel, who, thinking he is doing something original, merrily re-lives the previous life the other way up? And having lived that life, what is there? What but again the same theme, though perhaps still some other way up – perhaps the first half success, and the second half failure, or perhaps a steady growth toward success in one capacity, paralleled by a steady decline in another. In his essay, 'In Defence of Materialism', J.B.S. Haldane is most illuminating in explaining the mathematics of the inevitability of recurrence. Every event or life must keep on recurring for those with this belief. Thus what the Buddhist calls the *skandhas,* a sort of blueprint of life, inevitably 'reincarnates'. Clearly, it can be 'printed' different ways up, endlessly. No wonder Buddha regarded the prospect as one of endless suffering, and sought to break the cycle. It could only be ended by our ceasing to believe, since believing was the start of it. Especially should we cease to believe in seeming logical and reasonable; for being consistent, both in our own eyes and in the eyes of the community, is of the essence of all the ego's striving. People found themselves on believing. The content of a man's awareness of his ego is of self-validation by unending 'proof' of consistency in believing. If "What I say three times is true", how infinitely more true is what I have always said! And how infinitely more true and more right am I than anyone else! And although there are spheres in which many of us agree to share certain dogmas and opinions, there are indeed many areas in which we seek to be individual in outlook. What with this attempt, together with the faking of our egos to suit our purposes, is it any wonder that we are apt to die lonely?

If, during the course of our lives we challenged our own ego values sufficiently to learn to be without the flattery of community support, perhaps our ending might not be so solitary; for who will not seek out and follow the man who can stand alone? Is perhaps the message signalled by our Lord's very being that man *is* alone, and that he stands apart from the very values of the world, apart even from the best of the world, yes, and from the best of the world's values? Ego and community are one: they are but different ways of apprehending a tremendous falsification, a universal *maya,* whereby a man is ever prevented from being himself. The ego that would fulfil its destiny must die before death. In its resurrection it is seen as without that vainglory which is the mainspring of every old Adam; bereft of that, the ego's experience of itself is now that it is merely human; but as such, the new self has about it something one might describe as universality. Such a man we might send as a representative human being to some inhabited planet, knowing that, in spite of his marked individuality, people would not quarrel about his suitability for the role, and further, that however strange his spatial encounters, and however great his welcome home, he would yet remain the same George or John we had known. With his old ego dead, his reborn self knows its solitariness; community therefore can never more corrupt or wound him, and community itself, for him and to him, is thus changed. Where he goes people will either fail to notice him − for is he not *merely* human? − or they will themselves begin to be merely human, and community will begin to be a communion.

We can now see what it is that differentiates the strong, valid ego from the ego that must die. The latter is, in origin, the self we would see mirrored in the eyes of others; it is puffed up by their actual and supposed good opinions of us; next it is further inflated by having proved itself better than they (or that they are inferior); and as a last stage, may exist merely as a series of poses to deceive. As against this, the reborn ego, going beyond sociality, race, or faith, and acknowledging both personal kinship with all, and status for all to equal its own, is so strong with this human-wide sodality of the spirit that it is indifferent to opinions about itself. Moreover it knows its being is the same as that of nature, the cosmos, God; its sustenance is from all eternity, instead of from the crowd. And a man whose being is thus no longer contingent is so assured in his strength that he is warm, and he loves. He is like a child, who in the beginning is indifferent to others' attitudes, and yet is friendly, and loves one or two especially; and even if they injure him, he forgives. This is the small child, whom we are told to be like if we would enter the Kingdom. We see it all in the Gospel story. Christ, being of a God who was for all, brought us the great sodality. With such spirit animating Him, he was of course beyond hate or self-pity, even when they treated Him as an outcast and a malefactor. The warmth for all that was in Him was born of a strength and assurance that was independent of others' attitudes to Him; therefore quite naturally, when they were about to crucify Him, He prayed: Father, forgive them, they know not what they do.

He demonstrates the ego we should all seek, would we transform community into communion. First we note the determination in His prolonged refusal to be drawn till He judged His hour had come. Once it had come, we note how He retained the initiative all the way as He went up to Jerusalem, and then in pressing on towards His arrest and to the confrontation with Caesar's representative. Throughout He presents a picture of outgoing strength and tenacity of purpose, the power of positive action and forthrightness.

Alas! In place of the tremendous individuality that is the core of this ego, many Christians but ape Him, or seek to. Their repression of their aggressive drives goes to the point of eliminating the assertion necessary for strong action, and they have so much guilt about their sexuality that their positive and creative powers are replaced by the negativity of moral masochism. Worst of all, the attempt to love an enemy is based on simple denial of an opposite attitude, and therefore becomes sanctimoniousness.

The Oedipus story is of the universal community row, the tale of any family row; and we all daily prove its truth. The least vestige of a triangle situation, and the unwanted third must be dispatched, to leave us on the familiar horns of a frightful dualism, myself and the other, in which the longed for unitary state of unchallenged egotism is gambled and fought for in the chancy game of devour or be devoured. How true a tale! Yet is this man's truest?

We have already remarked on what some would call mankind's truest tale, that of the hero who hurtles right out of the community to his death — and to the creation of glory. It is told again of the scientist who risks his life and reputation for the new; or, to pass to another plane, of the penniless young blade who sacrifices his ego, pleasure and his standing among the gilded young for the sake of a family he will sweat to rear; of the mother who has abandoned the gaiety and smart freedom of singleness to risk her life for a new life; of the sperm that risks all self-life by taking with it no means of nourishing itself, and with the goal of its hard-competed race the creation of another being and not its self-perpetuation.

Ah! Christ, do you forever climb the senseless hill?

One, two, and then at three years, familiar though this seems, nevertheless unannounced we have switched thought to a different scale of reckoning. As we move up to three years, and then onwards, we need only to persist to find ourselves involved on the on the endless course of counting; but we were launched on this only on arriving at three: at two, there was no sense of a logical pull onwards to three. Our direction had not been established: we might as well have reverted to one. From the level of what may be merely personal, even infantile, we leap to the scale of the infinite repetitions and variations of the universe. The unseen, the Father, having been followed by the divine and yet incarnate Son, we then have the Holy Spirit manifesting communally.

First the unmanifest source of my being, my forgotten infancy, through which intimations of immortality jostle with the tremendous primitive obscenities of nature; then next my divided adult self, open to all events, yet closed to them by my criticism. Thus, part of me still the submerged mystery of my epic child self, yet another part of me active and critical, and forever faced with the dualism of problems. My heart, its palpitant, fearful flesh, is split, and its everlasting problem of oneness with the beloved. Here indeed is the dreadful home of Oedipus, and here always the crucifixion; for from this dilemma there is no escape within the confines of life. But I am not confined to these two selves, the private and the personal; there is also the public self. If through the Christ in me I am truly one with my source, and can remain one only, isolate, so that my spirit maintains its identity through the murderous stress and cross-purposes of its dual nature — and its consequent opposition to the world — then thereafter the Comforter, the third, will renew me in fellowship with all. For though it may oppose the ways of the many, the community, as the Apostles, like their Master, warred against the *status quo*, it will establish me in a communion of understanding with all. Martin Heidigger in *Being and Time* points out that people become a man's enemies when he seeks to be authentic. The community is 'the crowd', which is given to 'idle talk' and 'ambiguity', by which man is 'tranquillised' and led into 'temptation' and 'self-entangling'. Over against this experience of community we must set the experience of community as a communion, by which the individual is salved from anxiety, despair and isolation that lays him open to the temptation of the crowd.

But this is conditional on the maintenance of identity. Yet as we know, the Father forsook Him, and Christ Himself died. Both His hidden source and His adult, conscious life, what the ego relies on and yet fights, as well as the ego itself — the two terms of the everlasting human conflict — both disappeared. All that was left until the Resurrection was His body, the mere form of His life. And there is a sense in which we may say that, for a period, it is merely the form, the empty behaviour pattern, that survives a full experience of the devastation of any major problem, for intelligent self-direction is gone. Anyone who thinks he is so normal, ordinary, or well-adjusted that he can go through life without such devastation is either a clot, or is deeply, perhaps incurably, repressed; or he has had a rather full dose of the mummification that is called psychiatric treatment. We cannot even, and should not, avoid swinging between euphoria and phases, not necessarily of depression, but at least of counting the cost: moments when the soaring spirit has gone. And we must relinquish it, together with the vision it brought, if ever we are to see clear-eyed into a new truth. *Stirb und Werde,* die to become; this was of course Goethe's dictum. And though indeed our first such 'death', because of the ego's resistance to and horror of it, must needs be shattering, yet we learn to yield to it in such a manner that peace of mind persists. Death of the ego in this sense is obviously a precondition of any meaningful renewal. The deepest life in us, that which would live fullest, must therefore, in some sense, depend on the death instinct, must reach out towards death, or towards that which is spiritual.

Adler points to the power-striving that, he claims, originates deep in the pre-sexual life of the child. Freud's tremendous truth points to sex that divides (*secare* = to cut) our whole life. Stekel's insistence on the prevalence and intensity of sado-masochism may perhaps portray a sphere in which the two outlooks meet. But then we must see every psychological problem as one of ecstatically overcoming or being overcome, and full ecstasy is unconsciousness, a death of the ego. Jung facilitates thought by his concept of the universal unconscious; but by making this a sort of extension of the submerged self, he loses the third term, and with this, the crisis of destruction that leads to it. The terrible core of Christianity is missed, and hopes for the millennium, if Jung ever had any, fade into depression about our future. (I do not dismiss Jung. On the contrary, I have a high regard for him, particularly for his 'philosophy', his mythological and esoteric additions to his therapy; they are a valuable enrichment to the prosaic, positivist view of contemporary culture. Jung's therapy, however, is not to be compared with the Freudian, if only because of all that it fails to deal with; for instance, Jung has very little to say about the father.)

It is by the hands and feet that Christ is crucified. Psychoanalysis takes us again and again to the orifices which are situated in the head and torso, and has not a great deal to say about the extremities. The crucifixion is the drama of the individual, who unites his own duality within himself, opposed by the public. It is the crowd, rather than Pilate, which crucifies Him. The hands and feet are not indecent or private, for with the former we work, and even the latter are social, for metaphorically at least, they enable us to take our stand in life, or follow the steps of our career. Our activities, our function, are our public self; by these the law and societal life takes cognisance of us. By these we are tied to the daily round, the treadmill called community whereby each becomes a hand – never a person.

Our Lord's head and side are also wounded, by thorns and a spear, but it is the crucifixion and not these wounds that are the real means of His death. The head, however, has considerable public importance, for though – unlike many women – a man does not usually gain his livelihood so much by his face as by his hands, nevertheless others know him by his face; and in his head he thinks private individual thoughts that will seem to motivate his actions towards us. The breast may, in the case of a man, be exposed without indecency, and here traditionally reside our feelings for our fellows.

Below the belt Christ is unwounded. It is in the belly that the universal and therefore private needs are located. Here every man requires animal sustenance, here he yearns for the biological universals which are below the scope of community dictate. A man's need for food will remain whatever the government.

Lower still, in His privates, which are the emblem of the whole root and myth of man, Christ is untouched. But I write of what Christ is to us, rather than of what actually happened: it seems clear that the privates were indeed the object of particularly sadistic attention.* However, for us, the Christ drama is primarily one of life and death, not a sexual drama. Certainly the prime concern of all religion is death, and its fertility rites are firstly to continue life, and then sensual in motive. And it is the public spectacle of crucifixion, and not the private loss – of castration – that has moved the world. It is our function and status – women's place in the home and men as soldiers, and so forth – in the community and the cultural values thereby created, that have given sex the vastly greater place

*See 'Note' at the end of this chapter.

it takes in human affairs than in animal life, where it is usually seasonal.

Groddeck's alternative to the Freudian view of circumcision is here relevant. He questions the view of this rite as a symbolic castration on the ground that the sources of potency are untouched by circumcision. The operation is a removal of the containing or feminine part of the member, and is thus clearly a symbolic attempt by patriarchalism to make the man more male, more single. By this, man would impose his image of himself on his organism. 'Man' would? It is the self-conscious ego that does. Here we see dramatic expression of the will to isolate from nature, the given. The organ by whose function the ego most readily melts and merges with the life processes is maimed to bear that isolate ego's stamp. And is not the whole Gospel story a story of singleness, isolation? Christ is two, God and Man, yet does His works only by being one, one with the Father in himself. And His destiny is that He must stand alone, deserted by both man and the Father. It is, after all, by uniqueness, not by acceptance of communal values, that creativity appears.

Fear of nature, or of other people, fear of consequences, is really inconsistent with the distinctively human quality in man, in the sense that in the degree to which purposiveness is apparent, such fears and dangers are faced, dared. More characteristic is his fear of seeming odd, which is ultimately the fear of madness. Part of this is his tendency to be treacherous to a belief or an ideal, to some expression of what he regards as truth. Whether such cravenness results in adherence to a religion or in agnosticism, what undoes us is projection of our judgement on to the crowd, and submission to it, rather than defiance of 'Pilate's jibing question' (Groddeck).

But clearly such fears are far from the crude fear of nature. Nowadays, nature's body is raped for the knowledge with which to defy and master her laws, and her rule over us; by the intimacy of our knowledge of her, we achieve superiority over others who know less.

Oedipus and its triplicity again! But Groddeck claims that even the Oedipus complex is only a symbol. To regard some sort of tribal, family, or communal row as generative of our human quality is merely to retroflect the enigma of our destiny back on to nature and the community, and to make these into repositories of what may be confected by the ego. As Freud takes us beyond the pleasure principle, he seems to portray the neurotic conflict as more and more a battle between man and himself. This brings the death instinct to the fore. It is by his death instinct, and his own battle with it, that man becomes himself, and is then able to bring to the community that which makes it a communion. Only by death could the Son of Man exist for us.

We love to sleep, for then the vessels relax, and the blood smooths and feeds every twitching nerve till it is inert. But all day long, the more we wake, attuning to every stimulus, only to drive on to further vantage points, all the time heightening sensitivity and awareness of nerve and brain and spirit, we undo the life-giving work of sleep and the blood. It is thus death that gives human meaning to our existence: the life of the blood on which the tribal community is based would drown spirit and individuality. Community is the stumbling block, and the test for us all; can we exist bereft of community-made beliefs sufficiently to tread the austere path blazed by Freud? For communal truth is basically utilitarian, and may be made to lean towards either the vainglorious or the humanitarian. However in both cases it is over against the supreme values manifest through creativeness, revelation, poetry; for these manifest in individuals; over against, too, the validity of a life lived in awareness of the unconscious; yet without such leaven, community at its best is mockery and an unutterable bore, and as such, is death to any life of the spirit.

That communal life fails to extinguish Christ is due to its inability to tackle Him on the plane of His own reality. This is made clear in the symbol, as Groddeck explains. It seizes Him with wood, the stuff of His early craft, taking Him by the hands and feet, as though He lived by work, by community value. But wood is *the* substance with which (till modern times) things were built or made, is, to the unconscious, a universal symbol of the mother, who is the primary source and custodian of what is communal, who *is* the hearth and home, and the stability of all that is social, as surely as man is destroyer, arbiter and the mediator of spirit.

But Christ will be taken from the cross, and by His ascent, leave behind and below Him all that it would mean to Him. And He was destined to the words: 'Woman, what have I to do with thee?' In this we see that the incest taboo is loaded with more than its merely sexual significance, and is given a more fundamental value. His spirit leaves behind and below the one who stands for the value of substance, and who, by having given Him earthly and communal substance, would claim possession of and therefore power over Him. (He must be isolate.) Thus does He dramatically state the prerequisite of His new commandment: Love is for love's sake, and not for power's sake.

(Since the religious restrictions on sex arise from the primary incest restriction, this view is of vital importance to those wishing to live devout lives. What the Christian is really required to put out of his life is the ego feeling of power and possession usually associated with sex.)

By resurrection, and still more, by ascension, Christ eludes the community's intentions, thus showing that He cannot be seized by matter, nor taken by His communal members. His reality is not as a communal being, a worker, but in spirit. His truest resurrection is in the spirit of man, where He lives forever by His word. The beginning – and the culmination – of everything human is in language. Christ is the word of everyman, the pattern and meaning of every life. It is by virtue of this pattern and meaning, both in ourselves and in others, that we distinguish ourselves from the animals, and make the human communion out of our powers of communication. Thus the essentially human reality is of meaningful consciousness rather than of biological existence on the plane of sex or work.

Whether it be in wood, or in a life lived (and death), does any genuine life symbol, or equally a spiritual symbol (i.e. one that is unique, and sufficient among its kindred and in its own sphere) cover in its uniqueness its entire semantic field? Does it express a full potential? As Groddeck once put it to me, to the infant and to the small child, the relationship of symbol and that which is symbolised is one of identity. To this we may add the following reflection: whether in the vital matters that here concern us we ever attain to any higher principle of apprehension than that with which we start our lives, is questionable. The soundness of Groddeck's dictum will be increasingly evident the more the symbol replicates its original in a seeming livingness, an attribute that the child insists on in all that is meaningful to it. A living and perfect symbol, that is to say a life lived true in both spirit and fact to the life pattern of the Messiah, would be the Messiah incarnate.

Did the Incarnation complete wisdom? Is that what the Incarnation is, a new, full awareness? Is then all conflict resolved, if we could but realise it? Is it merely for us to recognise, to acknowledge, perfection?

Then, we cry out, there is an end to differences and definitions, and no more inquiry about the difference between difference and identity. Distinctions are gone; there is nothing new under the sun. It is time for sunset, for death. Indeed nirvana has been translated 'blown out' — like a candle. It would seem then that the stage is set for a new crisis, for who would accept such a sort of nirvana?

But are there not endless worlds to conquer? And is it not only egotism that is blown out, for have we not seen this as the proud aping of Christ? I acknowledge His atonement; it is His, and I no longer need to split myself in the enactment of crisis. I go forth to a world renewed: like one drunk at sunrise, and shouting at the sun, and drinking its brightness till my shouts turn to the laughter of release and ecstasy: and everything is worthwhile, and I am strong, and everything sings and is once more meaningful. No, it is meaningful as never before. In truth 'He is the meaning of the earth' (Rudolf Steiner) and its life. And if, when it is the afternoon, or towards evening, I am calm again, yet still the air is sweet to breathe, and soft on my cheeks; and the meaningfulness of all is that joy will always come again, and more, and always more and more. I too atone, by participating. I renounce my grievance and my grieving, and at once there sounds the voice of Christ: Enter thou into the joy of the Lord. Of Him my only organ of knowledge is worship.

What now is our position?

The unconscious meaning of war is man's need to come to grips with the problem of death.

To believe in death as an ending of consciousness is as absurd as to believe in the hippogriffe; for both are outside all human experience. As though we could experience non-experience, be conscious of no consciousness, have a pocketful of no money! By its very nature, consciousness is immortal, every moment of it.

We never come to grips with the real problem by dealing with death externally, as an event. Indeed we may start coming to terms with the external event only by approaching it subjectively. We should seek to understand both the significance for life of death as a spiritual and recurring annihilation of the ego, and equally the deep inner processes that result in our being propelled towards the ultimate goal of death. Why, though we are all brought up with the doctrine that Christ died to give us access to the Kingdom, why do we nevertheless still feel that new life is born only by our courting or facing death — or at least danger? It is as though the hero in every heart felt it necessary again to redeem the world, or at least to risk death for the sake of new life, or a greater glory. To comprehend man we need the Gospel story; without this we are left acutely conscious of the inadequacies in the picture psychoanalysis has formed for us from the myth of Oedipus.

The advent of psychoanalysis has the same meaning for our spiritual understanding as the coming of world wars; we are forced to grips with all that is involved in the life-promoting and death instincts.

Though we need our sexuality, and desperately need to be able to number it among those things that are meaningful in our life, and although the Oedipus story is true of all of us, the truth of immediate significance is our impious tendency to re-enact the gospel as psychological tragedy. In this we each divide and undo ourselves in futile striving, whether in repressing ourselves to counterfeit virtue, or in 'dying' for someone instead of loving him. We even become Judas to Christ, whether the Christ we discover in ourselves, or as discerned in the hearts of others; and at once we seem compelled to betray the ideal, the true-loving, the genuinely sacrificial. A proper understanding of these procedures brings a certain liberation from them; we need no longer enact tragedy; we can love and enjoy one another. The force of the death instinct will then go to steady the pivot of our judgement, ensure both mannerliness and sustained attention by constraint of impulses, so direct fear as to produce awe and reverence, and generally fortify our sublimations, releasing tenderness and the spirit's power of self-transcendence. The remainder of the instinct's aggression is to be turned outward, and to become the drive and tenacity in daily work, the forthrightness enabling a man to speak his mind, and the power to stand up for himself and his cause.

Since in a world of uncertainty, death is our one certainty, it may well be regarded as everyman's true purpose, his one sure goal. Those who, in addition to facing death, can discover this purpose in themselves, in a spiritual sense, and can realise its personal and universal meaning, transform time for themselves, and thence the quality of all emotion. For such realisation and acceptance of death and its meaning is the beginning of an experiencing of timelessness, of freedom from that desperate sense of urgency which constitutes anxiety. What is required is, on the one hand, an identification with the death instinct, a sense of working towards the ego's death,* symbolised by Christ's hurrying Judas towards his fell project. On the other hand, there will be no realisation of meaning in all this unless it is accomplished without diminution of all the usual life urges. As at birth, so on and throughout, both life and death are incarnate and active in us. Forever is there the crucified man in the heart, and our spiritual perception of His resurrection. Equally present is the blinded limper, outcast and driven on his downward course by the untiring furies; and burning in his heart to the very last is the over-zestful life urge that was his beginning. But is it not the death instinct that tames the Oedipal in us? The attempt to be without it makes idols of the self and its world, the community, and so also of Christ; it makes a nonsense of all virtue and holiness; it renders life a bondage to the sequence of mere causality; and our entire existence is transformed into alternations of boredom with gloom and worry, relieved only by anodynes. Much of our living is an organised denial of the death instinct; our prime concern is to 'ostrich' away this inner traitor. Yet eschatology is an essential for understanding the here and now, and is not without the fullest pragmatic significance on the level of the psychotherapeutic: a proper acceptance of death, while the love of life remains rich, is the certain path, not only to freedom from anxiety, but also to the resolution of doubt and ambivalence, and to their translation into faith.

The message of the hour to us should be that even Thanatos is to be brought under Psyche's sway. We no longer dare deny to consciousness a proper knowledge of the death instinct. How long before a majority agree that the unspeakable results of this instinct's unconscious out-turning would seen to demand of us that we give the meaningfulness of intimacy to community — as, at times, in Christendom's first century — and that such community, now as then, should ignore frontiers? It was by the widening of tribal allegiances to include gentiles that the human communion was founded. Communion: but we can hardly consider it without again realising the significance of the three. Having realised something of the Incarnation, of the secret spirit in the public form of

---

*Dreams of dying, or of approaching death, are valuable experiences of the death of the old Adam, our egotism.

man, we are bound to seek communion, that secret, spiritual bond between man and man, the Holy Spirit. Having learnt to count three, we are confronted with endless numbers – in this case – of other men. The family, father, mother, son, is indeed the starting point, the model of all community; but the endlessness of the human communion is never even entered into until all the three are fully equal, and yet fully individuate, a state of affairs precluded by Oedipal passion. In other language, the members of an ordinary family each in his own way fail to qualify as integers. To bring communion into being Christ had to redeem man and demonstrate the freedom attained by full individuation, and thence the possibility of a non-passionate love, *agapé.* Such a thought implies endless hope.

With the ending of both the great wars of this century there were hopes that victory would redeem so much death by inaugurating a new deal for mankind. Yet have we not well learnt that expectations of a heavenly reign should receive a purely mystical interpretation?

As the culmination of the analytical procedure, to meditate on death with life in the heart is to generate hope. Thus Roman Catholics, last thing every night, imagine the crucifixion, and compose themselves at the foot of the cross. Alternatively we may dwell on certain well-known words:

> . . . and desire shall fail: because man goeth to his long home, and the mourners go about the streets.
> Or ever the silver cord be loosed, or the golden bowl be broken, or the pitcher be broken at the fountain, or the wheel broken at the cistern.
> Then shall the dust return to the earth as it was: and the spirit shall return unto God who gave it.
> Vanity of vanities, saith the preacher: all is vanity . . .

After due meditation, we may perhaps for a time at least fully accept the demise of the vainglorious ego, whereupon a new light will conjure forth visions of timeless intensity of living. In the light of moments like these we are unable to renounce hope for the world, and must continue to toil at the foundations of the new Jerusalem.

A note on 'Death'

Parts of this book, especially the foregoing essay, are meant to reflect certain states of mind, rather than to be taken literally. Thus, for example, I have no wish to support Freud's notion of the death instinct; yet it is an expressive term conveying something of those paradoxical movements of the soul that sometimes appear in poetry and mysticism – or perhaps I should rather say, in those who still struggle to attain to the mystical level. For the true mystic is at his true moments serene, by virtue of his conscious integration with divine nature; and his mind is balanced by the ethical bonds of his communion with his fellows. Through troubled worlds he walks a level path, though known to no feet but his; and the tumbling world may think he tumbles worse than all. Yet even in the heart of one such as he, we may find a resolution of opposites that once clashed: indeed paradox is everywhere, and is the essence of all our finer feelings, such as true love, which is an amalgam of the longing to possess and of sacrifice or self; or to take another instance, awe, a sensibility compounded of fear and venerative love, or adoration. Many regard religion itself as paradoxical, not merely because it sees the end of life as the beginning of eternity, but because of the nature of its values and aspirations: Christ certainly appreciated the paradoxical, in this sphere, a fact well illustrated in the formulation, 'He that shall save his life shall lose it'. Tranquillity itself may be the product of a conflict. As Morwenna Donnelly writes in her *Beauty for Ashes* (Rider):

> And this stillness is
> As a spark of truth
> Struck
> In the clash of a paradox

I should perhaps add that I use the word paradoxical in its ordinary sense, and not in the special and limited sense given to it by Pavlovians to describe an abnormal condition of the brain in which weak stimuli result in more marked responses than stronger ones.

For an account of the central nail in the cross, to go under the crutch, see Charles Guignebert's *Life of Jesus* (History of Civilisation) (Kegan Paul Trench Trubener & Co.) 1935, p.479; but one must be wary of some of these secular writers on religious matters. Only ten pages after his remarks about the central nail, Guignebert, speaking of the women Mark tells us watched the crucifixion, suggests that since the Evangelists needed evidence, they must have invented these women. When it suits his book to accept a text as it is written, he does so; when he is not thus suited, without the pretence of evidence, he thus declares the text invention. He rushes on jubilating: "What must happen did happen; what must be said was said." And then: "The whole Gospel tradition clearly collapses in the face of the positions here established" (*sic*).

If so proud a boast is permitted, I too would mention a great triumph: aged five, with one blow of my wooden sword, I defeated a crowd of pursuing demons.

Forsaking All: in the Steps of the Forsaken

The white sea horses foamed,
And the white sea birds followed,
Wide winged, along the wake
Where the white sea horses ran.
      Tonight I have left my love.

Far, wild, and unimagined,
The course the horses ran,
As far and unimagined,
As the way my white love takes.
      Tonight I have left my love.

I walk on the lonely waters,
Direct to the wide world's call,
Away in the gales of midnight —
Away where my lady listens?
      Tonight I have left my love.

Farewell my vanished lady,
Who left as I might have left you.
Now streaming and reaching after, with
My tears I call you back — for farewell.
      Tonight I have left my love.

Is there leaving, or crying after,
Or listening, or hearing, or even sound,
Is there love, or love's death, or fulfilment,
Where the white horses carry our hopes?
      Tonight I have left my love.

The fragile and terrible horses,
The relentless flight of white birds,
My feet on the surging waters,
Without track — and the wide world's call.
      Tonight I have left my love.

Before me a breaking star now shatters
My sightless dark. Breaking and breaking,
Still breaking, its whiteness,
For this instant, illumines my sight.
      Tonight I have left my love.   (1942)

Part three

THE ACTUAL DIMENSION OF THE MATTER

9

AN UNUSUAL DREAM

I once asked a member of the Society for Psychical Research whether he thought that the main body of the membership was beginning to reach any sort of definite conclusion on the question of survival. The Society has, after all, been in existence since the end of the last century, and must have attracted many intelligent people who have been devoting a great deal of thought to trying to solve the problem. My friend replied that there was a substantial body of the membership definitely convinced that we did survive death. But on the other hand, there was another body of members who were pretty sure that we did not, and between these two were many who simply worked away at the procedure for sifting evidence, members who were interested in the problem, but who still preserved an open mind. I asked him about the proportion and size of these different sectors, and after making various reservations, he said that perhaps it would be correct to guess, though rather wildly, that the three of them were roughly equal. It is an interesting reflection that after so much inquiry, opinion may still remain balanced. It is also of interest to me to notice that believers and disbelievers tend to be impassioned in their statements of view; indeed one only has to recall hearing two such people argue to realise the intensity of the passion which is involved. I shall hope to discuss the motives for this in my next chapter. At the moment all one can say is that those on either side would appear to find it necessary to produce this passion to make up for the lack of conclusive evidence pointing either way.

With opinion so divided among the informed, one tends to ask oneself what one thinks. Perhaps I as an uninformed person may consider that I have a right to an opinion? For myself I must ask, is there a possibility of a psychological view of the truth? You will ask how a psychologist can possibly take cognisance of a matter so much beyond his scope? Yet in my circumstances, I feel that I am bound to ask that question of myself. In approaching the problem, one finds one's attention is necessarily directed to the people involved, and the effects on them of believing one way or the other; and it is of interest to note that the effects seem bad whichever way the belief goes. Sectioning the great whole of our experiencing, or of any aspect of our experiencing, is something in the nature of an act of violence, particularly if, for want of adequate reason, we are in any sense motivated by arbitrariness in our act. The unconscious is ambivalent, it always sees two sides to everything. To come down on one side or the other involves an act of repression, and repression is hurtful.

To attempt to preserve for ever an open mind is for ever to restrain our appetite for a solution. However rational such a procedure may seem, this also is hurtful, in the sense that it involves the maintenance of constant tension. To be for ever working at a problem and never to reach a conclusion seems contrary to nature. On the other hand, the cowardly avoidance of serious thought about the matter, a matter that we are all in a basic sense seriously concerned with, does not save us from belief; it simply lays us open to being possessed by such random beliefs as come our way from the environment.

I recall a philosopher making a *mot* on sexuality: sexuality is that sphere in which, whatever you do, or don't do, you are wrong. Does this apply also to believing? But perhaps all I am doing is to present another formulation of the doctrine of original sin, the view that one is wrong to start with, that believing is being biased, but that nevertheless one is almost bound to take sides.

Let us question believers on either side. We should ask a materialist first: Why do you believe in non-survival? His answer will be probably an expostulation that surely it is obvious that with the death of the body life ceases, just as when a dynamo stops no more electricity is generated. This will seem so obvious to him that he will feel that there must be passion to avoid seeing his view. It may also be pointed out to us that unless the human being had an end, he would have no shape in time. He would simply be part of the ever-continuous processes of nature, and so could not begin to assume the first requisite for that uniqueness which we know as personality. Those with faith in survival may well object that all this represents a very objective view, and may claim that it is only an objectively conceived self that, like all objects, must have an end. Moreover it will be justly said that it is not by feeling my time limit that I experience my own personality. Experience of time is always experience of anxiety or of boredom. My most real moments, moments when I am most myself, most experience my personality, are my eternal moments; in timeless moments I most truly exist. But there is a much stronger argument here: I have no experience of the cessation of consciousness. Even during sleep some thread of consciousness continues; I am aware on waking that I have slept well or ill, long or deeply. Looking at the matter objectively it is remarkable how few people, in spite of the random movements of sleep, fall out of bed. However, that takes one away from the centre of the problem, which may perhaps be expressed in the question, How could I possibly experience non-experience? And to be asked to believe what I have never experienced, and which of necessity must be outside the range of all experience, is like being asked to believe in pink elephants. Indeed it is far worse, for there are many who have indeed seen these wondrous beasts. (As I write I have discovered that Goethe spoke of the impossibility of conceiving of a cessation of thought and life. One might have guessed he had said it. He also warned of the difficulties involved in building on this.)

Thus it may well be said that the materialists must have had a great deal of passion to maintain the belief in death in the sense of cessation of consciousness. They were ignoring a vital aspect, a vital view of the problem, the experiential view. And the use of this word at once reminds me of Bertrand Russell's well-known dictum: experience is the neutral stuff of existence. Experience, be it noted, not matter, nor substance, nor objectivity. The reality of this table, of a woman's hair, of dustbins, atom bombs and politics is our experience of these things. Lord Russell's formulation has been subjected to criticism, and philosophy has moved on to other considerations, yet it must always retain great significance for all who, like psychologists, are concerned primarily with the experiential. Of course experience includes observation of other people, or we may put it that there are two sorts of experience, subjective experience and objective experience.

With these considerations in mind, I should like now to present to you certain strange dreams. I must, however, first mention scientific evidence suggesting that the kind of dreams I shall describe are impossible. I refer to well-known evidence that dreams are dreamed in periods of time that are, very roughly, appropriate to our sense of the duration of experience in the dreams. By observing sleepers, subjecting them to certain tests, and waking them at a particular moment, observers claim to have established the following positions. People dream during four or five periods a night. Before dreaming, the sleeper settles himself like a viewer before a screen, and is then still, except in certain cases where there are appropriate movements; for example, if somebody is dreaming of a of a tennis match, beneath the eyelids the eyeballs may be seen to move from side to side. If we wake the dreamer during these movements, it is claimed that he can tell us the dream of the tennis match. If we wake him by means of pouring cold water over him, it is said that he may report a dream in which the match is interrupted by a thunderstorm which wakes him. Thus the progress of the dream is regarded as a process that takes place in time. Subsequent experiments carried out by E.Moskowitz and H.J.Berger at the University of California with the aid of electrodes placed at the corners of the sleepers' eyes, have now rescued me by undermining these threatening positions. Among other discoveries was a subject whose eyes had been moving from side to side but who yet reported a dream of an upright row of buttons she had been studying from top to bottom. It is thought that the eye movements are not related to dreaming, but to the coordination of the eyes.

There is in Addison's *Spectator* writings* an account – of course openly sceptical – of such a dream, in conjunction with an analogous story about a dream or vision of Mohammed's. The former is quoted by the Right Rev. C.W.Leadbeater, in his little book, *Dreams.*

Addison writes:

"A sultan of Egypt, who was an Infidel, used to laugh at this circumstance in Mahomet's Life, as what was altogether impossible and absurd: But conversing one Day with a great Doctor in the Law, who had the Gift of working Miracles, the Doctor told him he would quickly convince him of the Truth of this Passage in the History of Mahomet, if he would consent to do what he should desire of him. Upon this the Sultan was directed to place himself by an huge Tub of water, which he did accordingly and as he stood by the tub amidst a Circle of his great Men, the holy Man bid him plunge his Head into the Water, and draw it up again. The King accordingly thrust his Head into the Water, and at the same time found himself at the Foot of a Mountain on a Sea-shore. The King immediately began to rage against his Doctor for this Piece of Treachery and Witchcraft; but at length; knowing it was in vain to be angry, he set himself to think on proper Methods for getting a Livelihood in this strange Country: Accordingly he applied himself to some People whom he saw at work in a Neighbouring Wood: these People conducted him to a Town that stood at a little Distance from the Wood, where, after some Adventures, he married a Woman of great Beauty and Fortune. He lived with this Woman so long till he had by her seven Sons and seven Daughters: he was afterwards reduced to great Want, and forced to think of plying in the Streets as a Porter for his Livelihood. One Day as he was walking alone by the Sea-side, being seized with many melancholy Reflections upon his former and his present State of Life, which had raised a Fit of Devotion in him, he threw off his Clothes with a Design to wash himself, according to the Custom of the Mahometans, before he said his Prayers.

Spectator, no. 94, 18 June, 1711. Addison quotes from *The Turkish Tales.* The British Museum General Catalogue of printed books up to 1955, published in 1963, lists *"The Persian and Turkish Tales,* complete translation from the French by W. Petit de la Croix, assisted by A. R. Le Sage, and done into English by Dr King and others". It will be noted that this work was published a few years after Addison alluded to *The Turkish Tales.* Presumably he meant the French edition, unless there was an earlier English one.

For both the text of this quotation and the references I am indebted to my friend the Rev. Nevin Drinkwater, B.Sc., F.M.A. and Miss Niamh O'Kelly, M.A.

"After his first Plunge into the Sea he no sooner raised his Head above the Water but he found himself standing by the Side of the Tub, with the great Men of his Court about him, and the holy Man at his Side. He immediately upbraided his Teacher for having sent him on such a Course of Adventures, and betrayed him into so long a State of Misery and Servitude: but was wonderfully surprised when he heard that the State he talked of was only a Dream and Delusion; that he had not stirred from the Place where he then stood: and that he had only dipped his Head into the Water, and immediately taken it out again.

"The Mahometan Doctor took this Occasion of instructing the Sultan, that nothing was impossible with God: and that He, with whom a Thousand Years are but as one Day, can, if he pleases, make a single Day, nay a single Moment, appear to any of his Creatures as a Thousand Years."

I myself once had such a dream. Though unfortunately I cannot find the notes of it, the main outlines of it are very clear in my mind. I had dozed off; somebody who was in the room with me left the room for a few minutes, and on returning woke me. It was during those few minutes that I had the following dream. The first part of it seemed as long as the life I had already lived; I was then in my late twenties. I dreamed my whole life over again, but backwards, like reading a novel starting with the last chapter, and working backwards chapter by chapter.

The outcome of each incident of my life was thus that my purpose was always reduced to nothing, my attempts to resolve problems, to produce results, were all undone, and always I was back where I started, and then further back, my will again still further undone. Chapter by chapter, I was increasingly reduced to impotence: and so, back and back, with every hope reversed, right back to the earliest years of my life, back through memories of childhood long previously forgotten, till finally I reached the frustration, the impotence of infancy. The experience was an agony, was utterly crushing, was complete destruction of my sense of ego.

At the moment that this was finished, I reverted to my then actual age, and at once started to dream again, this time living my life forward, on lines which seemed to grow logically out of the actual life that I had up to that point been living. Step by step, my life unfolded in logically credible sequences that led me on to more and more complexities. I was abroad a great deal of the time, particularly in the Middle East. My life's involvements became intolerable, and in the end my experience seemed to draw me on to the point where I committed a murder. I can still recall the unbelieving, incredible sense of horror that what I had done was irreversible, that there was nothing, no action which could mitigate, let alone undo, the situation. There was nothing left, nothing at all but inescapable guilt. I was spared punishment because the disease from which I suffered finished me while I was in the condemned cell.

The intensity of the unrelieved horror of my experience was given not a moment to evaporate. At once I was back at my then actual age, and had started still another dream. Once more, I was dreaming forward again, dreaming another possible life, which also developed logically from the life that I had in actual fact been living. And this life also was experienced in full detail, experienced actually as reality, each day, each hour of it lived through as one lives in ordinary daily life. Its lingering dreariness hung on as I dragged my way through all its dire inevitability, till in the lonely squalor of my old age, weak and ill, I forced myself to the window ledge of my attic. I can still feel that ledge, and then the headlong rush of air which preceded the sense of a worldwide explosion.

But instantly I was back again in my late twenties, and away on yet still another dream, again dreaming forward in a logical development of the sequences of my actual life. But this time I dreamt a life of success and happiness, a life where everything went my way, a life in which my plans were fulfilled, the work I had set my heart on grew in my hands to something that went beyond even my own hopes. The savagery of love that had undermined me in my life in the Middle East and the bitterness of love that had poisoned me in the life that ended in suicide would have been incomprehensible in this third life, in which love was full, sweet and unstinted.

Since then I have often found that my life seems to be made up from strands of all three of these dream lives. At first I was stunned by this. My judgement was awry, and I found myself associating with unsuitable people. My life was strange to me; it was swept along by alien currents, trends from the dream. And then there were moments of realisation that I was enacting, living through, a bit of the dream. Such moments of awareness came now and again; mostly there was simply the feeling that my life had changed. It was as though I were in a strange environment, or did not know the ropes.

It was years before I freed myself from these disturbing conditions, gradually, digesting the experience, and discovering myself in a new sense. It was as though I had returned from the dead, where I had known a wisdom alien to the life I led, and to the self I had been, as though I had to be broken and changed to its requirements; and then had to re-grow my being. But everything that is spiritually my own, everything of true worth that I have found for myself, derives from that great dream. Still it enriches and instructs me: without it my life would have been a husk. Though the gifts of the gods may blast or wither us, if we can at last bear them, they will transform us. Some claim that the true function of the brain is to shut out experience of vast phases and aspects of our pneumo-physical cosmos; if we value our comfort we may be glad that it mostly functions so well.

During that phase of my life, I had been actively exploring procedures for inducing a change of consciousness, and was then experimenting with fasting. Just at the end of a six weeks' fast I had had what we used to call sunstroke, the effects of which on my fasting organism were dire. I had strange symptoms, and seemed to lose much fluid, and I became so shrunken that, as a friend remarked, my hat came down loosely over my ears. It was this condition that occasioned my dream. Perhaps under such stress, the brain can no longer shut out as usual. In making the disclosures in the foregoing sentences, I am well aware that I lay myself open to anyone wishing to employ the fallacious but "familiar reductive method of explaining away anything remarkable in terms of some originating circumstances" (Charles Davy).

As a psychoanalyst I must point out that this dream could, like any other dream, be analysed; but to analyse a dream does not adequately render an account of it. To make this point I will cite another dream, that of a patient of mine nearly twenty years ago. I had been involved in a street accident, and when the patient arrived, she found me propped up in my chair, with an injured hip. She brought with her a dream she had written down, in which she had witnessed my accident. There it was described on the paper before me. I analysed the dream as one might have analysed any other dream, and found that it indeed had a latent content which was compatible with that of her other dreams. But merely to say that does not in any sense account for the manifest content of the dream, which very clearly showed an actual telepathic awareness of what had happened to me. In spite of certain obvious interpretations suggested by different parts of my own big dream, the dream as a whole, together with its relationship to my subsequent life, must surely remain unaccounted for in terms of psychoanalysis. (But perhaps that is an unwise claim that will be punished by a wealth of derogatory interpretations.)

The fact is that in what could not have been more than two or three minutes, I had a dream in which there were some 150 years of detailed experience. Indeed, in a sense, it contained more; for I soon found that if I dwelt on the dream, its strands of experience tended to interweave in such ways that I seemed to be beginning still another dream. I suppose that I might have gone on spinning out experience more or less indefinitely.

While it was all very fresh in my mind, I read somewhere, or was told of, one of those accounts of somebody who had been *in extremis,* and who reported that his whole life had flashed before him. One of the best of these accounts is that of Admiral Sir Francis Beaufort. (The judgement made on each of its acts is an integral part of such experiences.)

> Thus, travelling backwards, every past incident of my life seemed to glance across my recollection in retrograde succession, not in mere outline, but the picture filled up with every minute and collateral feature... The whole period of my existence seemed to be placed before me in a sort of panoramic review, and each act of it seemed

to be accompanied by a consciousness of right or wrong, or by some reflection on its cause or its consequences; indeed, many trifling events which had been long forgotten then crowded into my imagination, and with the character of recent familiarity.

Darwin in his *Autobiography** makes a very relevant observation:

I . . . fell to the ground, but the height was only seven or eight feet. Nevertheless, the number of thoughts which passed through my mind during this very short, but sudden and wholly unexpected fall, was astonishing, and seem hardly compatible with what physiologists have, I believe proved about each thought requiring quite an appreciable amount of time.

De Quincy relates a comparable experience. Accounts such as these will perhaps lessen the incredulity some may feel about my big dream being crowded into a few minutes. It would seem that the unconscious must exist in eternity: the study of dreams shows that events in earliest childhood may still be being experienced alongside those of today. We must conceive of some deep plane of the psyche, where there exists all at once the totality of individual experience; and it was there that the contents of my big dream must have existed. For ordinary consciousness to become aware of such a sequence, it would, of course be necessary for the whole to be translated into ordinary time terms: that is to say, a more or less instantaneous perception, all at once, of this content of the unconscious would be experienced by ordinary consciousness as taking place over an extended period of time.

One seems to have read something like the above as an account of what is involved in ordinary dreaming. In the terms of such an account, there is absolutely no reason why the dream should be limited to any particular length.

It occurred to me that my own dream, like those flashes of complete memory *in extremis* that I have mentioned, might be a foretaste of death. I asked myself whether death is such a stopping of time, a timeless moment involving more or less endless experience? Unfortunately I did not rush into print, and in due course found I had been forestalled by the late Professor Ian Aird, in his posthumously published autobiography, *A Time to Heal.* He writes:

'Every material and scientific signpost points to the finality of death. Yet I believe that we are immortal.

'For me it does not seem impossible that in our final moment our brain is subjected to such a unique and violent physical and chemical sensation that we can cram eternity into our death throes.

'Relativity teaches us that an hour or a year may seem to pass in a few moments. Why should there not be this great mental cataclysm of sensations and thoughts and dreams which makes our end an eternity?'

Professor Aird's statement of belief that we are immortal, which he presents in such a way that we may feel it is an inference from what follows, seems to me a misconception, a confusion between the subjective and objective. We are concerned with a timeless moment, with eternity, not with everlastingness.

Subjectivity has a claim to reality (of its kind) which is at least equal to that of objectivity. For Groddeck indeed it is greater. He speaks of the world of the real as distinct from the world of the factual. The world of the real is the world of fantasy, of hopes, of dreams, which we incarnate and express as plans. And indeed is not this world for us the criterion whereby actual experience is judged as having been good, right, or wrong — judged according to whether it involves fulfilment, or otherwise, of the dreams that give meaning to our existence? These dreams are of our achievements, and of their effects on our personal relationships; they include symbols — though the latter also of course, exist objectively. And it is to be noted that in the world of symbols Groddeck includes even the Oedipus complex, itself a type for the problems involved in relationships with more than one other person. Berdyaev also emphasised the importance of subjectivity, and told us that through it lay the way to the spiritual. Let us not suppose that that which is measurable, whether in terms of space or of time, has sole claim to reality. To the religious, God is of the essence of reality, but God is no-thing, and the way to His kingdom is, we are told, within. Thus if I say that death involves no survival, yet no cessation of consciousness, I am according value to the claims not only of the materialist, but also of the religious. To speak of this as mere verbalism would be to miss the confrontation of two worlds, the private and the public, for the experiential is the real, whether its content be — momentarily — private or public.

In substantiation of this view, and lest we accord undue reality to the world of public consciousness, let us be mindful of the significance given by Jung to the consideration that perceptions are unconscious, and only apperceptions reach consciousness. Thus we are conscious of data only as selected and arranged — by ourselves, though we must be powerfully influenced in making the selections and arrangements (i.e., in our manner of building our apperceptions from our perceptions) by the *Zeitgeist*. By these means unique events are constantly stereotyped for the grouping required by organised society, to the point where man has to have poets so that the uniqueness of individual events may not be altogether forgotten. That the reality we accord to the eternal moment of death is other than the measurable reality of public consciousness is indeed far from a disparagement of that intensely living moment.

In this view of the moment of death, it is as though the formula produced by Einstein for very different purposes held. Thus: if we could move at the speed of light, we should have no more space, but time would become infinite. Consider the application of the formula here: in the timeless moment of death, though we can then no longer move about, and therefore lack space, and are no longer to be located in a body, we do have a seeming infinitude of time. It is of interest here to reflect on a passage in a lecture by Professor D.E.Littlewood to the British Association last year on the subject of cosmology and conformal transformations. Conformal transformations are kaleidoscopic means whereby the same data can be accounted for in such different ways as to produce different pictures of the reality concerned. In discussing a boundary of one such possible version of a universe, Professor Littlewood said:

> All stars and galaxies recede from us and approach this boundary with speeds which increase almost to light speed in the neighbourhood of the boundary. In spite of this they never reach the boundary, as time passes more slowly near the boundary and stands still on the boundary itself.

Though, of course, this is only a mathematical picture, it is nevertheless significant for our purposes. At its ever unreachable boundary the passage of time would cease. Such a boundary, though beyond the reachable, i.e., the spatial, and being also timeless, would be no mere nothing; on the contrary, we should have to conceive of it as infinitely potential. Thus our subjective view of the timeless moment of death is of no wasteland dropping over a horizon of nothingness. Rather we must think of a state of beingness raised to supreme intensity, of a potentiality that is eternal. Nevertheless there will be those who will still protest against the subjective view; and for these there is a curious answer, though to present it I must lead you through various considerations, as follows.

It will be recalled that in the first section of my big dream, that in which I was living backwards through time, there was a complete elimination of all sense of will. The last three sections each grew by logical sequences out of the life I had actually lived, and the experiences of the past thirty odd years of my life show that the dreams were only extrapolations of what subsequent experience proved was actually possible to me. I am here making reference, of course, to my earlier statement that, throughout my life, since that dream, I have found, again and again, that strands of experience of all these dreams have appeared in my actual existence. The dream thus presents life not as a field of action for free will, or for will of any sort, for any kind of purposiveness. However, Mr Charles Davy remarks: "Your actual life has been woven from strands of the three 'future' dreams. Who has done the weaving? One could take it that some (perhaps unconscious) part of you has been active in choosing which strands to use for the actual pattern." We must, of course, agree with Mr Davy, yet unconscious choice is different from ordinary conscious choice; it seems effortless. In it there is no experience of our willing this or that. And since in this sense I can therefore alter nothing, there is no place for any tussle with the nature of things, with nature. The reality encountered in the dream is therefore no more subject (myself, will) nor object (nature), but the experience of human relationship. To appreciate this we must rid ourselves of the old view, which the behaviourists have attempted to revive, that our impressions of other people are as subjective as the sense impressions made by objects are supposed to be. A number of psychoanalysts have become convinced that the emotional response produced in us by our patients is a true organ of knowledge of the patients. Wilhelm Reich adumbrated this view. More recently it has been put forward by Professor Rosenfeld in the Kleinian volume on *New Directions.* * Professor Rosenfeld seems to be telling us that to understand what the patient is really communicating to the analyst, the analyst must be able to understand the feelings produced in himself in response to the patient, must regard his power of response as a 'receiving set'. In a footnote the Professor quotes a similar statement by Paula Heimann, which emphasises the point that this response of the analyst is a means of understanding the patient's unconscious. Thus, in a new sense, other people do indeed get under our skins. We have penetrated each other's boundary; our isolation has been seriously breached.

Freud, like Stekel − and of course, Jung too − was convinced of telepathy. Indeed any sensitive analyst who has not wilfully closed his eyes to the problem must, I think, be constantly aware of the telepathic relationship that exists between himself and his patients. And nowadays, the developments of Professor Rhine's pioneering work have placed the fact of telepathy on a strong basis. In a privately circulated paper, the surgeon Mr Griffith Evans, commenting on a recent statement by G.E.Hutchinson to the effect that ESP experiments conducted by Soal and Goldney have a probability of 1.10^{25}, remarks that there are indeed few experiments known to science with results that give anywhere near so high a degree of certainty.**

We seem to be driven back to the view propounded by Thomas Reid, the old Scottish moral philosopher, the philosopher of common sense, who claimed that with perception we stepped over the barriers of spatial separation and intuitively penetrated to a knowledge more than sensory. At least, we do this in cognising each other. Thus we live in each other's pockets. To attempt to treat another human being as an object is wrongheaded. We exist in our togetherness, and the world is its product.

---

*Pages 192-3.
**1969. Of course latterly it has again been asserted that the whole matter is in doubt.

Our world, the world we actually live in, is our human agreement on our world; our so-called objective world is very largely the product of our intra-subjective agreement on the nature of reality. And, obviously, this agreement changes with the flux of epochs. I have seen it argued, partly on a linguistic basis, that the Greeks had a different colour sense from ours; Owen Barfield in his *Saving the Appearances* has plausibly suggested that the quality of quaintness in medieval art truly reflects medieval man's picture, or perception, of the external world. We may say that the outstanding fact of experience is the human communion. No wonder Tarzans* are less than the animals that rear them. Thus beyond both the objective and the subjective, there is ever the personal world, the world that is the product of human intimacy, indeed that is human intimacy.

Now we may consider the relevance of this consideration to our timeless moment of death in which all the experience of one's life, together with its extrapolations, is dramatised. In 1941 the Ven. A.P.Shepherd,D.D., Canon of Worcester, published a book on time, after which he was told by a friend: "Your idea that the whole of our earthly life is recovered after death as a unity and as an actual experience is the same as Rudolf Steiner's." (Canon Shepherd referred to this in a letter to me as "the metamorphosis of time experience — with the cessation of physical consciousness — from successional to continuous time". By 'continuous time' I think the canon means the state of affairs in the unconscious, in which what happened in childhood is as real as what is happening now. We can see this in dreams, which commonly embody childhood's experiences mixed up with today's.)

Rudolf Steiner described the after-death experience as one of in-escapable intimacy, a world in which we live in full awareness of each other, unable to shut off consciousness of the reproach in those who felt that in life we had not loved them adequately, unable to hide from them our own feelings, a life in which all the hidden emotions in ourselves and others are constantly experienced by all concerned. Of course, there are other theosophies which have comparable views of life after death. Various religions have purgatorial pictures that are perhaps comparable to Steiner's. Beliefs in literal hells and heavens would seem to follow from an

---

*Recent opinion about so-called wolf children is that they fall into at least two animals: a few do develop noteworthy abilities.

Recent opinion about so-called wolf children is that they fall into at least two categories. The earlier view mentioned in my text, is that the position was bedevilled by parents abandoning autistic children, which, when found by others, were assumed to have been reared by animals. Some cases of normal children that were in fact brought up by animals, when found, were said to have developed various skills: for example, of one of these youngsters, it was claimed that he had learnt to run at fifty miles per hour. — Such an assertion naturally arouses ones scepticism about these alleged skills.

unwillingness to accept the idea of a non-objective after-life; whence the false notion of a timed and thing-like survival. But, apart from a few fundamentalists, I do not think that religious people believe in that sort of thing. However, the point is that Canon Shepherd arrived at a view which he later found Rudolf Steiner had also arrived at.

To state it briefly: death should be conceived as the gateway to a more intense experience of what I have just been describing as our supreme reality, the world of human relations. This is a world in which, in order to attain knowledge of the highest, God, perfection, we must love our neighbour. As the Gospel puts it, "How can a man love God whom he hath not seen, if he do not love his brother whom he hath seen?" This is a world in which, according to St Paul, we are nothing without charity, have our existence by means of charity — not money nor brawn, nor for that matter, will. Conation has ceased, and with it anxiety, the essence of our personal time sense.

If Canon Shepherd and Steiner are right, then, though we can still perfectly well maintain our view of death as the experience of the eternal moment, its essence is not, as I had supposed, subjectivity, but intimacy. But whichever of these it may be, at least it is certainly not objectivity. Steiner's account is one in which experience is ineluctable. Will is inoperative, as in my big dream will was made inoperative, there is therefore no possibility of a tussle with the nature of things, with nature, i.e., objectivity. Both the subjective and the objective are devoured, swallowed up by the intimate.

The objective world is indeed the standard of reality in this our daily life, but it is a field in which only an aspect of ourselves is involved. I believe that, as a psychologist, one may have a view of these ultra-mundane matters, and that by considering the various aspects of the personality, and considering which aspects are involved, one may bring an increased meaning and fulness to such deliberations.

I have spoken of three aspects of the self. To make myself fully clear, I should like to conclude by saying more about these three aspects. When alone, I feel and behave in certain ways that must at once change when another comes into the room. If neither person devours the other, nor throws the other out, we establish a relationship called intimacy, in which we feel and behave in ways that are at once disturbed if anybody else (or any group of people) comes into the room. When alone, my private self remains, as when I sleep, or in my day dreams; it is this self that may experience the real, the everlasting glory and validity of mysticism; this self that was active in Einstein's *a priori* thinking out of his theory of relativity; this self which gives both the joy and the innocence to infancy. When Freud spoke of the infant's actions as polymorphously perverse, it was, of course, Freud who was being perverse, though for the then commendable and salutary purpose of destroying obscurantist sentimentality. It would take the infant years before it could work through the experience of intimacy sufficiently to be at all genuinely aware of the real subjectivity of the other, which awareness is what we require in a good human relationship; many years of strife and suffering, with some rewards, before it could have any real concept of public standards, in short of objectivity. To condemn its motivations, as Freud did, by a word that is meaningful only in terms of the public self's conscience, is to treat it merely as an object, to deny the whole of its actual experiences. Romantic tradition rightly speaks of the infant's innocence; the private self is private, is undeclared, is innocent.

The standards of the public self are inappropriate not only when applied to the private self, but also when applied to the personal self. One thinks of the joke of a judge speaking of a woman's evasiveness. Repeatedly he complained that she refused to give a plain Yes or No to his plain question, Did you love your husband at the time when he was being unfaithful to you? Such a monstrous application of the standards of the public self, of objective justice, to the sphere of the intimate, by no means exaggerates the gulf that exists between the two. For the public consciousness there must be — as near as we can get to it — unequivocal truth in the objective sense of the word. Very rightly, we require unqualified, objective truth, need to know simply whether an event took place or did not take place; objectivity is of the essence of the matter. But though measurement and justice are here our natural desiderata, when it comes to the sphere of intimacy, what is just, or accurate, or perhaps I should say what is right, has a different quality. Doing 'the right thing' by a girl usually involves avoiding the impartiality of merely just treatment; it involves showing her favouritism. And we feel that a woman treats her man porperly not by giving him his deserts, but by making him feel good. Indeed the intimate self has its existence over against the public, and certainly by denial of the claims of the private self, which, if it intrudes into the reals of intimacy, becomes mere ruthless egotism.

I have said that where we were concerned with the public self, with justice, we were concerned with one definite, logically required answer to any problem; we needed proof, we needed to know whether such and such a thing happened or not. We needed the truth. There is a similar one-pointedness, a singleness of purpose, in the requirements of the private self; its fantasies and dreams have their happy endings, their particular goals; which of course is why, when the private self intrudes into the domain of the intimate self, it manifests as pure selfishness. The intimate self, however, is different from either of the other two, in that it is for ever divided. It may be heavenly and delightful in its intentions, yet horribly human in its actions. In it are born the intensities of love-hate which, unresolved and persisting through the Oedipus complex, then sour and embitter public life, falsifying truth and justice. In it also, however, are born all that is tender and warm in our communal life. It is because of its duality and its eternal conflicts, therefore, that this sphere of intimacy is Freud's particular domain. Perhaps such tensions are never resolved in this life, and perhaps there is no perfect intimacy. Given that Canon Shepherd and Rudolf Steiner see true, then the resolution of its problems is to be found in death. This of course is an old thought, and the ardours of intimacy's conflicts are such that sentiment has dreamed of death as embodying sentiment's happy ever-afterwards. Thus we have Southey's lines:

> Too oft on earth a troubled guest,
> At times deceived, at times oppressed,
> It here is tried and purified,
> Then hath in Heaven its perfect rest.
> It soweth here with toil and care,
> But the harvest time of love is there.

But alas, or perhaps happily, the love-hate of the intimate self must be conceived as seeking its resolution through the greater intensity of an endless moment of death, endless orgasm, endless tenderness, endless sorrow, endless shame. Canon Shepherd's and Rudolf Steiner's views, like those of other religious formulations, is one of purgatory and heaven rather than of Victorian sentiment. The spirit's reality is not that of the plush drawing-room; it is as hard as starlight, and as burning as sunshine, and as limitless as the sky.

For those who would follow the experiential way, the only attitude is loving, for only love opens a personality to full interaction with others. Fear inhibits, aversion alienates, dominance subdues. As love welcomes the inescapable intimacy, and so makes it heaven, to those with unloving hearts, such an intimacy must be purgatory, or perhaps hell.

As has been indicated, our experience of each of the three selves may be adulterated; this is commonly because of our use of a self that is inappropriate to the circumstances, or for other reasons, such as that circumstances call for the use of different selves at the same time. We may perhaps be unfamiliar with any of the three selves in its purity. The unalloyed experience of the private self is timeless, for there is none other by which to time it. The unalloyed experience of the personal self is eternity; for it is that that every true love is pledged for: "love is *passion infinie* per se, and by no means 'time's fool', as Shakespeare expressed it in such impressive fashion."* The unalloyed experience of the public self is

---

*Dr Ludwig Binswanger, 'The Case of Ellen West', English translation in *Existence a New Dimension in Psychiatry, and Psychology,* edited by Rollo May, Ernest Angel and Henri F. Ellenberger (Basic Books, 1958), p. 313.

Dr Binswanger himself described three aspects of the self; but instead of basing these on our sense of numbering, or counting, he took them from language (starting with Buber's 'I-thou'). The resultant formulation was not quite adequate, so that he had to produce a fourth, which however was not fully on a par with his previous three.

endless endurance — as of the rock of ages, of Peter, and as man's hope for the *polis* he builds; for our conception of all such examples is that they should endure on and on, and however long that may be, yet still longer — which is a way of defining infinite lasting.

A consideration of what I have been doing will show that I have been making conformal transformations, if we may use the words in a non-mathematical sense, of my material, giving different accounts of the same data in such wise as to produce alternative pictures of the reality concerned. Thus I have been able to present a case for saying that though at death there may be no survival, yet there is no cessation of consciousness.

But this is not all that I have been doing. Among other things, I have also sought to suggest something of the extent to which, in our different states of consciousness, we select and arrange our data in accordance with different criteria.

These two steps are essential in the procedures of transvaluation.

Notes on 'An Unusual Dream'

(a) The Subjectivity of Our Sense of Future Time

Erwin W. Straus, in a profound and illuminative article, '*Aesthesiology and Hallucinations*',* writes:

> Action is understood as a coupling and integration of reflexes. The motor reaction necessarily follows the stimulus in a measurable time interval. In acting, however, we are directed in anticipation towards a goal. When a hand is stretched out toward something, the retina has always been struck previously by light rays. And yet I stretch out my hand towards something that stands before me as a future goal. This personal time system cannot be converted to the objective one. Future is always *my* future; future exists only for experiencing beings. In the conceptual system of physics, events are determined by the past; physics does not acknowledge any action into a distant future, there is no open horizon of possibilities. Only the relationship before-after is admitted in objective deliberation; both temporal moments, however, are observed and understood in retrospection.

---

*Pages 150-1, in *Existence, a New Dimension in Psychiatry and Psychology,* ed. by May, Angel and Ellenberger (Basic Books, 1958).

This close connexion between conation and our sense of time at once suggests that we only have to relax fully, and time will vanish. And indeed it does so, every time we go to sleep – to return, partly, in dreams. (The yogi's ability to still all conative strivings would thus seem to be the perfect means of doing what is claimed for yoga, taking us out of time into eternity.)

(b) Steiner – Blavatsky

I am not myself a follower of Steiner, yet because of my absorption in mysticism I cannot but be interested in him as a great seer, though he has been described as an 'occultist' rather than a mystic. My reference to him, rather than to a proponent of some other theosophy, is not to decry the others. Steiner's special claims to interest in this book, are first, his Christianity, and second, that like Groddeck, he was enormously influenced by Goethe. He worked while still a young man, for a number of years in the Goethe archives; the outcome of his insights into, and preoccupation with, Goethe's conceptions were that these became the basis of the whole of his spiritual-scientific system. Moreover he holds a key position in that he had an orthodox scientific training, and integrated his seership with his knowledge in such wise as would seem to widen enormously the bounds of knowledge.

His weakness is in this, his very strength. The great All would appear to be knowable; indeed Steiner decries our sense of the unfathomable. (See several places in 'The Metamorphosis of Phenomena', a section of the introduction to *Goethe's Conception of the World.*) Is there a place in all this for the central experience of the mystic?

Countess Helena Blavatsky was, by a long start, the first modern exponent of theosophy; obviously exponents of other versions of this are deeply indebted to her. Some, such as the Gurdjieff Ouspensky people, fail to acknowledge their debt. In Dr Steiner's case people draw their conclusions from the fact that, originally, he was General Secretary of the German section of the Blavatsky theosophists, under the presidency of the late Dr Annie Besant.

This is not to deny that he had his own visions or perception in his earlier years, as of course he had later. Moreover he sowed seeds in the thought of some of his followers that are producing a very notable harvest.

(c) Troward on Forgiveness

No student of religion and mysticism should neglect the writing of Thomas Troward of which William James wrote "Far and away the ablest statement of the philosophy that I have met, beautiful in its sustained clearness of thought and style". But although clearly a presentation of a known position, its individuality establishes it as an original creation. In his *The Creative Process in the Individual,* and again, in abbreviated form, in his *Bible Mystery and Bible Meaning,* Troward anticipates Steiner. He arrives at his position by inference from and extrapolation of what was then generally known about the 'subjective mind', which Troward assumed survived bodily death. In the latter work, in his chapter on 'The Forgiveness of Sin', he writes:

> "Now if, as I apprehend, the condition of consciousness when we pass out of the body is in the majority of cases purely subjective, then from what we know of the laws of subjective mind we may infer that we live there in the consciousness of whatever was our dominant mode of thought during earth life.

> "We have brought this over with us on parting with our objective mentality, as it operates through its physical instrument the brain, and if this is the case, then the nature of our experiences in the other world will depend on the nature of the dominant thought with which we have left this one, the idea which was most deeply impressed upon our subjective mind.

> "If this be so, what a tremendous importance it gives to the question whether we do, or do not, believe in the forgiveness of sin. If we pass into the unseen with the fixed idea that no such thing is possible, then what can our subjective experience be but the bearing of a burden of which we can find no way to rid ourselves; for by the conditions of the case all those objective things with which we can now distract our attention will be beyond our reach.

> "When the loss of our objective mentality deprives us of the power of inaugurating fresh trains of ideas, which practically means new outlooks upon life, we shall find ourselves bound within the memories of our past life on earth, and since the outward conditions, which then colored our view of things, will no longer exist we shall see the motives and feelings which led to our actions in their true light, making us see what it was *in ourselves* rather than in our circumstances which led us to do as we did.

> "The mode of thought which gave the key to our past life will still be there, and no doubt the memory of particular facts also, for this is what has been most deeply impressed upon our subjective mind; and since by the conditions of the case the consciousness is entirely subjective these memories will appear to be the re-enacting of past things, only now seen in their true nature stripped of all the accessories which give a false coloring to them.

> "If we have carried over with us, not perhaps the full assurance of actual pardon, but even the belief that forgiveness is possible, we have brought along with us a root idea whose very essence is that of making a new start.

> "It is the fundamental conception of a new order, and as such carries with it the conception of ourselves as entering upon new trains of thought and new fields of action — in a word the dominant

idea of the subjective mind is that of having brought the objective mental faculties along with it. If this is the mode of self-consciousness then it becomes an actual fact, and the *whole* mentality is brought over in its entirety; so that those who are thus in the light are liberated from imprisonment within the circulus of past memories by the very same law which binds those fast who refuse to admit the liberating principle of forgiveness.

"It is the same law of our mental constitution in both cases, only acting affirmatively in the one and negatively in the other."

Troward, however, sees hope for those of the dead who are imprisoned "within the circulus of past memories". This help may come from 'some of those (dead) who have brought over their *whole* mentality', and from "those who are still in the body, for the action of mind upon mind is not a thing of physical substances. (Thus) we can see a reason for prayers for the departed." He goes on to speak of "the many instances in which ghosts are reported to have besought the intercession of the living for their liberation".

10

THE MOMENT OF DYING
AND OUR IDEAS ABOUT AN
AFTER-LIFE

What do we mean by survival of bodily death? We may ask this because of course different religions give very different accounts of it. The Jews had a good covenant: they had suffered and struggled for it, and had established a principle of consistency; everywhere there was one God, who always pointed to the one true course of action, a course that was always possible. It was a good covenant in the sense that it was thus possible for the good Jew to live within its terms, and yet still have ample freedom. There was no reason for the Jew to suffer excessively from bad conscience. I believe it is largely because of this that the Jewish faith has so little to say about an after-life.

For the Greeks, as we know, life was indeed desirable. Its sunshine, poetry and lusts claimed the incarnate spirit as their own; and death was a limbo. But, on the other hand, almost any act of freedom was liable to offend some god; man was constantly judged for having risen up above his own station, and was to be crushed by the great, gay gods who, like revelling parents, could endlessly enjoy all they forbade their children. Thus with plenty of punishment this side of death, and all that could be desired at hand, there was no need for either a doctrine of a harsh hell, or for an infinite heaven.

For the Hindus and Buddhists life in a tropical climate with no sanitation was hard, so that there was great scope in the after-life that was provided to them. But for the soul who had endured such a life, the ideal of perfection was non-being (Brahman), or nirvana. Yet the Indian's guilt remained unresolved; his prison was inescapable; he must ever return in repeating incarnations — perhaps a more refined punishment than that of many a hell.

Christianity is, of course, monistic, and offers a way of love; on the face of it, therefore, one might think that it provides a ready means for the resolution of guilt. But the historical nature of its mission commits its followers to action, and war becomes an easy temptation. It has bred a striving, active culture, which has explored and fought nature, and constrained the rest of human kind. This has brought us great rewards, and the principle of rewarding is expressed in its seraphic heaven; but the guilt from all its striving action has accumulated to make a terrible hell.

Now turn for a moment to a more primitive people, the American Indians. The Reverend Professor E.O.James assures us that the American Indian simply does not know religious guilt; though he might possibly be somewhat guilty for not having danced sufficiently for his god, his guilt would stop at that. Thus there are no arrears of guilt to be worked out in hell after death. But since life is harsh, the after-life promises a reward, the happy hunting-grounds.

Thus, as indicated by my random examples, mankind conceives death as a gateway to the domain of conscience. In short it is a state of being in which the feelings that we have not worked out on other people can now be resolved. Is not the very basis of consciousness social, and guilt primarily the problem of "man not having loved his brother whom he hath seen"? As a psychoanalyst, I must regard death as a symbolic return to the parents. The happy hunting-grounds are the mother's body on which the infant played and fed, the very same that we approach up the milky way, and via the pearly gates. And the principle of judgement and punishment represents the father. He confronts us, often as gatekeeper, though more commonly as a judge. There is a scene of judgement, a grand trial, after which we may, or may not, enter heaven.

This great judgement scene portrays the depths of every human heart. Reinhold Niebuhr, the Lutheran theologian, described man's longing to meet a just judge as fundamental to human nature. Man seeks a judge who will know his true worth, understand his motives, and who, on the other hand, will be able to restore man's sense of worth where this may be wanting, by giving him, if necessary, Augean stables to cleanse of all of what turns out to be his own filth. This longed for, awesome trial is integral with all our conceptions of death. With this to face, it has always been felt of decisive importance to die a good death, to be sent forth in a good way to meet the ordeal. As psychologists, we know that the manner of waking in the morning conditions our whole day. During sleep we go into deep troughs of our consciousness, and then rise up to crests of near-wakefulness; if we are awakened while in the depths of a trough, we shall be drowsy, and not at our best, throughout the day. Analogously the manner of our birth, the intensity or otherwise of its traumatic effect on us, conditions the whole of our life. It thus seems perfectly reasonable that the manner of dying should be considered important for the whole after-life. We may recall the thoughts that check Hamlet from avenging his father's death on his uncle while the latter is praying: "Death in such a moment would be a blessing to the deceased's soul, which would then rise on the wings of prayer straight to heaven . . . now he is praying: And now I'll do 't:- and so he goes to heaven . . ."

What is the manner, or the actual process, of our dying? According to Groddeck, in dying, attention sinks deeper and deeper within, away from the demands of the world, its stress, irritation and hurts; it sinks down to remote levels of being, always in search of pleasure. In the pre-natal existence, all supplies, of course, arise from a point inside our own skin, brought there by the umbilical cord. Is dying, perhaps, the search for an inner source-point of goodness, perhaps that same original point? With this withdrawal from the periphery to a point within, the experience of death could be described as that of a turning of the self outside in. Thus it would be complementary to what I believe to be the experience of being born, an experience of being turned inside out: coming out into a world where everything arrives from the external. Is death, perhaps, a way back to those clouds of glory through which the poet brings the newborn? Certainly it would appear to be a complete withdrawal into that state of private consciousness, or subjectivity, which I have quoted Groddeck as calling the world of the real — a world which is the source of all our plans and hopes, and which also provides us with a touchstone for the worth of all experience. Perhaps, as indicated in the last chapter, this is a preliminary to the soul's entry into the world of full intimacy. But whichever of these may be the final condition, at least it seems we cannot subtract from the reality of the death state, that moment of eternity, by seeking to make it less real than the reality of ordinary daily life, of the public consciousness, where reality is ironed out as apperceptions are modelled to group, societal, and *Zeitgeist* requirements.

The essential significance to us of this ideal of intimacy or perfect human relationship may be seen in the effect of these beliefs on us. Let us ask ourselves the question: what are these beliefs for, beliefs that is to say, in survival or non-survival? Let us put this question to ourselves in the same sort of way as one might ask what our breathing is for: Or perhaps we might modify it, and put it in the form: what are we to do with these beliefs? The fact is that life in the here and now is experienced differently by those who believe in an after-life; if the human body houses an immortal soul, the human person is sacred in a sense in which other creatures are not. A spiritual principle, conscience, the voice of the father God, decrees a new status for the person. But though indeed Christianity gave to personality what Rome could never give, and thereby foredoomed slavery to become a crime, we must recall that it was humanism that brought the consideration of other people's feelings to the point of freeing us from torture as an overtly approved procedure of authority. And humanism was not concerned with any doctrine of survival; its motivation, rather, was that of a mother who would care for her children. Indeed underlying the humanist attitude was an awareness of the frailty, the impermanence, of human existence.

With such considerations in mind, we might well say that belief, one way or the other, about the problem of immortality exists in order to support or modify our way of behaviour, and our attitude to human personalities, our own as well as those of other people. The beliefs we have been considering would tend to move us toward the ideal of heaven, of blissful intimacy.

Yet beliefs concerning the subjective and the spiritual would have the reverse effect on us when couched in the thought language of public consciousness. Consider, for example, the belief in materialism. This is, in many ways, very like fundamentalism; but though it has in it the advantage of being more rational than fundamentalism, it has the immense disadvantage of being so much drearier than the latter, for want of miracles to enliven the scene. Both doctrines really involve an objective view of what, to each, is the most significant aspect of human existence; indeed they involve an objective view of the self. But regarding oneself as an object means that one is not being self-possessed; there are the viewer and the self which is viewed, instead of being possessed. This position of alienation of the self leads to fear for it, for one is not with it to defend it. Whenever there is guilt, therefore, fear of the judge is augmented. Freud pointed out that the precondition of suicide was to regard the self as an object. The self may be thought of as actually embodying the quality of a hated parent, or the suicide may feel that his act is an abolition of the parent's handiwork. I have often felt the wisdom of the old-time coroner's regular addition to his verdict, "while the balance of his mind was disturbed", for taking a purely objective view of the self does indeed involve a disturbance of the mind's poise. And this is of the very essence of guilt; to become guilty, the self seemingly slips out of its subjectivity, and regards itself through the eyes of the condemning judge.

In a posthumous article in the October 1962 number of the *Liberal Catholic*, the late Bishop Robert King, who claimed to be a clairvoyant, gives us his account of a suicide's after-life. He tells us that the moment when suicides have severed the cord of life there is an

> "overwhelming desire to get back into the body no matter what life holds. . . They are quite conscious of what has happened. By their own act tied to the place where it happened, they keep on going through it all again — over and over — from the start to the moment of suicide. . . A girl had thrown herself over Waterloo Bridge . . . she lived the incident over and over again, the walk down to the bridge from the Strand, the intense emotion, the throwing herself into the water, the momentary sensation of peace. Then, back once more to the Strand — and so it went on . . . It must have been an eternity of time. We made enquiries and found that it was about four months of our time".

From such an account it would seem that the suicide is completely identified with the last significant environment, as someone, perhaps a patriot, is identified with his country, or as a man may be identified with the kind of clothes he is habituated to wearing — and of course with the role that goes with such a way of dressing. The self is then part of the objective world; no longer a subject, it is an element in the content of what I have called public consciousness. I mentioned the way of behaviour that goes with certain clothes, for the self can lose itself completely in a manner or a role that is systematically played. One might think of ghosts as such behaviour patterns broken off from the personality as a whole. One has heard the theory that just as the body takes time to decay and break up, so it may well be with the mind; there may be partly decayed fragments of mind floating around where their former owner's thoughts or desires normally played. Thus a ghost would be a self-objectivication, a self — or an aspect of a self — that had become a mere object, without content. Their pronouncements accord with this view; judging by such spiritualistic communications as I have read, I would say that though these may purport to come from great and noted characters, their content is quite incompatible with such supposed sources. However, it seems to me to be of the essence of spiritualism that it is an attempt to approach spirit objectively, as though it were knowable in objective terms, or by an objective means. Bishop King's statement, and the view of ghosts as part-decayed fragments of mind, are objective accounts of that which can be approached only through the subjective. Let us then revert to a subjective approach to the problem; and first let us return to the big dream I spoke of previously.

Starting with a consideration of the big dream, we were led on to an account of the content of what we conceived as the eternal moment of death. This was a re-experiencing of all human relationships that had been made during life, with their every implication brought out by their being now re-lived under conditions of inescapable intimacy, such that nobody could conceal any thought or feeling from anybody else. We can imagine that whenever this great review, or reliving, of events did not flow freely, there would be an experience as of a sort of knot of tension, a sticking point, where the scene would become motionless, or, as with a spoiled gramophone record, produce a repetition of the same incident more or less endlessly. But this dreaming, or re-experiencing of the events of life would necessarily, like any other form of mentation, be liable to have telepathic effects, even telekinetic effects. As when an object is stuck in one's gullet, or when the stool is too hard and large to be passed, there is anxiety, so similarly at the sticking points in the great reviewing, or when the reviewing was held up by the gramophone-like repetition, there would also be anxiety, thought would become frantic. Some then of all this experience of reliving would be bound to get communicated to living minds, though the communicated form of it would, of course, not be timeless, but spaced out in time. And, surely, those parts to be communicated would most probably be of moments when the experience had been intensified by the frantic feeling, that is to say, the stuck points and the gramophone-like repetitions. These stuck points, the knots of tension, and the motionless moments in the review, the reliving, would, when communicated to a living mind, and therefore spaced out in time, very likely seem as though they were the product of a decayed fragment of mind, and their mental content — any 'message' that it contained — could not be expected to be the expression of the highest level of intelligence. The spoiled gramophone record effect when communicated, and expressed in terms of public consciousness, would indeed seem rather like Bishop King's account of the *post mortem* state of the suicide.

It is to be noted that we are now talking of the partial re-objectivisation into timed experience of the content of an eternal moment, which itself was the subjectivisation in the timeless moment of a lifetime's previous experience of experience, that is to say, that was timed and objective. We may here think of how an entire plant may be 'crammed into the twists of nucleic acid in a seed, where it may then exist indefinitely in its potential state. When the conditions for the seed's germination are provided, the potentialities 'unwind', or 'expand' into the timed and objective existence of the plant's life cycle. Or, since there is still structure in the seed's content, we may think of the amorphous pap into which all but a few cells of the grub dissolve in the chrysalis, and from which the butterfly is later shaped and given life. All the creature's life potentially is organised; it is 'uncoiled' to spin out its time-shaped form in growth and movement, the behaviour by which it now exists.

This exemplifies the sort of process that I have been describing as the life events are 'crammed' into an eternal moment, and then, in some sense, and in some degree, as we have seen, unspin themselves into actuality, and reappear in the field of public consciousness as, for example, in actual hauntings. I have been talking about experience disappearing from the timed realm of what is publicly acclaimed as real into a realm of pure, or mere consciousness, and then at least in part, reappearing on the objective scene.

Now, in the account given of the *post mortem* strivings of the suicide by Bishop King, the suicide is seen as constantly shying away from the eternal moment of inescapable intimacy, which we have postulated as the true home of the dead. In our inferences based on the big dream, in particular on the 'undoing' of will in its first section, this condition of inescapable intimacy must be conceived as one in which, as we have seen, action is impossible. The very nature of the experience involved, must therefore be here considerably intensified precisely because there is no possibility of our usual escape from emotional or subjective reality into action. Now the suicide, in Bishop King's account of him, is constantly seeking to generate an act that will undo his act of suicide. It is this that I have described as his spoiled gramophone record; it is this that Bishop King describes as constantly returning into the place of the action of the suicide, and constantly repeating the process. Such everlasting unrest must preclude all that digestion of the life experience which must, surely, be the normal process, if any of our postulates and inferences are acceptable. There is thus no possibility of gain in wisdom, and therefore of happy acceptance of the inescapable intimacy, of the whole experience at last becoming the fulfilment of all dreams of delight. In short the nature of the suicide's crime is flight from human relationship, untimately, flight from the supreme reality of love.

Such is the end result, the full logical outcome of the application of the objective view of the self. In passing we may perhaps hazard that a comparable falsification and ill result would accrue from the logical consequences of the objective view when applied to other people also. Essentially this view has the same purport as the suicide's flight, the repression of love, of our supreme reality.

We have spoken of the culminating experience of the eternal moment of death as the joy of perfect intimacy, in short of unrepressed, uninhibited loving. Perhaps the clue to the nature of this is given in the Gospel statement that there is no marriage in heaven. Here we must follow Professor Norman Brown in his *Life Against Death,* and see this as implying that there are no longer any sexual parts, or part feelings, and that this state of affairs would throw us back into the condition of the infant before the libidinal organisations have been established, to a phase when the mind-body as a whole is erotic in an unspecific sense. And although it is of the nature of love that one person is loved more, incomparably more, than all others, and although this state of affairs must persist, and be intensified in the phase of inescapable but joyous intimacy in the eternal moment, yet also, with the ecstatic innocence*of the infant, the experience of a loving inter-relationship with others will so co-exist with the loving of the one true beloved that the dark, and often ruthless, exclusiveness of earthly lovers that becomes, and is experienced as, marriage, would no longer be possible. This is not because the joys of individual intimacy of two people have been destroyed, or in any degree mitigated, but that this same quality of intimacy, though in more diluted form, has been extended to include all others with whom there is contact.

---

*In what other terms could we characterise the experience of the fetus as it floats in rarily disturbed satisfaction, perhaps, kitten-like, playing sometimes with its cord? And even if birth disturbs this, and if bad family conditions thereafter seem to make all Melanie Klein come true, nevertheless all this is to be understood only as a perversion of the original sense of delighted innocence — our paradisal nature which forever awaits re-discovery.

Perhaps this is the true meaning of communion, in which the essence of intimacy is no longer confined to the relationship of two, but achieves communal reality, and in so doing creates a new community, truly a communion. Incarnated on the plane of actuality this would transform the objective world of public consciousness. Perhaps something like this happened among the Agapetae, those early Christians who commonly radiated a joy unquenchable even by the demands of martyrdom. In such moments, perhaps, is the atom 'spun' from infinity into actuality, the chaos within the chrysalis stirs towards organisation, what was un-conscious in the artist's heart becomes explicit and incarnate in com-munally meaningful form. This secret life and meaning is the same as what otherwise often receives only a somewhat subjective expression, as through the innocence and ecstasy of the infant, and (as I have sought to suggest) in the moment of dying. Since, as we have seen, there can be no will, in the sense of no power to motivate action, in the eternal moment, since indeed the organs of action, such as hands and tongues are gone, the eternal moment must be one of pure experience, tending toward the experience of delight. But all this brings to mind Groddeck's account of dying in which consciousness sinks away from the world of action and striving, down to the levels of a deeper experience, always of pleasure, levels of pure experience, for here also will's means of action are wanting. This sinking within, to a point within, is, indeed, comparable to a return to our pre-natal orientation. We pass away as we came in.

There are those without carefree memories of childhood, and who never catch up with the march of events. Their time hangs heavy; or if not in gloom, they live in fear. Unless by some gift of spirit they can turn their course, age for them will be only their cantankerous childhood again, or a weary resignation. Could we say these have not found their souls; or is it that they really are as soulless as they look? At the end they seem only to disappear; having never lived, or achieved, nor left any marks in events, nor a significant trace in any memory, they are perhaps then truly dead.

Another sort of person, in looking back towards his beginnings, recalls the long endlessness of those pristine years, before time was ever anxious. Dreams of infancy may employ imagery that seems to stretch out memory even farther, into dreams of prehistory, or even of another life. By comparison, present years are puny, and their passage often irrelevant to the urgent business of the untiring daily strife to win life's prizes. Or the 'prize' may be in gains foregone for love . . . But at last, when suddenly, as it often comes, when a man is all at once aware of the weight of his accumulated age, his years seem a tinkling merry-go-round, inanely round and round, disregarded: Now so little time is left to him that he may forget time, as hindsight recalls the timelessness that, for wholly other reasons, he first possessed. The early diffusion of the psyche had, in maturity, given way to the achiever's single-mindedness, but now the world his senses space around him shrinks or narrows, so that the spread of his mind's interests must find its scope within: Thus, back come even earliest memories, with renewed appreciation of their value, a new awareness of their delight, intensity, or even poignancy. Next, just as memories displaced perceiving, so does their felt essence begin to displace memories; then consciousness contracts, or turns even farther inwards in search of the quintessential of all that pleases;* around this, as the last seconds race, his whole being is concentrated, contracting to an all-pregnant point, or focus** of infinite meaning. Across time's threshold, as he breaks life's boundary, a vista opens, in which his whole life is there before him, revalued *sub specie aeternitatis.*

Some, snatched back from the brink, or in great crisis, may glimpse and recall this eternal moment, but this can be done only by transposing it into the briefest flash of autobiographic memory. Yet its entirety can only be present to the time-bound mind if it is apprehended as a sequence, and timed at the speed at which it was actually lived.

---

*Groddeck taught that the apparent signs of distress sometimes seen at a death are commonly deceptive; the dying man's focus of consciousness is drawing away from these comparatively superficial manifestations towards ever deeper levels; and this all the time in quest of pleasure.

**An accelerating body approaching the speed of light contracts, and its mass – or, more loosely, its density – increases to infinity. It is not suggested that a human life will rigidly reproduce the acceleration of an inert body. On the contrary, there will be both psychological and physiological variables. Regarding the former, we all know how the existential speed of living varies with our moods, from lightning-fast to leaden-footed. Regarding the latter, Martin Geschwind (in *Untersuchungen über veränderungen der Chronognosie im Alter,* Basel, Diss. med., 1948) has drawn attention to our sense of acceleration of the speed of time in the year after puberty, and again some time after middle life.

11

REINCARNATION

If I can recapture the spirit of a past occasion, why should not my spirit recur when my life is of the past?

Yet the essence of personality is its uniqueness, and how can the unique recur? Berdyaev points out that in regarding a human face we are aware of something that looks out from a plane other than its environment; the impression it makes on us is different in nature from that made by all else in the world. The fact is that whereas nature is meaningful to us because every aspect of it relates to all the rest, in the look of, the impression given by, a human face, we are vouchsafed a glimpse of a world in which uniqueness rather than similarity grants significance. Is to consider reincarnation to demand of the unique that it should somehow destroy its own quality in becoming part of the world of endless recurrence?

A great many years ago I read an article by J.B.S.Haldane about the mathematics of recurrence as applied to the theory of reincarnation. He was emphatic that, epochs hence, there must be such a general recurrence of events. Of course this is different from the ordinary idea that human souls reincarnate into a world that will in basic ways remain unchanged, while developing in other ways, and different too from the conception of the ancients, with which Nietsch has familiarised us, that throughout the ages, each of us endlessly repeats his life. Haldane's idea, like that propounded in the Vedas, is that everything *in toto* will recur. In any case, after vast cycles of time, my replica will again grace our earth. Yet will it be me? How would one know? How could it establish its identity as me? If, by some trick of time, I could confront it, how could I prove it a usurper, and how establish my own claim to be the genuine me? I might easily find myself in an embarrassing position, and crying urgently for Wells' time machine to rush me back to the safety of my own epoch.

When the Dalai Lama dies, the Tibetans are at pains to discover his successor, the infant in whom he is thought to have reincarnated, though I suppose now that the Chinese invaders have raped the land, this procedure will have been discontinued. A likely child is examined carefully for certain bodily signs, but he is also required to recognise certain objects. In short, the principle of memory is invoked. Similarly, those interested in seeking to verify the principle of reincarnation will always prick up their ears if they hear of a case of a person seeming to have memories of long ago. I recall reading of the careful investigation of someone who spoke a dead language, and ignorant person, the circumstances of whose life would have seemed to preclude his having studied this rare and little known tongue. It turned out that he had been a servant in the employ of a professor who had studied the language, and had unconsciously picked it up by overhearing the professor practising it; he was able to repeat it when in a hysterical condition. I understand that there are other cases of this sort of ability which have not been so readily accounted for. The idea of a racial unconscious is invoked, but this is a difficult concept, providing a tenuous argument for explaining away the concrete evidence of a seeming memory. Such evidence appears to have great claims on us. It is our usual lack of any memory of a former incarnation that undoubtably is a major reason for our tendency to discredit the belief. Most people remain unimpressed by the argument that, in lieu of memory, we reincarnate with a built-in capacity, or a talent; after all, they reflect, heredity can account for an ability. But actual memory seems very different. Altogether, when all else fails, memory often provides us with the most decisive evidence in cases of doubtful identity, for example.

A professor of philosophy to whom I put the problem of my replica and myself at once went to this same point. "How could a mere replica of you," he asked, "have the same memories as you have? The replica would not have lived your life, had your experiences."

In passing I would note that Rudolf Steiner touches on this aspect of the matter in taking the biography as the real manifestation of a man.

My professor friend continued: "If you questioned your replica about his past, you could soon show him up as an impostor."

From an external and essentially public point of view, one might comment that his great difficulty would be that — excluding forgery — he could not have the same passport as I have, which means that my mother could not have brought him forth at the same time as she was bringing me into the world.

My professor friend continued: "You perhaps have your father's walk, or your mother's way of laughing. How could your replica, not having had your parents, have these habits? Is not personality, to a considerable extent, compounded of such traits?" Of course, here we are no longer dealing with memory in the ordinary sense, but with what has been unconsciously preserved and filed away in the form of habits.

But now we have man's existence in time competing for reality with the spatial self, and obviously this will not do. Let us try again without the idea of a perfect replica. Imagine the return of a missing person, now physically changed, perhaps defaced, mutilated and suffering from loss of memory. Would we accept him as the same person? This was my professor friend's criterion of sameness: what will people accept as the same person? During the Communist trial of Gary Powers, when we were all wondering how much his mind had been worked upon, his mother, after a certain utterance of his − I forget just what he said − suddenly felt able to assure us that it was the real Gary who was speaking. In this connection we might ask why we say of a man that he is, or is not, himself today. We imply the existence of some sort of real self, as distinct from other appearances. When Mrs Powers recognised the real Gary, had she noticed a trait in him comparable to my father's walk or my mother's laugh in me? Or did she notice a sign of some essence of personality, a uniqueness that is not acquired? We are born with a certain personality, our mothers are apt to say, and this is protested with an emphasis that is sometimes more convincing than their accounts of this uniqueness. Perhaps a mother sees with Berdyaev's eye. Should we accept this view, then the problem is merely one of recognition. If the spirit of me is some undefinable, yet recognisable essence, replicas are mere fakes if presenting themselves as me, however well they impersonate me.

A term such as 'essence', meaning a mystery, or something indefinable, is unfashionable today. More fashionable would be an attempt to break down whatever is referred to into a few definable terms, thereby commonly dissolving the mystery into incidental or spurious concrete phenomena.

The fact is that we may have perceptions too elusive or too Protean or too unlike anything else for us to describe. Thus many people will tell us they are aware of the 'atmosphere' of a house; and yet they are unable to describe just what they are referring to.

But perhaps we should get away from essences and back to a consideration of what we would accept as the same person, noting as we pass that there may be a problem about our 'we' that mothers, at least, are apt to have their own criteria for. However, there will be many rigorous critics who will tell us that to take refuge in so indeterminate an expression as "some indefinable yet recognisable essence" may look like a confession of failure. Truth, ultimately, is what can be agreed upon, and proof therefore is only a method of presentation which will gain credence. Thus there would be no meaning to the statement, "He is really the same person, but nobody can see this (know it, or prove it)", because there would be no way of demonstrating what we are claiming. In other words, it is not possible to show what is referred to in mentioning the sameness imputed both to him and to his alleged former self. Nevertheless our immediate reaction would be to commiserate with such a person: suppose he is genuine, how bitter for him that no one will acknowledge his identity! But take a more extreme case, a sole survivor of a devastated area, a man who is not only physically unrecognisable, but whose whole mind and nature have grossly deteriorated, and who, also has completely lost his memory. What is recognition, or the want of it, going to mean to him? Do we still commiserate with such a person if his identity is not acknowledged? Imagine him still further reduced, to a mere mass of functioning protoplasm. Is there now any meaning to a sense of commiseration with him because people will not acknowledge his identity? He is no longer 'the same' to anybody.

My point in this is to present you with this question: what do we mean by 'the same person'? Would the wretch we have just described, who is the 'same' only in a biological and legal sense, actually be in any personal sense the same? Could a former intimate feel toward him as if he were the same? If he is unrecognisable, without a passport and otherwise unidentifiable, the answer must obviously be no. But grant him at least his identity. Though to associates he might still mean nothing, to a former intimate the case might be somewhat different − or perhaps not? One final question. Would he be still able to say, with any sense of meaning, I am I? (Note that I am considering the problem of this recognition, or acceptance, in terms of all the three states of consciousness adumbrated in my chapter on the unusual dream: public consciousness, intimate consciousness, and now, private consciousness.) I recall a very bad attack of influenza I had when I was fourteen or fifteen. My temperature rose quickly, and I was put to bed that night with a considerable dose of aspirin, which sent me into a deep sleep. During the night I was moved without being waked; my parents took me to sleep in their bedroom, which they rearranged to accommodate me. Later still, I awoke, and in the darkness did not recognise the rearranged room. I myself was different in that, so far as my awareness went, I was floating up somewhere near the ceiling; moreover, though I am sure that, with an effort, I could have recalled where I had gone to sleep, and indeed all the ordinary events of my life, yet momentarily I was without such memory. Nevertheless, in spite of being thus without my bearings in both space and time, I did not panic at all, because I knew that I was I; that was the only thing that really mattered.

Can it be that memory, commonly regarded as the basis of personality, and indeed vital for the public self − both for knowing itself, and for establishing its identity with others − is yet by no means so essential for the private self? (This last, we should recall, is both seed and essence of the whole.) Public consciousness is timed, and memory is our record in time; but the private self has something of the quality of a dream, and is timeless.

If it is the self of the public world that for you is the real and significant self, you may ridicule this 'I am I', and call it a nonsensical affirmation without real reference. But from the point of view of the private self, the answer to that is, 'Rubbish!* This private consciousness is of primary importance to us, and its affirmation is a prime source of all our strength, our will. Indeed the will inheres in this private, subjective self, and exists in it alone. Psychologists, studying the self objectively, have disintegrated the will into several quite distinct aspects of our being, and have shown that, objectively speaking, will is a meaningless term. Indeed its meaningfulness is to the private self alone; however, in this sphere, its significance is so great that it will be manifest so long as there is enough of a man still left to say, I am; and it is in the character of his willing that we discern what we call the spirit of a man. Perhaps it is this that we mean when we speak of the *real* self, when we say, That is the real Smith, or the real Gary. But of course in order that we might be moved to make such a remark, he would have to be expressing his willing in terms of some visible action. Mere willing would not do, he would have to perform an action that would bear the stamp of his spirit, display the manner of his willing.

How could we be aware of him in this sort of way if he were not exerting his will – had perhaps lost the will to do so? Perhaps such was the plight of the wretch we spoke of a moment ago, who it would now therefore appear, since he now lacks even will, has no claim to any place in the human communion, which is to say, to any human identity. Yet surely, like myself as a boy with influenza, he could still affirm his own identity, at least until the last stages of his disintegration in death? And though he might be too far gone for us to accept him as an intimate, or even an associate, yet the knowledge that he could make this affirmation would prevent us from being able to treat him as an animal or a mere thing. However to grant him a personal and spiritual existence because of such a purely private, subjective and unverifiable action is, surely, to regard his principle of existence as an essence that is in no measurable or demonstrable sense definable. I believe that, if actually confronted with him, we should all do this, yet in doing so we should be acknowledging what is merely the spirit of him, that which bloweth, or willeth, where it listeth; in other language, his potentiality of a human existence.

If such is, ultimately, the real stuff of a man, I need no longer, before I can reincarnate, await the millenniums required for the laws of chance to produce my replica, and I can again comfortably show my face on earth without the risk of seeming bogus, and this even though my memory has utterly faded, and although the self that reincarnates will be merely a shadowy 'I', with its ridiculous "I am I", that is, its asserted self-awareness. The 'I', indeed! A nothing-but-awareness associated with a potentiality of

*See 'Notes' at the end of this chapter.

that other disintegrated nothing, will, the power to assert, the potentiality of deciding, of willing!

The mode and external nature of my new life will depend on the circumstances of my reincarnation, which will, doubtless, have been pre-selected by my manner of living now, and will therefore be a means of expressing me. And working in this mode and external nature of my new life, I, my will − my sort of will − will generate all the rest of the future me. Thus that remotely future being will be redolent of my spirit, indeed be wholly expressive of my spirit; what will have reincarnated will be my spirit.

What had been the real, daily-life me had ceased. Then the mere spirit of a shadowy-nothing me is, mysteriously, to become a real daily-life me again. Like a candle snuffed and re-lighted; and this time, no mere haunt, or echo, of my former self.

Perhaps, on the other hand, the whole bridge between the actual me and the fellow in the future is so shadowy as to be meaningless? If I hanker after the plain view of the ordinary believer in reincarnation, then certainly this bridge is a no-bridge, and I have merely been destructive, and had better have held my tongue. Be that as it may, it will have been noted that I have been able to reach this position by distinguishing between, firstly, the biological and legal view of the mutilated man, secondly, his claims − whether actual or potential − to a place in our social and personal world, and thirdly, the purely private or subjective existence we were prepared to accord him.

It is to be remarked, however, that our willingness to accord him this was almost wrung from us by a commiseration which induced us to grant that his biological and legal claims to human status were, after all, valid. Equally, however, there remains a vital sense in which the general acceptance of anybody as human depends on an acknowledgement of his spirit. And in such acceptance we experience a sense of certainty. Yes, indeed, and if we come to think of it, was it not his spiritual power, his power of self-affirmation which, but a moment ago, seemed decisive for our attitude to him? Clearly this takes precedence over the legal aspect of the situation, or at least it is what underlies, or gives rise to, his having been accorded any sort of claim, legal or otherwise, to human status.

Thus what some would speak of as merely subjective takes precedence over all else; once again we see mere consciousness as primary. Perhaps here we might gather together some of my earlier observations about this merely subjective self. And first I would emphasise the unquestionable and overwhelming reality of my own timeless moment, in which I lived through about 150 years of utter reality. It will be recalled that I cited Groddeck who referred to this subjective world as the world of the real, thus distinguishing it from the world of the actual. He pointed out that it originated the symbols to which he accorded such high importance, and among which he finally suggested we might include the Oedipus complex itself; that from it emerged all our values, plans, and the meaning of our loves and strivings, that it was the very criterion of all we met in the external world; that it is the world of the child − I would add, still more of the unborn − and that it is this same inner world that is sought again in age, and more intensively, in the process of dying. One should add that the mystical and religious sphere of reality, the Kingdom of Heaven, is also, of course, within, where being is no longer timed.

Since, as we have seen, the spirit of a man may be thought of as manifest in his willing, if will leaves him, there will be no more manifestation of the spirit, in short, life will have left him. Bereft of will, the spirit could exist solely as the spirit of understanding. We have already seen that this understanding could manifest only as an experiencing of the consequences of the life that has just been lived, by re-living, and very fully reviewing, that life in the uninhibited intimacy of death's unending moment. On its way to the perfect intimacy of love, it would thus feel, all the time, under the judgement of all who acknowledged the full claims of love. As the spirit worked through all familiar permutations and possible representations of its life experience, the psychological tensions would gradually be eased to the point where psychological existence as such would cease. The spirit then, no longer manifesting by means of subjectivity, would lose interest in it, let it fade into a cosmic sleep; and the spirit itself would now embody only divine love, that is to say, exist in a state of unalloyed intimacy. What then, logically, could be the next step?

But before considering that, let us revert to our former procedure, and ask, like good psychologists, what the idea of reincarnation is for. At best, it may inculcate a greater degree of responsibility for the way one lives one's life. Those with marked antipathy to the doctrine are sometimes those who cannot bear to think that the way they spend their lives matters; living in the belief that one's life is only one in a developing series may encourage one to build for the future. Besides, there is the hope for another chance, and the feeling that if in this life one does one's best, one may get off to a better start next time. For many there is real comfort in this thought; yet a different view of it may be taken. Mr A.P. Sinett, who was perhaps the real means whereby theosophy got started in this country, on first hearing a lecture on reincarnation, remarked, "I fail to see what comfort it would be to a crossing sweeper to know that if he swept his crossing with assiduity, he might in his next life be a cheesemonger." I remember the tremendous impression made on me when I attended one of the early performances of Elmer Rice's *The Adding Machine* in London about 1923. If I remember it aright, the story concerned a clerk who is sacked from his job because an adding machine has been introduced. He commits suicide − but no; he shot his boss. Later, in hell, he finds himself condemned to relentless labours on an adding machine. Just at the end of the play, he discovers his real punishment; the Devil appears and announces:

> "It is time for you to go back . . . back to earth . . . Do you think they are going to go to all the trouble of making a soul just to use it once? . . . Why, man, they use a soul over and over again — over and over until it is worn out."

In the war, I knew a doctor who had idled his life away in increasing poverty. He comforted himself with the thought that he had had wonderful incarnations in the past, and would do so again. "This time," he said to me, "I am just shuffling my way through life." The comfort of the belief had in this case produced the reverse of responsibility to himself. Shortly after our talk a flying bomb fell on him; it seemed somehow poetically appropriate that so soon after his shameful avowal the course of his life should thus be obliterated.

It will be noted that I have introduced the idea that the way one lives in this life will affect one in the following life. This of course is the familiar idea of karma, which always goes together with the belief in reincarnation when conceived as a path of self-development. As a man soweth so shall he reap. In this life we plant the harvest, or the famine, of a future life. Karma is often portrayed as a mode of divine justice. But among the Hindus are varying notions of reincarnation, one of which (already mentioned), is like that of the eternal recurrence of the Orphic tradition. It was evidently with this that Buddha was concerned when he spoke of the everlasting wheel of birth and death; yet his followers often seem to think of it as a way of self-development. However, he devoted his life to discovering, and then expounding, a way of escape from this unrelenting wheel. To him, therefore, it can hardly have appeared as a mode of the divine justice, but rather as a monstrous trap.

Groddeck points out that the blindfolded figure of Justice cannot see which way the scales dip, that the search for justice in life is fantasy-motivated. Justice would certainly have a mountainous task if she had to rule in face of the plain fact that the wicked flourish like a green bay tree, and of that other equally clear fact that whom the Lord loveth he chastens. Nevertheless, there are many warm supporters of the doctrine claiming, in spite of these considerations, that it explains the apparent injustice of life, even the apparent injustice of God.

In the degree to which one admits the ordinary process of cause and effect in the affairs of our daily life, one would have no difficulty in accepting, and indeed would naturally expect, that the same causal principle must extend as long as a personality exists, whether that be for the length of a lifetime, or for the length of many lifetimes. In this sense, one would admit that the doctrine of karma was no more than a statement of the obvious. But to give it passionate credence in order to spare God, or life, from the charge of injustice obviously presupposes an infantile view of God as some sort of projection of a parent figure from the unconscious, or of life as a glorified nursery, or welfare state. It would be sounder to worship a god who makes it rain on the just and the unjust, and whose idea of peace is so remote from our own that it passeth understanding. In the nursery it is preferred that all should have only two sweets apiece rather than that some might have three, and others only one. Absolute justice denies the uniqueness of individual requirements, which are always more here, less there, and otherwise elsewhere. If it bent itself to these, we should cry: one law for the favoured and another for me: In other words, we should not name it justice. Such a justice may lead to callousness: among the passionate believers, a friend may often be left to suffer because it would be wrong to interfere with his karma. Obviously there must be something wrong with a doctrine that so readily lends itself to such smug sadism. Perhaps the most important criticism of the doctrine arises from considering the injustice of its justice: what was deserved by that unique being, my former self, would be quite inappropriate to the needs of the equally unique self of this life; what would have rewarded me in one kind of society, may well burden or punish me in another. Besides, suffering is the more crushing if I must own it as my own fault; and pleasure is not greater because earned; it is a gift that is pure joy. It is only the ego that thrives on rewards and punishments, and the meaning of death is, surely, the loss of the ego as the self becomes pure spirit. The old 'I' must always thus be obliterated, a fact which, if we accept reincarnation, would surely be sufficient explanation of the lack of any memories of former lives. The endless moment of death is in its essence an experience of intimacy; love and the ethics of love consist of favouritism. Even Jesus Christ was not impartial: it is written, "Jesus loved John".

God's love is grace; to attribute to Him the I-love-you-as-much-as-you-deserve kind of loving would be a gross affront to the gracious Lover. Though karma, as indicated above, has an obvious, yet limited, truth, there are nevertheless many religious teachings implying that this is by no means as inexorable as the law of cause and effect. Christian science and its derivative, New Thought, which together so characterise the spiritual climate of America, preach that healing lies in getting above the rule of law, to live under grace. The whole of Buddha's teaching, as we have seen, was of the way out from the ever-recurring stringencies of the law. Ultimately, the Buddhist can escape by ceasing to be, whereas for the Christian there is the parable of the prodigal son, the doctrine of salvation by divine grace. The Gospel story is full of the idea of forgiveness; by a word of forgiveness people are healed of bodily ailments.

The idea of karma as a secret dossier carrying a man's record forward into his new life, carrying through death the means of interfering – by punishment – with his living, and of distracting him by rewards, is but another way of speaking of the great judgement, the great trial of the dead, told by so many faiths. As indicated previously, death is the gateway to the domain of conscience. To the question I put to you a little while ago: what are our beliefs for (beliefs about survival or non-survival, or the nature of survival of bodily death)? To this question the answer is that they are to enable us to envisage, at last, some ultimate way of dealing with our guilt, whether the meeting with the just judge, or equivalents of this meeting. And, as we have seen, the judgement provided by this eternal moment of death is the judgement of and by love, in the experience of inescapable intimacy, when all repression and denial are impossible. All our earthly loving is guilt-laden; its nature is partiality. The impartial love of God involves what to many is the injustice that karma is invoked to explain away. Yet it is divine love that forgives; our love singles out, separates its object, which it punishes or devours, the more so the more earthly it is. It is a spiritual love that heals and grants freedom; and perhaps the death experience is to spiritualise our loving till it is like divine loving. Such spiritual impartiality of loving would undo lovers' exclusiveness, yet so intensify loving – which in its nature is a supreme act of concentration, of focusing – as to preclude infidelity.

It should not be thought that the rule and justice of love is less thorough, less exigent, in its justice than the rule of law. Those who champion law against love seem to others more literalistic in their concepts of justice; indeed the further we progress on this path away from love, the nearer we approach talion justice, the primitive literalism that demands an eye for an eye and a tooth for a tooth. The notion of karma, with its seemingly almost automatic punishments to fit the crime has much in common with this primitive rule; indeed karma is retribution. Few would deny that our modern methods of justice are both juster and better means of securing the general rule of law than is the principle of talion. They are less efficient only in the matter of ensuring vengeance and retribution. Moving still further from the principle of talion, and closer to that of love, we find an even more powerful means of bringing justice into the world: the intimacy of any decent family exerts a tremendous force, not merely as a corrective, but far more, as a preventive of unethical behaviour. Indeed without the family and its rule of love, the law's rule could do little more than secure a purely external form of obedience to the state's edicts. Those who deprecate love's power, and plead for any form of authoritarian violence, from child-beating to fascistic beating of political opponents, are often frank in their avowals of the demand for retribution, if not vengeance. That these are themselves breaches of the harmony that law exists to ensure seems to concern such people as little as the objective evidence that violent methods are less efficacious.

When every permutation of all the themes of a lifetime's experience have been worked through in the great death dream, when this has been done on all planes, the plane of the thoughts involved, as well as the functions and sensations, then, surely, all sense of strain or tension, all negative attitudes will have been resolved into a state of blissful harmony. And since the total experience is in the realm of intimacy, this harmony will be the harmony of resolved personal relationship; that is to say, there will be perfect intimacy; this involves the creation of an atmosphere such that both parties to a relationship can fully enter into its spirit, without either being devoured or destroyed in any sense. Our name for such perfect intimacy is true or spiritual love. The closest expression of this that we know is in the good moments of the early mother-child relationship. The end of the great death dream would then find its earthly expression in such a relationship, that is to say, in the beginning of a new incarnation; and since the dream is timeless, conception could follow immediately on the previous death. This indeed is the Gurdjieff-Ouspensky teaching, based on the ancient Orphic doctrine. Conception would then be the materialisation of the culmination of the dreaming. But perhaps Southey is right after all, and intimacy is not at home on earth; for in spite of the foetus's more than merely close corporeal relationship to the mother – which must surely involve an especially close form ot intimacy on some deep level of beingness – it is, we must feel, solitary. Thus we may say that man's life begins as it ends. As the foetus grows, its experience of mundane intimacy must increase, till, at birth, the child reaches our human experience of intimacy, the early and intense joy of which is, however, to be so soon chequered.

But another interpretation is possible. The world of spirit that we have been considering is, in the fullest sense, outside time as well as space. As we know from the phenomena of ESP, the spirit can see through, not only pretences, but brick walls, and can read the past and scry the future. Perhaps we may say that for the spirit as for the unconscious, there is no such thing as time. We know that mystics experience a state of consciousness in which they may be one with the external, in short can span space, and so the doctrine of reincarnation may be a way of expressing our power to span time. Certainly if the spirit is timeless, reincarnation by it would not have to follow immediately on its prior experience of death. The old Hindu view that the various incarnations are spaced out in time, and thus form a series during which progressive development of the continuant is possible, is as conceivable as the Orphic view. In the Orphic view, each life would be a repetition of its predecessor; there would be a mere endless recurrence; whereas in the other view, the possibility of development obviously suggests change in the successive lives. I suppose that a choice between the two views would involve a choice between belief in determination or free will.

In passing we may remark that there are still other views of reincarnation. It is to be noted that there is nothing about reincarnation in the Rig Veda; India's Aryan invaders assimilated it only later from the Australoid aborigines they conquered. The original form of the belief, before the Aryans took it over from them involved the soul in incarnations in animal form, a belief that reappears in Mahayana Buddhism. Thus regression as well as progress was envisaged.

However, it is possible to take another, and totally different view of the doctrine.

I have known a number of Westerners who have been serious students of Hinduism, and some who have tried to follow it as a faith and practise its meditations. Of all these, one friend, now alas dead, stood out as having done both so wholeheartedly that one felt, when he spoke of these matters, as if a Hindu sage, a genuinely holy man, were expounding. He questioned whether we had been sufficiently careful in the translation of the terms of some of the ancient Hindu sacred writings. He thought that when these referred to what we call reincarnation, the meaning intended was more likely to have been, not so much successive incarnations in time, as the spirit's presence up and down, throughout, time. This was the counterpart in time of the well-known doctrine of the omnipresence of spirit, its actual incarnation, or manifestation, in every form of life throughout the universe. To our spatially limited consciousness, the nearest we get to the latter insight is a realisation of kinship with each of the myriad separate expressions of life that we could conceivably encounter. We do not, like the Hindu mystic, attain to the experiential realisation that all these beings are expressions of the one great spirit. The Hindu mystic, in attaining to his sense of unity with the great spirit, can feel that he is one with the whole. In a similar sense, as my late friend described it, the doctrine of reincarnation would reflect a mystical union with life throughout time, or at least throughout that part of time spanned by the human story. Each of history's and pre-history's phases would thus be present to the mystic in his experience of spiritual unity with the totality of our time. This last formulation clearly carries the implication that his ego, his experiencing 'I', persists, and persists with memory of the past.

It may be noted, however, that my friend was actually speaking of a timeless moment experienced by the mystic, the contents of which were of endless time. But in its nature, this was what my big dream was.

In the light of this, perhaps the significance of karma will also be clarified. Behind the notion of automatically earned rewards and punishments of a sort to be poetically fitting, or talion, is the suggestion that whenever I strive to organise my life, or any part of it, in any particular way, I thereby set in motion processes that will, though perhaps not till a future life, lead me to the experience of an opposite way of life. Given this on a background of progressive unfolding of the continuant throughout life after life, in an environment that is itself constantly changing in great cycles (the Hindu view), it would seem that, in due course, the continuant will have had all experience and thus be truly able to say of anyone *Ta twam asi*. This simply means that the doctrine of karma is merely another way of stating, though now in terms of time, the central Vedantist doctrine that Atman, the spirit, and Brahm are one. Thus the goal of every 'I' is the attainment of some sort of universality. The yogi would therefore seem to teach us a more intimate awareness of the realisation that there but for the grace of God go I. But this indeed is what the psychoanalyst would have us own: during analysis it is necessary to take responsibility for the universal, primitive urges in ourselves.

To this end, the karmic balance of cause and effect would not be thought of as spread out in time, but as existent in the eternity of the unconscious. And indeed in the unconscious the super ego does work in terms of nemesis and talion punishment. It is not asserted that the ordinary view is necessarily wrong: it could be merely that it needs amplifying; but at least karma can be understood without the literalism and the smug values sometimes associated with this. Karma is revealed as having a significance within the scope of the immediately experiential, and like all validly conceived doctrines, as a window through which we may look out beyond the timed, and into the eternal.

There is a valid sense in which the experience of the eternal moment is implicit in the only moment that there ever is, our present. Memory, our version of our past experience, as also hope, the means whereby the future gives meaning to our living, are indeed powerful aids to the development of the 'I', and as such are invaluable to us. Yet the self can go on developing, adding to, and improving, itself indefinitely, and still remain for ever, to itself even, a mere object in the sphere of public consciousness. To get beyond this form of literalism, and to know the real spirit of the 'I', and to let that spirit declare itself, is possible only in this present moment; and is always so possible whatever degree of development has been attained to, or not attained to. We can never decide to do it tomorrow, or in a year, or in twenty years. If the full significance of a moment can be apprehended, not in mere abandonment to it, but rather in seizing upon it, and making it wholly subservient to the purposes of the 'I', purposes that are more important than heaven and earth, and that sweep aside all our ancient wiliness about how to live to fight another day, in that moment, the true spirit of a man will blaze forth in full self-declaration. This is the meaning, for every son of man, of that central Christian doctrine, the doctrine of the incarnation.

We have covered a wide field in this chapter. At the outset, the mention of J. B. S. Haldane's article led us to the curious question whether a future replica of me would be me. From this we finally moved right over to the question whether the doctrine of reincarnation, properly understood, was a way of conceiving the mystical oneness of life throughout time.

Among the various doctrines of reincarnation we find mention of very different periods between incarnations; and as already noted, in some systems, no time at all elapses between death and rebirth. In general, however, whatever the frequency of incarnation, this frequency seems to be maintained fairly regularly, at any rate over a considerable span of incarnations. Although in some systems place is found for a certain proportion of young souls – which incarnate much more frequently than others – most of us, in most doctrines, would seem to have had many lives. Thus in the ordinary theosophical teaching, though young souls do indeed find their mention, in most accounts of experiences of the reincarnating soul, one finds oneself reading of what happens to the souls that take their time between lives. One is thus left with the impression that this is the usual thing. Though there are exceptions, for example, souls with special tasks which reincarnate without delay, it would appear that the great mass of humans have, throughout the millenniums incarnated at intervals of some number of hundreds of years. Intervals of seven hundred years are given as not uncommon; groups of mostly cruder souls have to manage on much shorter intervals, while nobler spirits may have intervals of as much as a couple of thousand years.

Given what I say, how are believers to account – in terms of the numbers of extant souls – for the population increase?

Are we to suppose that modern science, particularly hygiene and agriculture, called new souls into being, induced God to create them? If so, we must suppose that, in His omniscience, He foresaw science, and reckoned on the scientist acting in this matter as a stimulant to Him. We may also suppose that these new souls may seem somewhat raw. And indeed as one looks at the people in the streets, one may well feel confronted with evidence that this theory of fresh created souls is correct. I also feel a similar confirmation when I see my enemies.

There is a very different implication in the theosophical teaching that sixty thousand million souls were allocated to our planet from its inception. With such a figure in mind, especially when we consider how small the world's population was till recent times, we can only suppose that the vast majority of souls have been kept in storage. And this was not in order to have spares in case of wastage, for in this teaching, souls do not wear out; on the contrary, they mostly improve with age and usage.

In the light of this teaching, we are constrained to abandon the attempt to equate karma with any literalistic or egalitarian views of justice. For only the privileged few could ever have been in the position of being able to say "When I was a king in Babylon, and you were a Christian slave". The rest never had a chance of being around then – or in antiquity's other delectable spots.

A friend who is also a fellow priest wrote to me a year or two ago about the doctrine of the sixty thousand million souls in our planet in connection with a report that Dr W. Ross Cockrill had recently spoken of a world population of over six thousand million by the end of this century, and had reckoned we should need to treble our food production to ensure a generally decent standard of nutrition — a possible achievement, one feels. Yet is it? Alas! it seems a commonplace to read (*Times,* 26 September 1969) of the nightmarish growth of population in Britain which threatens to swamp available land and food resources by the year 2000. One may perhaps take it that, from then on, we shall begin to see the real truth of J.B.S. Haldane's prevision that everything conceivable will be done, and nobody will be able to stop it. A backward glance at 1969 would see it, no doubt, as a year of halcyon serenity.

But I will continue about my friend's thoughts on the sixty thousand million souls, and the prediction of six thousand million in incarnation by the end of the century. It next occurred to my friend that we need only assume the possibility that by A.D. 2000 medicine will have given us an average life span of three score years and ten, and granted that the average soul's discarnate period is nine times its life span, we could be assured that the population would soon have reached its limit without having exhausted this planet's food yield. But, of course, my friend went on, we may doubt whether medicine could do so much so quickly. Further, the period of seven hundred years — (70 x 9) + 70 — is given in theosophical teaching as a fairly usual period between incarnations only, my friend recalls, for ordinarily developed souls. Thus my friend fell back to the thought that we might indeed have to rely on contraception to prevent the population rising well beyond six thousand million and thereby perhaps making an impossible demand on our food sources.

It would have been pleasing to think that there was an inherent congruity between the limits of our demands on our planet and its powers to meet them. And, on second thought, perhaps we need not despair: once again God's omniscience to the rescue! He must have taken man's invention of contraception into consideration in His original plan: after all, contraception is thus the inbuilt natural regulator producing the desirable congruity. And this will serve the further laudable purpose of safeguarding egalitarian karmic justice from an invidious position. Consider the smarting sense of injustice among souls had population growth pressed beyond the limits of food supply: everybody always hungry, and yet the spectacle of the raw young souls, who had so far contributed so little, nevertheless, by means of their frequent incarnations, getting so disproportionate a share of the shrunken supplies!

One of my sons, catching my mood, remarks that the population increase might be due to the press of souls anxious to incarnate before somebody blows up the planet, or perhaps, in more sombre mood, we might think, before the sea; and with it all life, is poisoned. (See p. 179).

I trust that believers will forgive my levity, and perhaps even join my implied protest against those who are as serious about the minutiae of these doctrines as once were those others who argued about the number of angels who could dance on the point of a needle — if indeed this matter ever was argued.

One final irrelevance: what about clones? On the animal level, with primitive organisms, it is already possible to grow animals that are replicas by taking what have been characterised as 'cuttings'. (A cell nucleus from the embryo of one animal put into an enucleated ovary of another animal is the implanted 'cutting'.) Joshua Lederberg, a Nobel prizewinner, foresees that human beings may one day be produced in this way; indeed he is convinced that work is already being done on the project. Supposing you were considered a sufficiently desirable type to take cuttings from, and say, a dozen clones were grown from you — or fifty, and even more — would your name (inverting biblical usage) be Legion? In plain terms, would your soul, or your 'I', inhabit all those clones? or short of that, would it at least be true that all the clones would have the same 'I'?

The point I am really emphasising here is that personality is unique, and is therefore a once-for-all creation. At the heart of every personality there is mystery, and since therefore no personality can in any ultimate sense be given quantitative definition, even Professor Haldane's best mathematics cannot pronounce it repeatable.

I do not deny that we may reincarnate; indeed it is impossible to refute a doctrine such as reincarnation. But I do vigorously assert that the naively literalistic approach to it can easily divert us from any imaginative grasp of the ways of the spirit. An existential understanding of the doctrine must begin with the question: what is it that reincarnates? Through creative deeds an 'I' must be born that might feel not unworthy of continuity. Thus Goethe to Eckermann: "The conviction of a life after death comes to me from my own sense of activity. If I work without ceasing to the end of my life here, nature is bound to find me another form of existence when this one can sustain my spirit no longer." Such an 'I' could bear to recall any former existence, and could therefore suitably address itself to the problem.

Most conceptions of a continuant fail to take adequate account of the degree to which we are members one of another, and of the extent to which the 'I' — at best a flux — would have to be dependent on a metamorphosis to reincarnate.

Of course, once we are aware of the implications and difficulties of the doctrine, there is nothing to invalidate a methodical study of it. My great difficulty with it is the extent to which, in practice, one may find it a shield for thoroughly neurotic attitudes, and for a false, hypocritical 'I'.

Having said this, however, having warned against the dangers of a too facile belief, dangers of falsification on the levels both of logic and of the spirit, I will admit that the belief may be advantageous. It can be associated with a clear and innocent consciousness of the spiritual nature of the cosmos. Dr Arthur Guirdham* claims that its acceptance can be salutary. He writes:

"Sickness in general is an attribute of the human personality which is tethered in time and place by its lusts and ambitions projected into the future and by its regrets and recriminations relating to the past. On the psychic plane, freed from the trammels of time and space, the symptoms arising in the personality are dispersed. This open phase of psychic activity is revealed in the disappearance of the patient's symptoms, in the gross dislocation of the sense of chronological time associated with the recognition of the fact of reincarnation . . ."

Dr Guirdham further claims that the belief may be accompanied by extra-sensory capacities, such as telepathy, clairvoyance, precognitive dreams and the capacity to heal; further that "the repression of psychic gifts results in the production of psychiatric symptoms".

That the doctrine can be superbly presented will be obvious from the merest glance at the *Bhagavad Gita*:

Nor at any time verily was I not, nor thou, nor these princes of men, nor verily shall we ever cease to be hereafter.

As the dweller in the body experienceth in the body childhood, youth, old age, so passeth he on to another body; the steadfast one grieveth not thereat.

As a man, casting off worn-out garments, taketh new ones, so the dweller in the body, casting off worn-out bodies, entereth into others that are new.

I quote from Dr Annie Besant's translation: the clarity and dignity of her style facilitates portrayal of the material. The same can be said of her theosophical writings altogether, the core of which is the same doctrine of reincarnation, linked as in the *Bhagavad Gita* with that of the karma.

Dr Raynor C. Johnson** has assembled an interesting couple of quotations on karma. He writes:

The earliest allusion to the doctrine of karma is found in two of the oldest Upanishads.*** On one occasion King Pravahana teaches it to a Brahmin as the factor determining rebirth. On another occasion King Janaka says:

"According to his works, according to his walk, he becomes; he who works righteousness becomes righteous; he who works evil becomes evil; he becomes holy through works (karma), and evil through evil. As they say, man is formed of desire; as his desire is, so

---

*'Reincarnation in Clinical Practice' in *The Golden Blade*, 1969
** *Nurslings of Immortality* (Hodder & Stoughton) pp. 210-11, 213.
*** *Brihad Aranyaka* and *Chandogya*.

is his will; as his will is, so are his works (karma); whatsoever works he works, to those works he goes."*

The same teaching runs through both the Testaments,**   from which I quote one instance, "For with what judgment ye judge, ye shall be judged; and with what measure ye mete, it shall be measured to you again."

Dr Johnson claims that "there is no rigid 'law' of karma, no mechanical sequence of events, no cycle of mere recurrence, no history repeating itself; always there is freedom to choose . . ." To support this statement, he points to Buddha's emphasis on the motive and spirit of actions as being decisive of karma. He goes on to quote the *Gita* to show how the right application of the law leads beyond the binding effect of action, through its karma:

> He who seeth inaction in action, and action in inaction, he is wise among men, he is harmonious, even while performing all action.
>
> Whose works are all free from the moulding of desire, whose actions are burned up by the fire of wisdom, him the wise have called a Sage.
>
> Having abandoned attachment to the fruit of action, always content, nowhere seeking refuge, he is not doing anything, although doing actions.
>
> Hoping for naught, his mind and self controlled, having abandoned all greed, performing actions by the body alone, he doth not commit sin.
>
> Content with whatsoever he obtaineth without effort, free from the pairs of opposites, without envy, balanced in success and failure, though acting he is not bound.
>
> Of one with attachment dead, harmonious, with his thoughts established in wisdom, his works sacrifices, all action melts away.

Repeatedly we have had to ask ourselves, what is the 'I'? What is it that could survive death and reincarnate — if not a replica, then the mere *skandhas* (formula, code, or blueprint) of me? Some sort of 'essence'? Or the simple sense of "I am", though bereft of my memories? After death all sorts of aspects of me would have to change or disappear: thus, to take a very basic example, lacking a stomach, I should have to lose all appetite; there would be nothing left of hunger but the basic demand for the bliss of intimacy with the mother, a loving conation. But I need say no more here: by this path also we are led to an already familiar conclusion.

We can, however, add a comment to our inquiries. The outcome of them all is a realisation that the ego must be modified in one way or

---

*Charles Johnston has drawn attention to the likeness of this passage from the *Gita* to Revelation 22:5, 11-12.

**Matt. 7:2, 16:27; Rom. 2:5, 6; 2 Cor. 5:10; Gal. 6:7, 8; Psalms 62:12; Prov. 24:12.

another. In brief, the psychological meaning of this doctrine is that everyman's *magnum opus* is the task of coping with egotism.

A most noble view of reincarnation is found in Jewish mysticism, a view that goes far towards explaining many of the difficulties we have considered, and which points the way in dealing with the problem of egotism. Gershom Scholem writes on p. 282 of the third edition of *Major Trends in Jewish Mysticism*, Thames and Hudson.

> If Adam contained the entire soul of humanity, which is now diffused among the whole genus in innumerable codifications and individual appearances, all transmigrations of souls are in the last resort only migrations of the one soul whose exile atones for its fall..*

Notes on the Nature of Meaning

Any possible difficulty in seeing sense in the assertion 'I am I' is because we have been indoctrinated by such as C.K. Ogden and I.R.A. Richards with the superficial view that meaning is, essentially, reference to particulars, by virtue of which we learn what to do about this or that. Although there is truth in this view, when left without suitable qualification it amounts to a gross falsification. As an antidote to it, consider the implication of Groddeck's etymological work as expounded in *Der Mensch als Symbol*, much of which appears in *The World of Man*.

The true mode of verification is symbolic. (Groddeck's accounts of the symbol overstep Freud's literalism, and I do not think he would agree with Dalbiez's extrusion of dramatisation from the concept of the symbolic.) We know what to do with anything because its nature and form speak to us. Thus, in the presence of the sublime, I know divinity, and can only be myself, express myself, as the worshipper. And a symbol of the divine can animate my worship.

On another plane, the objects of the world present themselves to us either as implements or as containers; and we are moved either to use them, or to be borne or held in them. Thus all becomes sexual: knowledge of the world makes a man as impassioned about the deeds and events of his life as when with a woman. Indeed, again and again Groddeck shows that what gives us a sense of meaningfulness is, very commonly, the sexual

Major Trends in Jewish Mysticism, Gershom G. Scholem, Thames & Hudson.

symbolism of an object or situation; and further, that, in a very basic sense, it is by virtue of, or in terms of, this symbolism, that we apprehend an object or situation, know how to respond to it, and therefore what to do with it. Meaning is that whereby I realise myself as the lover.

Then also the object or situation portrays or suggests a nursery situation. We may then be moved by our orality, basically the urge to eat, or to fight for everything. Or the object is rubbish : we would defecate, abolish it, or do dirt on all. But another moves to grab what we reject, and forthwith it is value, a possession, money. And thus, as we learn war and possession, our world is endowed with a whole new range of significators. It is the will, released to appropriate action by the symbol, that gives meaning. In this sense conation underlies cognition, and by its action I become myself in the role of the hunter, the warrior, one of the world's workers. (However it must be stated also that since the infant's suckling, or the defecation of the nursery child are the erotised means of relationship with the mother, the will itself is a lover's.)

The unborn child I once was, and which still lives in my depths, may spread its paradisal world before me, so that the scene presents itself to my gaze as a symbol of universal peace, which brings release from all urge towards doing. Its meaning on every hand is the bliss that is now my being. Even worship — everything — is now changed, for I am myself without a need of role. Thus, though the symbols in terms of which the world revealed itself to me enabled me to become this or that aspect of myself, yet when the primary scene is re-created, I am myself without need of my multitudinous facets. Quite simply, I am I, or more truly, I am.

12

CAN I KNOW GOD?

This work is an attempt to see whether one can usefully discuss spiritual questions while using language that would be acceptable to a psychologist. An attempt to encompass the spiritual in such terms is bound, of course, to appear as an apology for religion.

From the outset I have made it plain that transvaluation is conceived as a way of thinking about eternity, and of all we locate in the eternal. It is the way, or manner, of thinking that is of the essence of the matter; it is this rather than merely what is thought that is significant.

I have distinguished three phases of consciousness: Originally there is private consciousness; and how distinctive this is we realise only as it is changed by the arrival of another person; if neither devours nor rejects the other, a condition of reciprocal acceptance, or personal intimate consciousness develops, if another, or a dozen others arrive, the intimacy is disrupted, and public or objective consciousness takes its place. I gave some indication of how people might get stuck in one or other phase of consciousness, and therefore be unable to participate in the kind of relationship for which a different phase of consciousness would be appropriate. But this applies not only to relationships, it applies to all that can come within our purview, and perhaps especially to our thought processes. Thus people might well conceive of God in terms of public consciousness, and therefore be unable to love Him except as an objective entity, who would everywhere represent an alternative to the reality of actual experience. But if they could transpose their consciousness of God so that He was apprehended in terms of private consciousness, we should find that the bundle of concepts, values and emotions they have in relation to Him would have been totally transvalued by His non-objective and interior mode of existence. Such-like procedures have underlain all our thought.

In the chapter about my unusual dream, I spoke of various types of dreams, particularly those in which many years of experience seemed to be lived through. As an example, I described one such dream of my own, in which the whole of my life was reviewed in full detail. In thinking about it, I was struck by the resemblance between it and the accounts given by people who have been *in extremis,* and have reported, "My whole life flashed before me". It is natural to wonder whether perhaps these experiences are a foretaste of the moment of death. My own dream, which took place in a sleep which lasted only a couple of minutes, included far more than a review of my own life; there were experiences as of other lives that I might be going to live, each of them experienced in the fullest detail, and as though spread out in natural time. Similarly the moment of death might well be one in which consciousness continues as active experiencing, perhaps more or less indefinitely. In effect, what would thus happen would be that experiencing would be transposed from the public to the purely private consciousness, in which time need not limit. In passing we should note that this sphere of private consciousness, though it has a different reality from that of public consciousness, is in no sense less real; it is the sphere of fantasy and hope, whence we derive the criteria whereby we shape and judge our external lives, and it is the sphere of all the interior life of the mystics. If then, in the timeless moment of death, we 'continue' to exist, that form of existence must be conceded to be a valid form of existence; we may agree of the formulation that though at death there may be no survival of consciousness, yet there is cessation of consciousness. (At death, we might say, time ceases to be an appropriate category.) I gave parallels from the field of science exemplifying the way in which action could pass out of the realm of the timed into potentiality.

When we asked ourselves what must be the content of this more or less unending, or timeless, moment of death, we were driven to realise that it was an experience of complete and inescapable intimacy with all with whom we were in any sense, positively or negatively, bonded during life. This would be a trial and a judgement, and according to whether or not we could rise to the demands of love, would produce either heaven or hell. Reflecting on this, we are confronted with the thought that the emotions associated with intimacy are what confer the sense of reality on experiencing. Further, we may ask ourselves whether alive or dying we experience, through our intimacy, a telepathic, or intra-subjective agreement on what really is and is not. If so, such an intra-subjective agreement, an externalisation of intimacy, would then constitute what reality is to us; in short, it would constitute reality. If God is love, that is, perfect intimacy, it is then meaningful to say that God is the stuff of reality.

It will be noted that the means whereby we have handled all the foregoing material has been the transposition first from the public to the private, and then from the private to the personal spheres of consciousness. Such movement is an essential procedure of transvaluation. However,

I shall shortly give other examples of its methods which will show that it is not mere transposition. Groddeck brought out a relevant implication of psychoanalysis by stating that in a patriarchal civilisation we were bound to believe in a first cause, and to regard it as personal. Further, he asked, though these were not his words, how it is possible for a man to change from the one true faith, the faith of his childhood? The child in each of us is the reality, the genuine self; to deny its voice in us, is to deny our much cherished aptitude to pronounce on the truth of matters not subject to proof. Which prompts me to ask whether it is perhaps because of faith's foundations in childhood that either proving or disproving God's existence is always absurd. Speaking perhaps to the emancipated, Groddeck said: find your childhood's faith in a new way. He did find it for himself by showing the psychological truth of the Gospels. But though he did this both movingly and with reverence, it has been felt that what he presented was an alternative intended to supplant the old beliefs, and to abolish God. But this presupposes a crass view of Groddeck.

Such lack of subtlety in this sphere is not uncommonly the product of fear lest God should be toppled. This may be either a fear or a wish, and the mere expression of either naturally prompts us – since we speak from the psychological point of view – to ask why anybody should consider abolishing God. Yet before we can ask the question, we are confronted by the obvious answer that we are all sufficiently guilt-laden to fear a judge. And of course it is the fear of God that troubles those who would divest themselves of belief. Intrinsically, what is important in a primary sense is neither belief nor unbelief, but our motives and purposes in these, what we do with belief - unbelief (and with the guilt and yearning that underlie both equally), whether our beliefs are to lash our fellows with, or to help us the better to love them. The criterion for spiritual beliefs should perhaps be that they vivify our communion with our fellows. This, as I see it, is the meaning of Christianity. Given that communion, we can all communicate irrespective of our beliefs.

Mr Charles Davy writes to me:

> "There is now a great vogue for emphasising that 'personal relationships are the heart of religion' (e.g., the Bishop of Woolwich and Wren Lewis). You say something like this yourself. I don't exactly dispute it, but I think it is incomplete. The Eucharist is not only a communion of persons, but a communion with bread and wine, fruits of the earth. The outcome of the 'personal relationships only' school would be to abandon the earth and all the realms of nature to the devil, or at least to science and technology. I was glad to find it emerging that you are aware of this yourself – towards the end of this chapter, you have a fine passage on communion with nature."

Perhaps I should have made acknowledgement to the Bishop of

Woolwich and Mr Wren Lewis, but it never occurred to me to do so, because I derived this idea from Groddeck. Indeed personal relationships are both the kernel and the meaning of everything. As Groddeck showed by his whole *oeuvre,* this truth becomes self-evident once we understand with Plato that *eros* is at the heart of it all. Groddeck traced its symbolism in *The World of Man* and in other writings on the It in science, art, and industry throughout man's world. Because in his very essence man is erotic he both perceives and fashions his world in terms of this symbolism. And he loves and desires the world with all its creatures, and his love claims it; and lo! it becomes, is, and always was his world, the world of man. And it is ever increasingly his world, in the measure in which his love for it grows. And this is his understanding with his fellows, that in the degree that they share it, it is Eden again: the love of man for man is thus the key to re-create all. It is love, which manifests for us as personal relationship, that is Lord.

From a psychoanalytical point of view, obviously, Mr Davy is of course very correct: I certainly would not place external nature beyond the province of God. But what I would do is to affirm that without communion between men, however much our faith be common, we shall remain a Babel of discord.

From a psychoanalytical point of view, obviously the quest for God must turn, not skyward, but within. And within, as we have seen, is a trinity, the three phases of . . . of what? What is it that is conscious in three phases? The answer given by Hume, and since then by all modern philosophy is, Not anything, nothing in any way identifiable. Hume followed Locke in the latter's criticism of the notion of causality which, he said, arose because we were accustomed to seeing certain events follow others. And so he proceeded, through a criticism of all ideas or relationships of necessity, to a denial of the notion of substantiality, and thence of the ego itself. Introspection reveals nothing but flowing associations, and the ego therefore has no existence; in man's core is a void.

We are at once driven to think of the Vedantist's view of the little self as a mere misperception. The reality, we are taught, is spirit, atman, or the Great Self, which however is one with Brahma. Brahma is not merely this, nor merely that, nor merely anything; in other words is beyond definition, and therefore in a sense is non-being. For us also, God, as spirit, is no-thing; spirit, as that which bloweth where it listeth, is indeterminate. This is clear even in our most ordinary usage of the word. Thus when we say the spirit of the troops is bad, we may mean nothing at all tangible; it could be that there is nothing for which the sergeant could 'crime' them, though their spirit is quite obviously bad. We may feel our reference to be merely to the underlying mood, or its manifestation somehow in their manner; perhaps we refer to an overall impression, the *Gestalt* presented.

We may like to think this is due to many small indications, each of which is in itself either too elusive to notice in isolation, or which can achieve significance only in terms of the whole. Spirit would then be that which does not fit into the categories of daily life, or common sense, and is therefore excluded from our apperceptions. Or if in fact the indications are unnoticed, it could as well be said that they are non-existent as not noticeable. The same remarks would often apply to our use of the word 'atmosphere', when we speak of the atmosphere of a place. In this sort of sense, a being who is pure spirit could be said to be non-being, meaning that we have no way of proving his existence. Our only way of cognising such an entity is through noting our own emotional or feeling states. In an earlier chapter I have remarked that certain Freudian analysts use their own subjective responses as a means of knowing what is really taking place in the depths of their patients. And long since, students of Jung have accepted this with little difficulty, while to ordinary people, who are not students of anything, it is usually obvious. If there are murmurs about 'the pathetic fallacy', I would remind people of a fact that is often overlooked, namely that it was, specifically, *violent* feelings that Ruskin condemned as falsifying our impressions of externals. Ortega y Gasset, contradicting Stendhal, affirms, "The lover's valuation is no more illusory than that of the political partisan, the artist, the businessman etc."*

Romantic love, as we know, is a very recent addition to mankind's sentiments. Was it developed as a way of better knowing the beloved? The will to have a new organ of knowledge would indeed be a very powerful motivation to self-development. Perhaps the oldest and most characteristically human of our sentiments, worship, might, in this way, be defined as our sole organ of knowledge of God. We might then define God as that which is known by means of worship, and by worship alone. This would have the same kind of meaning as the statement: "Music is that which is known by our musical sense, and by that alone." Worshippers, whether the great mystics or ordinary people, describe their experience of this knowing as an experience of love; they are overwhelmed by a sense of personal love. Thus God would be the source and stuff of intimacy, a position we approached earlier in this chapter. As a lover sharply condemns any betrayal of intimacy, so God would be the inexorable judge of sins against His nature. The great trial by love that we envisaged in the unending moment of death is, then, properly described as trial by God. In this way He is experienced as a judge. When the essence of the experience is intimacy, it must inevitably be personal, and God, who was non-being, no-thing, reveals Himself to the person as person. But so it is, also, on another plane, with the 'I': this nothing also finds its way into existence.

*Ortega y Gasset, *On Love, Aspects of a Single Theme,* trans. by Tony Talbot (Gollancz), p. 43.

In spite of what Hume said, the subjective sense of an 'I' of course exists, and is indeed the all-pervading essence of private consciousness, and – a point that is especially apparent to the psychoanalyst – the 'I's' very definite existence is the precondition of responsibility. Any weakening of the 'I' leads to what we should call excesses of the super ego, or of the Id, to use Freudian terms. Thus the 'I' achieves an existence that is valid in the sphere of our public consciousness by, and via, our behaviour. Every child knows that without the 'I's' assertion against whim, its behaviour will be wild.

Thus by looking within, into our own nature, we might indeed have learned something about God. Perhaps it is not surprising that man is said to be made in God's image. But such knowledge would not take us very far (nor does our possession of it derogate from the principle that it is only by worship that we could know God). I can credit another person with having a mind only by virtue of having myself looked within, that is, having knowledge of mind in myself is a criterion for recognising it in another. But there are obvious limits to such a way of knowledge; thus looking within does not give me such a knowledge of mind as to enable me to say that I know any other man's mind.

It should be noted that having first transposed our consideration of the 'I' from the objective to the subjective sphere, we move back into the objective, although on a different plane. Though the 'I' was first denied objective existence *as an entity,* it is now accorded this, but in terms of its behaviour and not its substantiality. Hume is still with us, in fact. We may, perhaps, note the further point, that in moving from the subjective, by means of its responsible behaviour, to a public existence, the 'I' must pass through a phase of intimate consciousness (the *'filioque'* clause).

This development of three personalities in the self parallels that of the three persons in God, so plainly stated for all in the Nicene Creed. It is here pertinent to mention the doctrinal basis of the division between our Western Church and the Orthodox which has persisted since the eleventh century. In the Nicene Creed we have "Who (the Holy Ghost) proceedeth from the Father and the Son", whereas our Eastern bretheren omit the *'filioque'* clause ("and the Son"). To my mind this reflects an attitude which also manifests politically: the Russians used always to have autocratic rulers, and did not early develop our system of intermediaries (politicians) to represent the people. The rule of the Tsar being directly over the multitude, the individual and his status did not really exist. I believe that this together with the gorgeous Byzantine Christianity, goes far to account for the special qualities of the Russian mind. The people with their minimum of rights and of status could not become wholly adult in the outer world, in relation to which they perhaps gave themselves up to moods and associated fantasies, yet in themselves, and in their personal relationships, they often more than compensated by their *sobornost,* a spiritual intimacy and a veritable brotherhood that is reminiscent of the *agapē* of the early Christians (*pace* some of our too learned critics of those blessed early times). Yet as must be plain, it was out of their child natures that *sobornost* appeared. And without the middle term in the procession of the persons of the Trinity, and all that reflected in their political life, there was no place for man, for the mature and independent individual. In spite of the harsh organisation of the state, a wonderful intimacy was created, yet not a plane of maturity where the full 'I' could best manifest itself.

We may now return to our major theme of God defined as what is known to worship. To take up our analogy, if music is that which is known by our musical sense, then not everybody who hears the notes played has necessarily heard the music. We can go ever further: though "music hath charms to soothe the savage breast", and though its rhythms may stir us, yet by being soothed or stirred we have not necessarily experienced the music. Similarly, we do not know the 'I' in its essential and secret subjectivity merely by observing it and its behaviour, nor even by being affected by that behaviour. Not the behaviourists, only the analysts can present to a man a picture of himself (the personal self) true enough to move him to self-creative development. And Groddeck, speaking as an analyst, repeatedly warned that we can never really know a man. Beyond the effects produced on us by the personal, is the mystery of its being: without objective existence, motivated by unconsciousness, an *Ungrund,* its true plane of existence is the plane of potentiality. As the source of being, this utterly private plane should be described as the plane of creativity. But the creative spirit is love, whether the sexual love shown by Freud to be so universal, or *eros,* to whom Plato ascribed all, or the *philia* that enables us to band together, and thereby produces civilisation, or, finally, Christ's caritative love, that re-creates the entire spirit of living. We can, then, find God only if we search appropriately and adequately, as Freud sought the meaning of sexuality in the depths of the unconscious; as Plato looked all through the very nature of thinking to ascribe its true place to *eros;* as Christ suffered the world and His passion to make *agapē* the new reality.

From this there ensues the obvious corollary that we do not know God if we look only to the appearances, or conceive Him in terms of externals. But the obvious nature of this truth has in no way inhibited the long history of spurious attempts to know Him. The resultant un-gods have constantly devoured us. In *Totem and Taboo* Freud has presented us with an imaginative account of a god's coming into being for men submerged in nature. It has been remarked that although nowhere do we know events to correspond with the tale told by Freud, he has yet presented us with a great symbolic truth. The imagined return of the murdered parent and the sacrificial propitiation of this ghost portray a detailed account of man's subservience to his guilt. It is gods such as these that have devoured the millions of human sacrifices. At their best, such primitive gods are conceived as arbitrary powers, like men with endless magical equipment, magical mechanics. The endless demands ot petitionary prayer rise up to them, and if the prayers are ungratified, the gods are punished: primitives will beat their images. Nowadays, the tendency is merely to ostracise God by denying His existence.

The religious people I know do not believe in this sort of objective God.

(After I wrote this sentence Canon John Pearce-Higgins protested against the forcing of Anglican clergy to assent to the Thirty-Nine Articles. Then, to my horror and astonishment, a committee of eleven clergymen in Nottingham agreed that there was "no room in the Church" for people such as the Canon. They confirmed their allegiance to all of the Thirty-Nine Articles "interpreted in their plain, natural, and intended sense". I had not realised that such crude literalism persisted.) Of course there have always been literalists about, and doubtless it was their existence that drove Emerson to remark that the spiritualist (of course he used the word before the modern cult of that name existed) finds himself driven to materialism. It is such as they that provoked the 'honest-to-God' reaction attributed to Adler: "When a man talks about God, I ask him to put his cards on the table". It is they who provoked the attack by the young peasant described by Dostoievsky, who took a pistol to church, and at the moment of the elevation, shot the Host. It is they who, by their mad attitude to the development of science, provoked the war of scientists on religion, and perpetuate it by their arrogantly maintained stupidity. As distinct from the God of the mystic, of the worshipper whose worship is filled with experience, these old gods all diminish the 'I'. Whoever prays for their helping hand is rewarded by a monkey's paw that snatches his individuality, his independence. Once helped by them, a man becomes helpless.

They are the products of the attempts to know God without worship. In such idolatries, the god is either a *deus ex machina,* Mr Paley's watchmaker, or a magical mechanic. In spite of the very forceful emphasis that I put upon the need to worship as an approach to knowledge of God, I do not wish to decry the place of reason. Once we worship, then we may indeed use our reason about Him, just as the musical person, truly hearing music, may then usefully think about the notes that are played.

However, before we leave the old pseudo-gods, we must take full note of paganism's nature gods. Under paganism, man was threatened on every hand by savage gods of unpredictable temper. There was no scope for the 'I's' sense of responsibility, and therefore no true ethics. Nor for that matter could there be true love; for love without a full sense of responsibility for the other is not even altruistic. And without true love, the human person lacked full human status; indeed he was the gods' plaything. Every wood, every stream, was haunted by a god; devotees made them more real by erecting images to them. No wonder the Jews' iconoclasm − closely echoing Hinduism's doctrine of God as non-being − which showed that God could not be anything that could be represented! Owen Barfield in his *Saving the Appearances**has covered this ground. Originally, God was still in the burning bush, as for Moses; but finally, for Elijah, He was neither in the wind, nor in the earthquake, nor in the fire, but was the voice of conscience. For the true overthrowing of the old sky-infesting host was by human individuation, when man became so much 'I' that he could be sufficiently responsible to become his brother's keeper, instead of leaving the task to his parents, to the gods − or to the devil. But this means that his brother was conceived as a person, that is to say, an incarnation of spirit, as distinct from a tool, a rival, or a leaning-post.

It is important for us to realise that science is a great ally of God in the battle against the old pseudo-gods. Any god still lurking in the thunder, in the earthquake, or in a fire, like a spirit haunting a place, would have been fiercely attacked by science as a threat to scientific monism. If God is anything, what He is not is a ghost. A ghost, though not human, is yet not a mere nothing; we might call it an incipient something, or better, an attempt to be something. But as spirit, God is no-thing. Yet science makes it possible to find God in nature again − in the external world, therefore, as well as in the interior life, though in a new way: this time without the risk of our being overwhelmed by nature.

To the religious man, science should be regarded as of prime assistance. It is like a sieve for sifting away the absurd from the truth; it teaches us to test. St Paul, of course, told us to test the spirits to see whether they were of God. In 1956 Basil Blackwell published a series of broadcast talks, 'The Institutions of Primitive Society' which contained an account by Dr Godfrey Leinhardt of the Azande use of a poison oracle on fowls. Dr Leinhardt showed how sytematically they tested the oracle, and concluded that the methods showed a genuine affinity to our scientific methods for determining truth. We should follow this primitive example, and invoke the touchstones of science to test our concepts and formulations, and indeed, even to guide us in shaping these. Let the need for absolute clarity here be my excuse for presenting the following obvious example. If I describe a mystical experience in terms of public consciousness, scientists would be the first to be enraged, but also the spirit will have been betrayed. If I heed the scientists' warning, and describe the same experience in terms of private consciousness, I have a better truth from the

---

*Pages 113-14. Those in sympathy with me here may feel that this book is of crucial importance, especially because it shows whither all this leads. We are greatly indebted to Mr Barfield for his profound and original work.

point of view of religion. Science should be felt by the religious as a gift of God to purify religion. It has made religious people think more, so that their religion has gained in significance, and has purged out of the congregations many a lip-service adherent whose membership adulterated the whole.

We cannot, however, go all the way with Professor Julian Huxley, great as is our regard for him; for it is not possible to worship the evolutionary process, any more than a man could fall in love with the female developmental, menstrual and psychological phases. His love requires the personality of a woman. In other words, the question of whether there is a God is, in an important sense, the same as the question of whether other people have minds. Some will claim that it does not matter very much what one believes about a woman's possession of a mind, or a soul, so long as one can fall truly in love with her. And, at first glance, my formulation, "Worship is the only organ of knowledge of God" might seem to fall into the same trap. To escape it, one has only to pause a moment to see that such an attitude to woman would lead immediately to concubinage, which of course does not involve real love; for in that relationship the woman becomes a chattel rather than a person. One should rather ask whether one can fall in love with a woman without believing she has a soul and a mind. It was because the troubadours accorded both to woman in very full measure that they were able to lay the foundations of modern romantic love. It is to be noted that male Muslims accord themselves souls; and that those who disbelieve in the minds of other people take their own believing seriously. Intimacy, of course, cannot be experienced except on the basis of the recognition of the personal nature of the other, whether that other be woman or the Divine.

Throughout his life-long intimacy with nature, Goethe gradually came to know her as a being like himself: all her life processes were expressions of one great archetype, the very same that man, her son, may find manifested in himself. Thus she too is discovered to be triple in all her phases. In his passion for nature, Goethe not only points to the archetype's expressions in his scientific works, but equally finds the same form structuring his lyrics. It was through his intimacy with nature that he was led to discover these objective patterns; through the same intimacy he was also led to an understanding of the plane of potential existence. Thus his *Urpflanz*, the archetypal plant form, was indeed the potential of all actual and conceivable plants. Whether the archetypal trinitarian image be conceived as divine, or as it is manifest in man, it is this same image that we should discover in nature, in order to have her make such sense to us as to enable us to have a personal relationship with her comparable to Goethe's. By virtue of expressing something of this relationship with her the romantic revival changed nature for us. In the degree to which its poets discovered for us our kinship with her, we modified the *Gestalten* we apply in perceiving her, reconstructed our apperceptions of her. Before the Romantic Revival, Switzerland was a hideous place avoided by travellers.

Mankind had to separate from nature in order to develop a true 'I', to become properly self-aware, and to discover nature, that is, the Freudian unconscious, in himself, where he has in some degree dealt with it. Formerly, his identity was overwhelmed by her and her gods. In order to individuate, he had to become involved in what we so rightly describe as the battle with nature. The truly human could be realised only in a degree of isolation from her. But now, with the new Goethean awareness of her, we can return to her, our source, for refreshment for our withered lives. And returning to her in the Goethean spirit of intimacy, we are moved to take responsibility for her, an attitude that is a full assurance against our being again overwhelmed by her. Concern for her good leads us to change her in a further sense. That great man, Luther Burbank, led the way in a tremendous partnership in which man aids nature in her own further self-realisation, producing the wonderfully enriched fruits and flowers that we all now enjoy. Will man now begin to take full responsibility for her by finding means to check the erosion of the earth's soil, restore it where it has been destroyed? For example, President Kennedy took action against the poisons of the earth as described by Rachel Carson in *The Silent Spring*, which threaten to poison us before the physicists can get at us with their bombs. In a spirit of true partnership with nature, man might be led to discover means of feeding humanity before discovering further means of exterminating it. In such a living communion between man and nature, in which the resources of the planet were properly husbanded and shared, man could find again an easy place in nature. He would discover the cosmos anew, in such wise that he would be no longer overwhelmed by what Wyndham Lewis used to call the 'snobbery of scale', whereby contemporary scientists would teach him to feel like less than an insect on a spot of mud in an unimaginably vast loneliness. Such a picture is a product of the little self, with its overwhelming parents projected into the skies to keep down the growth of the responsible 'I'. Such a picture is only a reincarnation of the old demon of paganism, which with its over-godded skies, could only iron out the responsibility from the 'I'. For in spite of man's efforts to free himself from nature's primeval dominion over him, nature continues to reassert this in new forms, and will do so till man takes full responsibility for so manifesting the spirit of developed intimacy as to transform his world of both community and nature and sets himself so to re-envisage and re-create society and the cosmos that the only significant reality will be, as for Goethe, the ubiquitous triple image and its spirit of love. Although we shall indeed not worship the evolutionary process in nature, we shall increasingly descry in her the signature and seal of the personal.

This is the final move required of consciousness, which we saw as originally private, which we understood in its intimacy, and which, as intimate consciousness, should now be transposed into the sphere of the universal, there to transform the merely objective and re-create nature. This would express the full meaning, cosmically, of the Incarnation. Without falling into paganism's error, we can find a valid sense in which nature can be conceived as, made to become for us, and finally experienced as, the epiphany of that which makes man other than nature. With this in mind, it can be said that community means only morality — duty and debt — till man knows that the heart of him is also nature's heart. Man is not freely himself and therefore cannot truly love his fellows till he can unite with nature without being submerged. Freud shows us how to live without feeling that we must forever repress the natural in ourselves: we can participate in its life without being overwhelmed. Mahayana Buddhists tell of a meditation intended to lead to a consciousness of unity with all life, but without annihilation of the real self. Groddeck claims that Goethe's great secret was the power, which we have lost, to unite with a larger whole without loss of the self.

But though we must hold to faith in the ideal of a new 'community' with nature as well as with each other, and though we need this ideal to give fuller significance to our living, we may yet feel that Southey is right, and that our loving is so guilt-laden as to preclude fulfilment this side of heaven; or at least that there is perfect love only in the content of that eternal moment that may sometimes be experienced in worship.

A Note on the Environment

My mention of President Kennedy's action against the poisons described in *The Silent Spring* brings to mind that only a few days later we read of the Americans filling our skies with small needles. What dragon's teeth are these? But such far past threats seem innocent compared with the far more imminent danger which looms ever closer. On 17 September 1968 the *Times* reported Lord Jellicoe, Chairman of the British Advisory Committee on Oil Pollution of the Sea, as saying that its pollution "by toxic chemicals and radio-active waste could be a more serious hazard in the future than the damage caused by oil from the Torrey Canyon". And the previous day, the *Guardian* had reported that the Inter-Governmental Conference of Experts on the Scientific Bases for the Rational Utilisation and Conservation of Biospheric Resources (Unesco) had concluded that "Within the next two decades, life on our planet will be showing the first signs of succumbing to industrial pollution. The atmosphere will become unbreathable for men and animals; all life will cease in rivers and lakes; plants will wither from poisoning." Already "the balance between man and nature has become radically upset".

On 1 April 1969, a letter appeared in the *Times* revealing a most horrible threat to our countryside.

Squeeze on Farming

From Mr. G.R. Judd.

Sir, I wonder how many people realise that the result of the Government's new squeeze on agriculture will be further frantic efforts by the farmers to become even more efficient. First and foremost, this will mean still more small farmers going out of business. For example, it is expected that by 1976 there will be a decrease of 60,000 in the number of holdings under 300 acres.

Secondly, the countryside will be transformed beyond recognition. Hedges and with them hedgerow timber will disappear (1,400 miles of hedgerow were removed last year). Parts of England to which access is keenly sought under the Countryside Act 1968 will become a prairie, and unsightly factory buildings will replace the old picturesque farmsteads to which we are accustomed.

The small farmer, and the countryside, are being sacrificed on the altar of cheap and, in many cases, poor food. Are we counting the cost?

Yours faithfully,
G. R. JUDD
Coval Hall, Chelmsford, Essex.

With the element of family control disappearing with the old farmsteads, large-scale strikes will break out, with dire results to farms. And the physical changes will doubtless lead to "dust-bowl" erosion and other evils. Meantime planners are hurriedly destroying the beauty of our towns to make place for the horrors of most modern architecture. There will soon be little difference between town and country, except that the latter will be emptier.

It is a bitter reflection on our manner of government that many of the dire effects which I have here touched on are being brought about without conscious intention, let alone consideration. Moreover, there is no one whose business it is to check or stop them. Indeed we have only to recall the tremendous official battles against such attempts — Stansted, Levens Park, and so on, and on, and on — to begin to feel that perhaps the only aims the country is organised to fight for are its own despoliation and 'uglification'. (Meantime, other countries fight to preserve their heritage.)

Is there some parallel in the depths of Albion's soul between our use of taxation to stifle our vital institutions (e.g., the London Library) and the apparently permissive attitude of successive governments to the increase of violence — by their near neglect of police recruitment?

Interminable Dreaming

After long roseate dreaming
I plunged to walk precipitously through ruined underworlds
Strewn with dark rock long concealed beneath large broken ice
That was by desert dust
Age-browned.
Multitudinous in cracked grots
I passed were dead dragons,
Mummified, cold embalmed
(In childhood's nightmare they had swallowed me),
And their dead glare of eyes,
Malevolent, cold-killed,
Was unreflected in the dust-browned ice,
Along the immense, malific, ice-formed caves . . .

Suddenly it was ended,
And through celestial marble arches,
Along the nightmare of my dreaming,
I entered China.

Amongst the mazing grain fields –
Stalk-browned by autumn –
A lissom road had stretched itself, and climbed,
And from each highest hill
Stretched further into never ending suppleness.

Beyond time,
In ecstasy's sharp agony,
I wandered on, and then on –
And later, still on ... .
And all the while my path
Was murmuring, droning to itself,
Of the endless change of ages –
Sounding with the eternity of pulsing flux,
The Tao.

At last, in pain and slowly —
Because divinely drunk
With explorer's bated fervour —
I mounted what I thought the final summit,
The goal of this long-wandering path,
Where my gaze would be commanded and rapt out
By the summoning beauty of some promised land.

On the peak
A patterned gateway, intricate,
Had barred the path.
(My heart's a shackled door.)

Through the time-split doors
(In vain I'd tried to open them),
I travelled with my eyes where the path was wandering
With the same directed freedom,
The unpremeditate intent,
Of the goalless wind . . .
A track that lost itself beyond the shining summits.
Ah to follow after!
Into unexplored aloneness,
Through undreamed dreams
And undiscovered majesty of mountains.
Unlimited extension . . . horizonless.

There drifted through the argent air
An echoing from Tao's eternity of change,
As it cascaded down the winding track
Beyond all hills of gold.

My powerless longing to unbar the doors.

(1926)

Part four

CULMINATION

THE MASS, A NEW VERSION

N.B. It will be observed that, as part of the rubric, there appear, interspersed throughout this text, both Greek crosses (+) and Maltese crosses (✠). The + is a direction for the priest only; the ✠ a suggestion for the people also.

ASPERGES

All stand.

All sing: Thou sprinklest me with hyssop, O Lord, and I am clean. Enable me, ever and again, to cleanse my heart of untruth.

The Priest sings: I look into myself, from whence comes my strength.

Congregation sing: I look to love, from whence comes my strength.

The Priest sings: I lift up my eyes to the hills, from whence comes my strength.

All sing: Glory be to the Holy Trinity, as it was, and is now and forever. Amen.

The Priest sings: Who shall go up on to the hill of the lord?

Congregation sing: All who are clean and true of heart.

The Priest sings: The Lord is with us.

Congregation sing: He is our spirit.

The Priest: Let us pray.

The people kneel.

In those places where an angel is mentioned in the older form, in this version of the Mass I have regularly spoken of a messenger, or a message.

COLLECT

All: While ever mindful of the suffering of all whose lives have been dislocated and wrenched from their control, yet with all our strength must we hold to the faith that, in keeping ourselves near to nature, good, and God, there is no need to take anxious thought for our well-being, or for the morrow, for, by the bounty of providence, and our own good husbandry, the means for fulfilling our needs and hopes are always at hand. Confronted with any lack or obstacle, we must seek the failure where we can come to grips with it, in ourselves. O Lord, we invoke Thy help in our resolve to sharpen our insight, and to guide our living directly towards vocation. Meantime the faith we hold to is that we shall thus avoid being such servants as burden Thy work by becoming incapacitated, or such blasphemers as, declaring that Thy creation and the life that Thou gavest us is not good, fail to enjoy Thy bounty. Thus also shall we be lured on by the growing fulfilment of vocation, till we can know worship as the meaning, intensity, and essence of all delight. Amen.

The people stand.

PREPARATION

INVOCATION

The Priest: In the name of the Father ✠ and of the Son, and of the Holy Ghost.

Congregation: Amen.

THE RESPONSES

Priest sings: I go to the altar of God.

Congregation sing: To the God Who gives joy to our youth, and a crown for our years.

All sit

Priest: We read the promise: Where two or three are gathered together in my name, there am I in the midst of them. Are we now so together?

Congregation: We are gathered together as we live, in the name of Logos, the Word.

Servers and
Choir sing*: Wisdom shall praise herself, and shall glory in the midst of her people.

Priest: Being gathered together in the name of Logos or reason, may we find such agreement as to be able to communicate and act in a true spirit of reason.

---

*(In the absence of servers and choir, the priest sings or intones the verses allotted to them).

Congregation: All our communications and actions will embody the way, the truth, and the life.

Servers and
Choir sing: As the Vine brought I forth pleasant savour, and my flowers are the fruit of honour and riches.

Priest: Will then the way we think and live be good simply because a couple of us, or a handful, agree on it?

Congregation: We shall live by Logos.

Servers and
Choir sing: I am the mother of fair love, and wonder, and knowledge, and holy hope; I therefore being eternal, am given to all my children which are named of Him.

Priest: Does living by Logos mean living by a reasoned agreement regarding what is the logic of events?

Congregation: We live by our common faith.

Servers and
Choir sing: Come unto me, all ye that be desirous of me, and fill yourselves with my fruits.

Priest: Does living by faith imply that there is nothing in heaven or earth to live by except the maya or convention created by our agreements regarding what reality is?

Congregation: All living is living together.

Servers and
Choir sing: For my memorial is sweeter than honey, and mine inheritance than the honeycomb.

Priest: Is there then only togetherness and human interaction, and no predestination for us all, and no free will for each separate person?

Congregation: In place of thought about life there is life.

Servers and
Choir sing: I said I will water my best garden, and will water abundantly my garden bed: and, lo, my brook became a river, and my river became a sea.

Priest: Would you then say that neither nature nor personality exist by themselves?

Congregation: It is their togetherness that gives meaning to our life.

Servers and
Choir sing: I will yet make doctrine to shine as the morning, and will also send forth her light afar off.

Priest: Does meaningfulness exist only for a person, or is it found within the framework of the scientists' truth, or in the laws of community?

Congregation: Significance is the reality we live. Its warp is the Kingdom of Heaven within, and its woof the glory of God without.

Servers and
Choir sing: I will yet pour out doctrine as prophecy, and leave it to all ages forever.

Priest: Can we, thus gathered together in the Name, define a formula by which we can communicate knowledge of this reality? Is it communicated in the descriptions of mystics, in doctrine, or by example?

Congregation: There is the holy communion of all our life and worship.

*Servers and
Choir sing:* Behold I have not laboured for myself only, but for all them that seek wisdom.

All stand.

All sing: Glory be to the Holy Trinity, as it was, and is now, and forever. Amen.

Priest sings: ✠ Our help is in God.

Congregation sing: Yes, our help is in all heaven and earth.

CONFITEOR

Priest: All things whatsoever that ye pray and ask for, believe that ye have received them, and ye shall have them.

All kneel:

All: O Son of Man, though we have often, like Peter or Judas, believed ourselves to be good or bad, we acknowledge that only God is good, and that the evil in our hearts is merely a vain posture, conceived in wilful blindness to Thy glory, and for our use against the community. Shuttered in, we are oppressed with our inadequacy; but our striving against it involves us in wounding others, and so leads us to shame and guilt.

This we may suffer till our agony would buy a sublime humility in Thy sight; or, in defiance, we would turn our bitterness on to others condemning our own sin, in them. Thus does our human nature cry for redeeming grace, whereby blame of self or others is replaced by responsible concern and lovingkindness.

Grant us, O Lord Christ, the sense to renounce both overt neighbour-baiting, and the insufferable role of constant good-doing; and grant the grace of kindliness, and too, the decorum of contentment in the cultivation of our gardens. And may we enjoy the ever-plentiful yield from blessed endeavour.

We recall your commandment that we are to be perfect even as our Father is perfect, and acknowledge that each of us has his own unique gifts, and place in life, for which he alone is perfectly fitted. We recall also the words of the Psalmist: I have said ye are gods; and all of you are children of the Most High. Wherefore, O Son of Man, we, made from dust, and yet divine images, invoke all heaven, and all the good God's creation to re-locate us, centring us again in life's very centre; and may He absolve us and redeem us from the shades and pangs of evil, as from all striving to be in the right, from fear of evil, or faith in hate.

Priest: By the grace of God, the Church ✠ confirms our absolution, it accepts us as nobody and yet perfect, and, in place of our fears and striving, offers us the timeless eternity of life.

Congregation: Amen.

Priest: Consider the lilies of the field, how they grow; they toil not, neither do they spin.

The Priest then faces the altar and the people sit.

Priest sings: Thou shalt turn again, O God, and quicken us.

Congregation sing: And thy people shall rejoice in thee.

CENSING

Priest: Thou art + blessed by Him in Whose honour thou burnest.

The censing of the altar takes place while the Introit is being sung by the congregation.

INTROIT

All sing: ✠ Blessed be the Holy Trinity, the undivided Unity, eternal immeasurable, to Whom be honour and glory for ever and ever. Amen.

Blessed is man's solitude, blessed is his love for another, and blessed the meaningfulness we create and discover in life by joining together in Thy worship. Amen.

The Trinity in our hearts knows our world as provident forever; for consciousness is without end, and is beyond all measure. Amen.

As it was in the beginning, is now, and ever shall be, world without end. Amen.

All kneel.

KYRIE

All sing: Kyrie eleison.
        Christe eleison.
        Kyrie eleison.

All stand.

GLORIA IN EXCELSIS

All sing: Glory to God in the highest, and on earth peace to men of good will. We praise Thee, we bless Thee, we glorify Thee, give thanks to Thee for Thy great glory. O Lord God, heavenly Father. O Lord Christ, alone-born of the Father, Lamb of God, Who takest away the sins of the world, receive our prayer. For Thou only art holy, Thou only O Christ with the Holy Ghost, ✠ art most high in the glory of God the Father. Amen.

Priest sings: The Lord is with us.
Congregation sing: He is our spirit.
Priest: Let us pray.
The people kneel.

COLLECTS

The priest reads any special collects, after which all join in saying:

All: From the struggle between the calls of freedom and duty, or any such opposites, grant us, O Lord, deliverance in the form of ability so to co-operate with the sense or logos of our lives' events as to overcome or transcend the irrelevant. Thus will our hearts and minds be rid of all factious desires to be for or against any part of that wealth of thought forever issuing from Thy Logos in man, our lips be able to speak whatever of Logos they find between them, and our actions so conformable to the Logos of all events as to be neither black nor white, but shining with the many-coloured promise of Thy rainbow. Amen.

Priest: The Church accepts us as rid of personal bias. To opened hearts and minds, scripture will always prove an open book, provenant of such truth and symbols as to throw our minds into creative ferment, and to still us in Thy peace. Scripture's word is indeed Logos.

Congregation: Amen.

The priest and people sit.

EPISTLE

The epistle is read by the priest, who concludes with the words "Here endeth the epistle".

The Epistle ended all stand and sing:

All: Our thanks for the Word.

GRADUAL

All sing: He that loveth wisdom loveth life: and they that seek her early shall be filled with joy.

Give me understanding, and I shall keep Thy law: yea I shall keep it with my whole heart.

MUNDA COR MEUM

Priest: Let the fire of the Holy Spirit cleanse my heart and my lips of all trace of pharisaism, egotistic divisiveness, or dominance, and of vain sense of rightness, that I may read the Holy Gospel with the inspiration of understanding.

Congregation: Amen.

THE GOSPEL

Priest sings: The Lord is with us.
Congregation sing: He is our Spirit.
The Gospel is read by the priest or the gospeller.
As soon as the Gospel is announced all sing:
All: Glory be to Thee, O Lord.
The Gospel ended, all sing:
All: Praise be to Thee, O Christ.

THE SERMON

(If there be a sermon, it follows here; during it, the people sit.)

CREED

All stand facing east and recite the Creed. It must never be sung or intoned.

All: I believe in the Son in man. As the notion of difference follows from that of wholeness, my Sonship inevitably follows from the perfection of my source.

This is not the result of any particular experience I may have, and in that sense, it precedes all experience, just as love, or love's fantasy, springs from the pride of my independence, whether I have met my love or not. Thus division, definition, differentiation, disagreement are of the same primary nature as unity or wholeness, and are as essential to me; for without bias, I should know neither the straight nor the curved.

Yet division presents an infinity of problems, and to solve them, I feel impelled to experiment with its possibilities. At once I am caught between the opposites of spirit and matter, male and female, the one and the many, the high and the low, the inner and the outer, the first and the last, the good and the evil, and I wake up to all their derivative problems. I experience these. I develop egotism. I make myself the arena of all problems. Because this is unbearable, I search desperately for some reality other than consciousness, even seeking to blame and damage others; and the harmony between my inner and outer selves is thereby destroyed. Next an apparent rebel, I am, condemned by all. In my agony of conflict and criticism, I find despair annihilates my egotism.

Of myself I can do nothing; yet by considering the lilies, I grow, and find life very good. But its new goodness is no more the old goodness than the denial of that, called evil: the new is the transubstantiation of all pairs of opposites into irrational delight.

I now value every phase of my experience, though I see that all my problems were inventions of my own. Faith always provides a third way that has nothing to do with independence on the one hand, nor, on the other, with necessity, sex, reason, or any element of a conflict. Thus after suffering every division, I have rediscovered my innate wholeness, which, I now see, could have been mine at any moment; and my irrational delight has become an integral part of that wholeness. Now, having learned love, I can freely enter into, and help in, all human problems, both of those who are easy by their faith, and of those who are dead to it. My present is as endless as my future once seemed.

And I believe in the Holy Ghost in man. From both my unity and my diversity springs the creative impulse that shapes my world-picture. This has taught me to predict the movement of stars and atoms, and still better, to move men.

I believe in the Holy Ghost in man. In the beginning of experience was the Word: He has sent us the Comforter. Through the community of those who can communicate, there is the holy communion of life, in which grow all those gifts of tongues, and fires of inspiration, by which the miracle of man's life was conceived, and is lived.

Through the universal church of man, dead eyes are regenerated. By this grace of God we learn to look with seeing vision, with the sight of faith, with the wonder of a child's gaze, on life, now seen resurgent, now and forever a new miracle. Amen.

Priest sings: The Lord is with us.

Congregation sing: He is our spirit.

OFFERTORIUM

While the offertory is taken, the choir may sing a song, which, provided it is not inappropriate to a religious service, need not be sacred music; or all may join in singing the following:

> Praise, my soul, the King of Heaven;
>   To his feet thy tribute bring.
> Ransomed, healed, restored, forgiven,
>   Who like me his praise should sing?
>   Praise Him! Praise Him!
> Praise the everlasting King.
>
> Praise Him for His grace and favour
>   To our fathers in distress;
> Praise Him still the same for ever,
>   Slow to chide, and swift to bless.
>   Praise Him! Praise Him!
> Glorious in His faithfulness.

Father-like, He tends and spares us;
   Well our feeble frame He knows;
In his hands He gently bears us,
   Rescues us from all our foes,
     Praise Him! Praise Him!
Widely as His mercy flows.

Angels help us to adore Him;
   Ye behold Him face to face;
Sun and moon, bow down before Him;
   Dwellers all in time and space.
     Praise Him! Praise Him!
Praise with us the God of grace.*

The people then sit, and the priest offers the host, saying:

Priest: Receive, O holy Father, this our offering of the host.

He pours wine and a little water into the chalice saying:

We mix water and wine, O Lord, praying that as, by His everlasting sacrifice, Thy Son shares with us our human nature, we, in following Him, may in some sort know ourselves as companions of His Spirit.

He offers the chalice, saying:

We offer unto Thee, O God, the chalice of eternal salvation.

He makes the sign of the cross with the chalice.
With bowed head he continues:

May our offerings be a sacrifice acceptable to Thee, O Lord God, for we recall and embody in this act, the spirit of all noble death and sacrifice; and our gratitude to Thee for endowing man with such nobility, becomes, in this offering, an offering of our purest worship.

He looks up and stretches up both arms in an act of invocation as he says:

Come *(he joins his hands again).* Thou Who makest holy, almighty and everlasting God: and + bless this sacrifice which is prepared for the glory of Thy holy name.

Congregation: Amen.

SECOND CENSING

The priest blesses the incense saying:

Thou art + blessed by Him in Whose honour Thou burnest.

He censes the elements and the altar. While doing so, he says:

Priest: Let this incense which Thou hast blessed, rise before Thee, O Lord, and let Thy grace come down upon us. Let out prayer be set forth as incense in Thy sight. Mayest Thou enkindle within us the fire of Thy love, and the flame of everlasting worship. Amen.

---

*By Athelstan Riley, 1855-1945.

LAVABO

The priest dips his fingers in a bowl of water, and wipes them saying:

I will wash mine hands in innocency; so will I compass Thine altar, O Lord; That I may publish with the voice of thanksgiving, and tell of all Thy wondrous works.

Glory be to the Holy Trinity, as It was, and is now, and forever. Amen.

The people stand.

ORATE FRATRES

Priest: Brethren, pray that my sacrifice and yours may be acceptable to God the Father almighty.

Congregation: May the Lord receive the sacrifice at Thy hands, to the praise and glory of His own Name, to our own benefit, and to that of all His holy church.

The people kneel.

Priest: Receive, O holy Trinity, this offering which we make to Thee in remembrance of the passion, resurrection, and ascension of our Lord Jesus Christ, and of Mary, ever a virgin. Let it be also a token of the indwelling Christ and Maid in Everyman's heart, that we may make of it an enactment of all that is true in the life of each one of us. Thus, by the symbol of this bread and wine, do we, here on this altar, offer our very selves, to be a holy and continual sacrifice in the communion of love ordained by Him we commemorate. Yet, O Lord, though this be a sacrifice that we long feared as death, since it costs all we knew as living, it is but a renunciation of the root of all despair, in exchange for the only fulfilment, a death of vanity, for the sake of communion and life; for in the moment that the old Adam in us at last dies, we find the new life of Thy ever-waiting blessing, and hear Thy Son's call: "Come unto me, O ye that be blessed of My Father. and possess the Kingdom which is prepared for you from the beginning of the world". In all delight we, therefore, pray that our lives may be joined in sacrifice with His life, the sincerity of our faith assuring us of our prayer's acceptance. Through the same Christ our Lord.

Congregation: Amen.

The people stand.

CANON

Priest sings: The Lord is with us.

SURSUM CORDA.

Congregation sing: He is our spirit. Sursum Corda.

Priest sings: Life up your hearts.

Congregation sing: We lift them up unto the Lord.

Priest sings: Let us give thanks unto our Lord God.

Congregation sing: It is meet and right so to do.

PREFACE

Priest sings: It is very meet, right and our bounden duty, that we should at all times and in all places give thanks unto Thee, O Lord, holy Father, almighty, everlasting God. Therefore with angels and archangels, with thrones, dominations, princedoms, virtues, powers, with cherubim and seraphim, and with all the company of heaven, we laud and magnify Thy glorious name, evermore praising Thee and saying:

The people kneel.

SANCTUS AND BENEDICTUS QUI VENIT

A bell is rung each time the word 'holy' is uttered.

All sing: Holy, holy, holy, Lord God of hosts, heaven and earth are full of Thy glory; glory be to Thee, O Lord most high.

Blessed is he that cometh in the name of the Lord. ✠ Hosanna in the highest.

PRAYER OF CONSECRATION

The Priest spreads his hands above the offerings, and, except where other actions are indicated, keeps them there till the consecration.

Priest: Wherefore, O most loving Father, we pray Thee to + accept this our oblation, and to + make it of Thine own + immortal nature. We offer it first for the universal church of man; likewise for Thy servant, Elizabeth our Queen, and for all our bishops, clergy, and faithful. We also call to mind all who are in any trouble or doubt (especially . . .) and our dead (especially . . .)

Almighty God, look down on us. We join with all Thy church in this our offering; do Thou + bless it, and + consecrate it, and + take it, that it may become to us Thy Son's very + Body and + Blood. Who the day before He suffered (*he takes up the Host*), took bread into His holy and venerable hands (*he lifts his eyes upwards*), and with His eyes lifted up to Thee, God, His almighty Father, giving thanks to Thee, He + blessed it, brake, and gave to His disciples, saying: Take and eat ye all of this, for

THIS IS MY BODY.

In like manner after He had supped (*he takes the chalice with both hands*), taking also this excellent chalice into His holy and venerable hands: also giving thanks to Thee. He + blessed it, and gave to His disciples, saying: Take and drink ye all of it,

FOR THIS IS THE CHALICE OF MY BLOOD OF THE NEW AND ETERNAL TESTAMENT; THE MYSTERY OF FAITH, WHICH SHALL BE SHED FOR YOU AND FOR MANY UNTO THE REMISSION OF SINS.

As often as you shall do these things, you shall do them in memory of Me.

After the last adoration, he holds his hands apart, and says:

Wherefore, O Lord, bearing ever in mind Thy beloved Son's eternal experience of a victim's passion and death, His eternal resurrection, and His eternal divine ascension, we do offer to Thee of Thy gifts to us, an impassioned + victim, a living + victim, a miraculous + victim, the holy + bread of life everlasting, and the + chalice of eternal salvation.

He stretches out his hands.

Do Thou look upon them, and upon Thy priest who offers them, with the joy of a Father Whose child offers Him presents from his family; and may these holy presents, which are also the offering of our life and our all, be pleasing to Thee.

Thus may the message of our oblation be borne in the fulness of its reality to Thine altar on high, that all who at this altar participate in the mystery of receiving the most holy + Body and + Blood of Thy Son, + may be filled with every heavenly grace and blessing.

He makes this last cross upon himself.

All this we pray, O Lord, through Thy blessed Son, Jesus Christ, for by His presence in every heart dost Thou so + hallow us, + quicken us, and + bless us that we are able to experience participation in Thy heavenly bounties.

He uncovers the chalice, then with the Host in his right hand, and holding the chalice with his left, he makes the sign of the cross over it three times, as he says:

+ By His continuous presence in us, + with that presence, and living always + in the reality of that presence, do we know our source in Thee (*he twice makes the sign of the cross horizontally, between the chalice and himself*), + God the Father almighty, and our unity in the + Holy Ghost (*holding the Host over the chalice he lifts both*) O Thou blessed Trinity, to Whom be all honour and glory, forever and ever.

Congregation: Amen.

COMMUNION

Priest: Let us pray.

All sing or intone: Our Father, Who art in heaven, hallowed be Thy name;

Thy kingdom come; Thy will be done in earth as it is in heaven. Give us this day our daily bread; and forgive us our trespasses, as we forgive them that trespass against us. And lead us not into temptation, but deliver us from evil. Amen.

COMMEMORATION OF SYMBOLS, SAINTS, EXAMPLES

Priest: We now call to mind and give thanks to Thee, O Lord, for the many glorious examples of Thy will made manifest. Thou dost awaken our minds with symbols to portray Thy renewal of our life and nature. Thus have we the Phoenix, which though it expires in the excess of its own life, forever flames to a new life of fabulous glory. And Thy nature is manifested in special ways in persons: thus have we Holy Mary, who by the symbol of her being is every woman, who though a mother, when again sought in love, is so renewed by it as to be a virgin at heart, thereby making heavenly that human loving which is so natural.

Our thanks are given, too, for John who, especially, sees personal happenings − our Lord's life − as enactments portraying heavenly intentions: for Paul, who in proclaiming love as the fulfilling of law, gave incarnate being to Christ's bride: for Francis, who in his Brother Sun, showed us what Akhnaton − for want of it − could not, the light of Thy truth in nature: for the princes of science who scry truth's very shape: for all creative humourists and artists, each of whom, in giving us his own motives for laughter and pathos, grants us organs for the discernment of truths we had otherwise missed.

Through all these, finding in ourselves something of the message of Thy Lamb, which was slain from the foundation of the world, we (*he makes the sign of the cross over himself with the paten*) + join ourselves wholly with the greatest exemplar of that sacrifice, our mother Thy church, who, though of this world, and suffering with it, yet transcends it, not only by enduring beyond the triumphs and failures of our empires, but because she embodies the faith, the hope and the charity of Everyman, is heart of all our hearts.

Through her whose special answering love for Him constitutes herself His bride, her who by giving true life, reshapes the lives of all who are born again by her baptism, through her, O Lord, we pray for the new life, the resurrection in our communion, of this, Thy Son's body, now (*he breaks the Host in half and then breaks off a small particle*) broken and divided for us.

Through her, O Lord, who mystically, is Thy (*with a small particle of the Host, he makes the sign of the cross three times over the chalice*) + Son's bride and + our mother, the + vessel of Thy Son's communion, which, by giving His very body to it, He makes our supreme reality, through her, we pray that in the symbolism of (*he drops the particle into the chalice*) dropping this particle of holy bread into the chalice of holy wine, our own immersion in His holy communion may be made with unqualified will. In truth, O Lord, we here re-enact his incarnation, as much in this chalice, as in Thy church's very womb, as in our own hearts; and in this mingling of seed with blood, manna with life, the part with infinity, our own with Thy universal consciousness, we pray that such harmony may be engendered between all the faithful that each, in his moments, may know everlasting peace of mind.

Congregation: Amen.

THE SALUTATION OF PEACE

Priest: O Lord Who hast instructed us: "If thy brother trespass against thee, rebuke him; if he repent forgive him", when it is our part to repent, grant, O Lord, that there may be in us enough of Thy truth to make our repentance take convincing form, whether in generous retribution, or in heartfelt service. And when it is our part to forgive, let us ever be reminded that forgiveness is not real until it has been ratified by the trespasser's forgiveness of us. We recall thy words: "if thou bring thy gift to the altar, and there rememberest that thy brother hath ought against thee: leave there thy gift before the altar, and go thy way, first be reconciled to thy brother, and then come and offer thy gift". We realise, O Lord, that only such an agreement can give an enduring peace, whether in our minds, or between people, and are therefore resolved that, with all with whom our best efforts in proffering the terms of brotherhood have succeeded, we shall always strive to make our rebukes such unbiased statements of the whole truth that both they and we may again be mystically incorporated by her whose catholicity unites all factions. And we pray, O Lord, earnestness and sincerity to the truth may be so strengthened, and our effectiveness thereby so increased, that, in the end, there may be no man who would tip or shoot an arrow to kill any Baldur, nor any woman whose breast would not weep her love for him.

Congregation: Amen.

The priest may give the pax to the server, who then gives it to the congregation.

Priest: The peace of the Lord is always with us.

Congregation: It is our spirit.

Priest: O Lord, in learning to make our peace with others, we cannot but make the gift of the whole of ourselves before Thine altar, where Thou teachest us what to our pride is the hardest of all arts, the art of receiving. For at Thine altar, O Lord, our offering becomes the means of our blessing, and finding that as Thou hast created an infinitude of plenty, our only choice becomes our duty, to receive, enjoy, and transmit Thy bounty. Let us receive our daily needs and our well-being; let us receive the talent for a love that is happy because it does not hate its own mistakes in its beloved; but most of all receive of the Kingdom of God, and his righteousness; for then without further petition, shall all these things be added unto us.

Congregation: Amen.

The people kneel.

While awaiting communion, or after it, the people may say privately the following prayer:

In this holy moment, grant us, O Lord, the stillness, the privacy, the utter peace of aloneness with Thee. May we be isolate, and single, and as separate as Thy stars, and present to Thee only and thereby renewed, and lifted up to Thy table, where in heavenly communion, all are known to each in spirit and in truth.

The priest says the following four prayers before and after receiving Holy Communion in both kinds:

Priest: May the embodiment of the world's compassion give me strength to love truly; may the body of our Lord Christ keep me unto life everlasting.

Priest: As the body of the archetype and pattern of man now becomes mine, so may the perfect image be manifest in my every deed.

Priest: May His Blood, shed for us, now so quicken my whole being that I may participate in life everlasting.

Priest: As the heritage of our earthly blood is always visible in us, so may my every action worthily proclaim the heavenly blood that now re-creates me.

After the priest, clergy, servers and choir have received Holy Communion, the priest invites the people:

All who will approach our altar reverently may now take communion.

The Communion ended, the priest says:

Now that we have divided and eaten the very body of the victim who forever bears the whole world's guilt, now that He is buried in us, now also that we ourselves by enacting His sacrifice with Him, have mystically killed our old selves, and are, in truth, dead to sin, may our resurrection, which is His in us, be manifest to ourselves in a new faith and joy in living, and to others in new works of our new faith. Thus, having with deepest heart, entered into the manifold symbolism of the Sacrament we have shared we shall henceforth make our every action a sacrament, that living may be to us a happy growing, and our growth be known to others by the sweetness of our fruit, yet remain always a heavenly blossoming in the sight of God.

COMMUNIO

All stand and sing:

Amen.
We worship our God,

The Man in the sky —
His body all worlds.
Not man; beyond sky and worlds;
His being our night.
Yet light is His first gift,
And his delight is our love,
His thinking ourselves.
Born again here today,
To be our renewal.
We worship our God.
Amen.

POST-COMMUNIO

The people kneel.

Priest: Let us pray.

Priest: Now indeed we have eaten bread together, but since our divine host shed His blood as a blessing for all faithful, we are more to each other than fellow guests; for in Him are we made brothers. May our brotherhood ripen to friendship. May the blessing we have received make us easy in our bearing, so that we give no offence, nor ever intrude on a brother, except by the favour of his friendship. Thus may we come to know communion and church as one.

Congregation: Amen.

Priest sings: The Lord is with us.

Congregation sing: He is our spirit.

Priest: Ite, missa est.

Congregation: Deo gratias.

BENEDICTION

Priest: The blessing of + God Almighty warm us to each other, and give us joy in all our doings. May it so ✠ sanctify our lives that we may become the means of its outpouring to all the sons of man. May our spirit be the Holy Spirit.

Congregation: Amen.

The people stand.

LAST GOSPEL

Priest: ✠ The beginning of the holy gospel according to John:

In the beginning was the Word, and the Word was with God, and the Word was God. The same was in the beginning with God. All things were made by Him; and without Him was not anything made that was made. In Him was life; and the life was the light of men.
And the light shineth in darkness; and the darkness comprehended it not. There was a man sent from God, whose name was John.

The same came for a witness, to bear witness of the Light, that all men through him might believe.
He was not that Light, but was sent to bear witness of that Light.
That was the true Light, which lighteth every man that cometh into the world. He was in the world, and the world was made by Him, and the world knew Him not. He came unto His own, and His own received Him not.

But as many as received Him, to them gave He power to become the sons of God, even to them that believe on His name: Which were born, not of blood, nor of the will of the flesh, nor of the will of the man, but of God.
And the Word was made flesh, and dwelt amongst us, and we beheld His glory, the glory as of the only begotten of the Father, full of grace and truth.

All sing:

O come, all ye faithful,
Joyful and triumphant,
O come ye, O come ye to Bethlehem;
Come and behold him,
Born the King of Angels:
O come, let us adore him,
O come, let us adore him,
O come, let us adore him, Christ the Lord.

God of God,
Light of Light,
Lo! He abhors not the Virgin's womb;
Very God,
Begotten not created:
O come, let us adore him, etc.

Sing, choirs of Angels,
Sing in exultation,
Sing all ye citizens of heaven above,
Glory to God
In the highest:
O come, let us adore him, etc.

Yes, Lord, we greet thee,
Born this happy morning,
Jesu, to thee be glory given;
Word of the Father,
Now in flesh appearing:
O come, let us adore him, etc.

Amen.

BIBLIOGRAPHY

Addison, Joseph, *Spectator*
anon. *Bhagavad Gita*
  Brihad Aranyaka
  Chandogya
Arnold, Sir Edwin, *Foundations of Tibetan Mysticism*
Barfield, A. Owen, *Saving the Appearances;* Faber, London, 1957.
  Worlds Apart: Faber, London, 1963.
Binet-Sanglé, Prof, *La Folie de Jesus:* Albin Michel, Paris 1929.
Binswanger, Dr Ludwig, "The Case of Ellen West" in *Existence, a New Dimension in Psychiatry and Psychology* (eds: May, R., Angel, E., & Ellenberger, H.)
  Basic Books, New York 1958.
Brown, Prof Norman, *Life Against Death:* Routledge, London, 1959.
Bucke, Dr R. M., *Cosmic Consciousness:* Dutton, New York, 1923.
Cadoux, C. J., *The Life of Jesus:* Penguin, London, 1948.
Carson, Rachel, *The Silent Spring,* Hamilton, London, 1954.
Darwin, Charles, *Autobiography:* Dover, New York
Donnelly, Morwenna, *Beauty for Ashes,* Routledge, London, 1942.
Fingerette, Prof, *The Self in Transformation*
Freud, Sigmund, *Collected Papers:*
  Totem and Taboo: Hogarth, London, 1955.
Geschwind, Martin, *Untersuchungen über vëranderungen der Chronognosie im Alter:* Basle, 1948.
Groddeck, Georg, *The Book of the It:* Vision, London 1950.
  Ein Kind der Erde:
  Exploring the Unconscious: Vision, London, 1950.
  Der Mensch als Symbol:
  Seeing Without Eyes:
  Der Seelensacher:

The Unknown Self: Vision, London, 1951.

The World of Man: Vision, London, 1951.

Guignebert, Charles, *Jesus:* Kegan & Paul, London, 1935

Guirdham, Dr Arthur, "Reincarnation in Clinical Practice", from the *Golden Blade,* 1969.

Haldane, J.B.S., 'In Defence of Materialism'.

Heidegger, Martin, *Being and Time:* S.C.M., London 1962.

Huxley, Aldous, *The Perennial Philosophy:*   Collins Fontana, London 1958.

The Doors of Perception: Chatto, London 1954.

James, William, *The Varieties of Religious Experience:* Longmans, London, 1952.

Johnson, Dr Raynor C., *Nurslings of Immortality;* Hodder, London

King, J. H., *The Supernatural: its Origin, Nature and Evolution:* Williams & Norgate, London, 1892

Leadbeater, C. W., *Dreams:* Theosophical, London.

MacLeave, Hugh, *A Time to Heal: The Life of Ian Aird, the Surgeon:* Heinemann, London, 1964.

Moffat, *The New Testament*

Ortega y Gasset, *Aspects of a Single Theme:* Gollancz, London.

Otto, Dr R., *The Idea of the Holy:* Oxford, London, 1950; Penguin, London, 1959.

Rosenfield, Prof, *New Directions;* Tavistock, London, 1964.

Sartre, J.-P., *Existentialism and Humanism:* Methuen, London.

Schonfield, Dr Hugh *The Passover Plot:*

Spinoza, *Ethics*

Straus, Erwin W. 'Aesthesiology and Hallucinations' in *Existence, a New Dimension in Psychiatry and Psychology,* eds. May, R., Angel E., & Ellenberger, H.: Basic Books, New York 1958.

Steiner, Rudolf, Goethe's Conception of the World:

Russell, Bertrand, A Freeman's Worship.

Taylor, Gordon, *Sex in History:* Thames & Hudson, London.

Troward, Thomas, *The Creative Process in the Individual:* Dodd, Mead, New York.

Bible Mystery and Bible Meaning:

Upward, Alan, *The New World*

Vries, Peter de, *The Blood of the Lamb;* Gollancz, London.

Wordsworth, W., 'Intimations of Immortality'